UNDERSTANDING OFFENDING AMONG YOUNG PEOPLE

Janet Jamieson

Gill McIvor

Cathy Murray

The Stationery Office Limited
73 Lothian Road
Edinburgh EH3 9AW

Applications for reproduction should be made to
The Stationery Office Limited

First published 1999

British Library Cataloguing in Publication Data
A catalogue record for this book is available from the British Library

ISBN 0 11 497261 3

ACKNOWLEDGEMENTS

This research would not have been possible without the assistance of many people at different stages in the research process. First we would like to acknowledge the support of the Scottish Executive who funded the work.

We decided at an early point in the study to anonymise the two towns in which the research was based to protect the confidentiality of respondents. We are grateful to the education and social work departments and police forces in Eastburgh and Westburgh for providing the necessary research access and to the individual teachers, police officers and social workers who were interviewed as part of the research. We are also extremely appreciative of the help given by the local secondary schools in the administration of the school-based self-report survey and for the office space and support provided by local projects in Westburgh.

The University of Stirling provided additional funding for the employment of sessional researchers to conduct some of the interviews. We would like to acknowledge, in particular, the contributions of Viv Campbell, Linda Dubhtaigh, Ailsa Cook and Ruth Emond in this regard and the assistance with specific aspects of data analysis provided by Kristina Moodie, Rebekah Pratt, Sandra Rodwell and June Watson. Secretarial support was provided by Sheena Conroy and Pam Lavery and much of the work of transcribing the many taped interviews fell to Morag Crumley, June Kerr, Liz MacDonald and Helen Scott.

Last, and most importantly, we would like to extend our warm thanks to the young people who took part in the study and who gave so freely of their time to talk honestly and openly about their experiences and views.

Janet Jamieson
Gill McIvor
Cathy Murray

November 1999

EXECUTIVE SUMMARY

Introduction and methods

This study, exploring the choices young people make with respect to involvement in offending behaviour, was conducted by a research team at the Social Work Research Centre, Stirling University from 1996-1999. A survey of self reported offending was conducted with 3rd and 4th year secondary school pupils and in depth interviews were conducted in two study areas with young people in each of three age groups: 14-15 years, 18-19 years and 22-25 years. On the basis of the self report offending questionnaire or on the basis of discussion about offending during interviews, young people were classified as:

- resisters: young people who had never offended;
- desisters: young people who had offended in the past but had not done so in the previous 12 months;
- persisters: young people who had committed at least one serious offence or several less serious offences in the previous 12 months.

Interviews were conducted with 92 resisters, 75 desisters and 109 persisters (50% of the sample were male and 50% were female) to explore young people's views and experiences of a range of topics: offending; education; employment; leisure and lifestyle; drug and alcohol use; relationships with family, friends and partners; neighbourhood, community and society; values and beliefs; identity and aspirations; the criminal justice system; and victimisation. Interviews were also conducted with seven police officers, seven social workers and five teachers about their understanding of young people and offending. The samples were drawn from two Scottish towns located in areas which had crime rates close to the national average. Westburgh had developed around heavy industry that had since declined and had male unemployment rates higher than the national average. Eastburgh was a new town whose economy had developed around new technologies and whose rates of male and female unemployment were lower than for Scotland as a whole.

Self-reported offending by 3rd and 4th year pupils

- Most 3rd and 4th year secondary school pupils indicated in the self-report survey that they had offended on at least one occasion but the types of offences committed were not, on the whole, very serious. However, girls were less likely than boys to have committed all but the least common offences and girls who did offend tended to do so less frequently than boys. Amongst boys, the range and severity of offending increased between 13 and 15 years of age.

Offending: attitudes and explanations

- In interview the youngest age group tended to ascribe greater seriousness to offences in which they were rarely involved and less seriousness to those which they perpetrated. Young people in the older age groups appeared to be more tolerant of property crimes of an essentially utilitarian nature (except where these involved a readily identifiable victim) and less tolerant of offences (such as street fights or vandalism) which tended to be associated with younger people. There was also, in the older age groups, a greater tolerance for violent offences among young men. Overall, persisters tended to take a less serious view of offending than did resisters, with desisters occupying a position somewhere between the two.
- Most resisters and desisters viewed offending generally as immoral or futile. Many persisters and desisters offered 'justifications' and 'excuses' for their own offending. However few persisters believed that offending was wrong unconditionally, often suggesting that the acceptability or otherwise of offending was contingent on a variety of factors, including the type or severity of the offence. Offending by others was more frequently attributed to upbringing or family (by resisters and desisters) and to drug use (by persisters).
- A higher proportion of the youngest age group considered no offending to be acceptable and resisters more often than desisters and persisters held such a view. Men and boys, more often than young women and girls, made reference to the personal consequences of offending. These included detection, punishment, diminished life chances and feelings of guilt.
- Professionals believed that relatively few young people were involved in serious offending but that there was an increase in young women and girls' involvement in delinquency and crime. The latter was attributed to an increase in drug misuse among young women and to contemporary cultural influences which encouraged girls' identification with attitudes and behaviour traditionally associated with boys.
- Professionals generally agreed that offending among young people was linked to family factors, peer influences, drug misuse, school failure and social exclusion while supportive families, self-esteem, education and employment could help protect young people from becoming involved in crime.

Offending and lifestyle

- Around three-quarters of boys and girls in the youngest age group reported having consumed alcohol and almost one third reported having used cannabis. Resisters in this age group were least likely to have consumed alcohol and drug use was almost exclusively confined to persisters. In the youngest age group, girls were more likely than boys to report having used drugs on at least one occasion.
- Overall there was an escalation in the severity and frequency of substance use by age. In the older two age groups resisters were least likely and persisters most

likely to report the use of illegal substances, with the experiences of young men and young women being broadly similar. Amongst the middle and oldest age groups alcohol, cannabis, and heroin were used more frequently than other substances. Self-reported addiction was most prevalent among persisters in the oldest age group.

- Common explanations for drug use included peer pressure, enjoyment, opportunity, curiosity, relaxation, recreation and boredom. Common explanations for non-use of drugs included the associated expense, the perceived danger, the illegality of drugs, choice, fear and the observed effects of drugs on others. Similar explanations were offered for the cessation of drug use, along with increased maturity and the assumption of parental responsibilities.

- It appeared that drugs were relatively easy to access and that young people considered drug use to be a relatively common practice among their peers. Cannabis was generally perceived to be less serious than other illegal substances; heroin use and addiction was regarded as particularly problematic. Persisters in the two older age groups were most likely to identify a link between their use of drugs and offending, especially property offences.

- The majority of young people reported initial alcohol use between 12-14 years. In the youngest age group persisters were more likely than resisters or desisters to report unsupervised and public use of alcohol. Use of alcohol was more common in the older two age groups and was often described as an integral part of social life. Those who did not use alcohol usually attributed this to their preferred use of other drugs. Regular use of alcohol was more often reported by young men, while young women were more likely to indicate that their use of alcohol was limited to special occasions and social outings. Although some boys and girls in the youngest age group indicated that alcohol use had contributed to their offending, those in the older age groups did not, on the whole, associate alcohol use with criminal activity.

- On the basis of responses to a questionnaire administered in the interview, persisters in all age groups were more inclined towards impulsive or risk-taking behaviours than were desisters and resisters. Among the middle and oldest age groups there was a greater inclination towards risky behaviours which were also illegal.

- Boys and girls in the youngest age group were most likely to participate in a range of hobbies. In the middle and oldest age groups young men were more likely to do so than young women. Across all age groups resisters and desisters were more likely than persisters to be involved in hobbies of a formal and social kind.

- Resisters of all ages were most likely to stay on at school until sixth year or to plan to do so, while persisters were more likely to have been suspended or excluded from school, to have left school at the earliest opportunity and to be unemployed.

- Education was considered by teachers to be a crucial factor in preventing offending among young people both through the ethos promoted by schools and through opportunities that education afforded young people in the future.

However, it was also recognised that schools could not fully compensate for the disadvantaged family background that many young people experienced.

- Most young people's aspirations for the future centred on employment, family life and other adult transitions, such as getting their own home. While most young people thought it likely that their aspirations would be fulfilled, persisters tended to be least optimistic in this respect.

Offending: relationships and social networks

- Resisters were least likely to report that other family members had offended while persisters were most likely to do so. Almost all resisters indicated that their families were opposed to offending and this was also true of most desisters and persisters. Many young people did not consider their families' views about offending to have made any difference to them, either because they considered their own views to be more important, because they had problems such as drug addiction which led them to disregard others' views or because their own opinions were, in any case, similar to those held by their families. Those who did think that their families' views made a difference – mostly resisters and persisters – also indicated that they shared their families' views or they had been brought up not to offend.

- The majority of persisters and desisters reported having friends who offended compared with only a minority – albeit substantial – of resisters. Most resisters reported that their friends similarly disapproved of offending, whereas offending was more often said by desisters and persisters to be considered acceptable by their friends. The majority of young people did not think their friends' views of offending directly affected them or how they behaved, either because they were independently minded or shared similar views in the first place.

- Girls and young women were more likely than boys and young men to have partners who offended. Persisters were most likely to have partners who offended while this was least often the case for resisters. The majority of resisters and desisters said that their partners disapproved of offending or shared similar views to their own. Some persisters also thought that their partners were against offending but others said that their offending was tolerated by their partners because they were offenders themselves. Although some young people did not think that their partners' views about offending made any difference to their own behaviour, where partners' views did exert some influence this was usually said to be in a positive direction.

- The majority of young people indicated that they felt 'part' of their communities – variously defined as the street, neighbourhood or town in which they lived – with there being no differences between resisters, desisters and persisters in this respect. Young people did not, on the whole, feel that their communities' views about offending made much difference to their own behaviour, though some suggested that community tolerance for minor crime and drug use may have contributed to their offending.

Young people and the criminal justice system

- The majority of persisters and desisters and just over one third of male resisters reported having had some involvement with the police while this was true of fewer than one in ten female resisters. Resisters were most likely and persisters least likely to believe that the police did their job well.
- There was a relatively common view that the courts were too lenient in respect of some crimes while at the same time being too harsh in respect of others. Perhaps surprisingly, persisters often believed that they had been treated fairly or given several chances by the courts. Overall, court outcomes were said to be a greater deterrent to further offending than court processes.
- Resisters expressed more negative views about the prison service than did desisters or persisters. Prisons were considered to be ineffective because they afforded prisoners too many privileges, were 'universities of crime' or gave insufficient attention to rehabilitation. Prisons were considered to be effective because they prevented people from offending for the duration of their confinement or because of their potential for individual deterrence.
- Although some young people were aware that the children's hearings system dealt with non attendance at school, the majority referred to it as a system solely for dealing with children and young people who had offended and few were aware of its child protection element. Whilst most young people expressed views about different aspects of the criminal justice system, knowledge about the children's hearings system was characterised by its vagueness, misunderstanding as to its role or ignorance of its existence.
- Resisters in particular lacked knowledge of the social work role in relation to children and young people who offend. Although persisters and resisters were equally likely to express positive views about social workers, this was more likely in the former case to derive from direct experience and involvement.
- Three-fifths of young people reported that they had been the victim of an offence, with experience of victimisation being more common among boys and young men. Domestic violence was more often reported by female respondents while male respondents were more likely to report episodes of victimisation outside the home. Female victims were more likely to report increased understanding of and sympathy for other victims as a result of their own victimisation while male victims were more likely to engage in 'victim blame' and focus upon the practical consequences of the incident rather than the personal consequences for the victim. Few persisters considered their own experience of victimisation to have affected their subsequent behaviour.
- Professional respondents recognised that relationships between young people and the police could be improved by better communication. They believed that responses to offending among young people by the police, social workers, the children's hearings system and the adult courts were effective with some young people but not with others, recognising that professional intervention was constrained by workloads and/or a limited range of options. There was universal recognition among professionals of the need for co-ordinated multi-agency initiatives aimed at preventing offending among young people, with the

development of initiatives to address drug misuse being according the greatest priority.

Understanding resistance, desistance and persistence

- Non offending was attributed by resisters to a concern to avoid the potential consequences of offending (such as contact with the criminal justice system and its influence upon employment or career prospects), to their upbringing and to a desire not to upset their families and elicit family disapproval. Similar factors – along with increased maturity and changes in friendship patterns – were also drawn upon by boys and girls in the youngest age group when explaining their desistance from offending.

- Desistance was explained by those in the middle age group with reference to maturity and to the experience of adult transitions, such as getting a job, having children, forming a relationship with a partner and leaving home. Maturity, a concern to protect or avoid hurting family members and lifestyle changes – such as the cessation of drug misuse – often featured in the accounts of desistance amongst the oldest age group.

- Persisters often related accounts of efforts they had made to stop offending or plans that they had to do so, with young women and girls in particular wishing to portray themselves as desisters even if they had offended recently. The youngest persisters were most optimistic about their ability to desist because they did not wish to invoke the consequences of being caught and often regarded their offending as a 'phase' they were going through. Young women in the middle age group were most likely to describe the use of avoidance strategies to facilitate desistance, such as staying in, getting a job, going to college or changing friendship groups. Drug addiction, especially involving heroin, was the most common explanation for continued offending among young people in the two older age groups.

- Professionals thought that the process of desistance was influenced by 'maturation'; finding employment; making lifestyle changes; forming relationships with partners; recognising the potential personal consequences of offending; and the deterrent effect of contact with the criminal justice system. By contrast, they associated persistence in offending with limited aspirations and opportunities for employment; the influence of intergenerational involvement in crime; institutionalisation by the child care and penal systems; and deliberate choices to pursue a criminal lifestyle for financial gain.

- According to the Rosenberg measure of self esteem, persisters among the older age groups had lower levels of self esteem than did desisters or resisters. Although young people overall tended to consider similar attributes to be appropriate for men and women, young men tended to adopt more stereotyped views of men and women and persisters also showed a greater tendency to adhere to gendered stereotypes. In response to scenarios exploring young people's values and beliefs, resisters were most likely and persisters least likely to respond in what might be considered the 'morally responsible' manner.

Conclusion

Offending among those in the younger age groups was usually a transitory phenomenon which derived from a desire to conform to pressures from friends to engage in a range of risk-taking behaviours that signal increasing independence from adult influences. Offending among the oldest age group was often associated with social exclusion and the misuse of drugs, pointing to the value of policy initiatives which aim to reduce economic and social inequalities and promote social inclusion. The deterrent impact of contact with the criminal justice system was largely confined to young people whose involvement in offending was of a relatively minor nature. Previous research suggests that young people's perceptions that criminal justice agencies have treated people fairly may have a greater influence upon their willingness to obey the law.

In undertaking this study we have become convinced of the importance of young people being listened to and having a direct voice in the formulation of local and national policies which impact upon their lives. The study demonstrates that the factors associated with offending among young people are complex, varied and defy simplistic solutions. A strategic approach to the issue of youth crime will, accordingly, require responses at the individual, the local and the national level if offending and related problems, such as drug abuse, are to be successfully addressed.

TABLE OF CONTENTS

CHAPTER ONE: INTRODUCTION AND BACKGROUND

INTRODUCTION

This study explores the choices young people make with respect to involvement in offending behaviour. It examines the relative significance of various factors (including social circumstances and opportunities, personal attitudes and characteristics and, where relevant, criminal justice interventions) to the decisions young people make with respect to resistance to, desistance from and persistence in offending behaviour with a view to identifying the implications for the development of effective strategies aimed at the prevention or reduction of offending behaviour.

EXPLAINING OFFENDING AMONG YOUNG PEOPLE

The link between youth and crime is one that has proved long and enduring. It is generally recognised that involvement in criminal activities is an integral part of adolescence for many young people (Graham and Bowling, 1995). In Scotland just under 40 per cent of all recorded crimes are committed by young people aged under 20 years of age and the total cost of youth crime to Scottish society is estimated to be at least £730 million per annum (Prince's Trust,1997, p.1). Theories abound as to the causes of offending and these are often fiercely disputed. It is now widely accepted, however, that monocausal explanations are insufficient and that criminal behaviour and its origins are complex phenomena which defy simplistic explanations and solutions. Contemporary explanations of offending among young people, such as the one advanced by Stewart et al. (1994), have drawn upon criminological theories which stress the importance of failure to adhere to socially agreed values (control theory), the blocking of legitimate opportunities to achieve socially agreed goals (strain theory), re-integrative shaming (Braithwaite, 1989) and commitment to alternative (deviant) reference groups (subcultural theory). Realist criminology likewise emphasises the multi-dimensional nature of the aetiology of crime, including, crucially, the impact of social inequality, while some criminologists argue that the aims of criminal justice policy should be linked with those of social policy in other fields and to 'some conception of what should count as a good society' (Stewart et al., 1994). Increasingly, too, the concept of masculinity is being invoked to explain a range of offending by young men (e.g. Buckley, 1995; Walklate, 1995; Mac an Ghaill, 1996; Collier, 1998).

RESISTANCE, DESISTANCE AND PERSISTENCE

It is possible to identify studies which have examined the determinants of offending behaviour (West and Farrington, 1973, 1977; Farrington and West, 1981) or which have sought to explore the reasons offered by young people for their involvement in offending (e.g. Graeff, 1993). Other recent research (e.g. Shover, 1985; Burnett, 1992; Leibrich, 1993; Hubert and Hundleby, 1993; Farrall and Bowling, 1997; Rex, 1997; Maruna, 1997, 1998, forthcoming) has focused upon the explanations offered by offenders for their decisions to desist from further offending behaviour. The present study attempts to bridge the gap between research which has focused upon causation and that which has concentrated upon the cessation of offending careers by focusing upon the choices made by young people of different ages with regard to resistance to, desistance from and persistence in offending behaviour and, centrally, the relative importance of a range of factors – including social circumstances, personal characteristics and the formal intervention of the criminal justice system – to the choices they make. The importance of studies focused upon 'relapse' into recidivism and desistance from crime has been highlighted in the draft recommendations to the Council of Europe from the 20th Criminological Research Conference in November 1993 (Hood, 1993).

The peak age of offending for young men appears to be around 18-19 years, though the peak age of recruitment into offending occurs somewhat earlier, at around 14-15 years of age. Many young men eventually stop offending altogether and will, by their early 20s, have effectively 'grown out of crime', although others will remain persistent offenders. In Scotland the peak age for *conviction* among women is also 18 years (Scottish Office, 1999a), though convictions for women remain fairly constant between the ages of 18 and 30, with a gradual decline thereafter (Social Work and Prisons Inspectorates, 1998). Data for England and Wales, by contrast, have suggested that the peak age for female offending is around 15 years (Farrington, 1996). The 14-23 year old age group, therefore, offers considerable scope for exploration of those factors which impact on the development, maintenance and cessation of offending behaviour. Research focused upon this age group is capable of addressing some of the key questions that Farrington et al. (1986, p. 151) have argued are necessary to gain a deeper understanding of the causes of crime: 'Why does crime [among young men] increase with age to peak in the teenage years? Why do [young men] stop offending at age 20? Why do people start or stop committing crimes? What is the influence of peers upon offending? What is the effect upon offending of events such as leaving school, getting married, and becoming unemployed? What are the effects of different sentences upon offenders?'. Answers to questions such as these are essential to inform the development of effective responses to offending among young people.

PREVENTING AND REDUCING OFFENDING AMONG YOUNG PEOPLE

Increasing attention has recently been directed towards the potential of various interventions to prevent or reduce the occurrence of social problems such as youth crime, school failure, drug misuse and inappropriate early sexual behaviour. In the UK, for instance, various reports exploring the phenomenon of youth crime (e.g. NACRO, 1995; Audit Commission, 1996; The Princes Trust, 1997) have advocated an increased emphasis upon preventive strategies. The importance of prevention has likewise been highlighted in Continental Europe where countries such as Sweden, Denmark, France and Belgium have established National Crime Prevention Councils (Ruxton, 1996) and in the USA by a Congressional mandate to evaluate crime prevention initiatives across a range of institutional contexts (Sherman et al., 1997).

The US Congress adopted a definition of prevention which focuses upon reducing the risk factors and increasing the factors which can offer individuals protection against involvement in delinquency and other behaviours (Sherman, 1997a). Risk and protective factors have been identified which relate to a variety of institutional contexts or domains, such as the family, school, community and peer group (e.g. Loeber and Dishion, 1983; Hawkins et al., 1992; Utting et al., 1993; Yoshikawa, 1994; Howell et al. 1995; Gottfredson et al., 1996; Farrington, 1996) and preventive efforts have likewise been variously directed. As Gottfredson (1997) has argued, preventive strategies are based upon the assumption that interventions aimed directly at reducing risk and increasing protective factors will reduce the incidence of youth crime.

There is broad agreement regarding the nature of the risk and protective factors for delinquency and other problem behaviours and agreement that the risk and protective factors for different types of behaviour overlap to a substantial degree. However, most of the relevant empirical research has been conducted in North America (the Cambridge Study of Delinquency (e.g. Farrington and West, 1981) being a notable exception). The cultural distinctiveness of Scotland – including its socio-economic characteristics, its historical and contemporary identity and its unique legislative system – requires that the relevance and relative significance of empirical and theoretical insights derived from other jurisdictions be carefully considered with respect to their transferability to the Scottish context.

Although there is some consensus as to what constitute the risk and protective factors for delinquency, the empirical evidence with respect to the effectiveness of social crime prevention initiatives is less clear cut, partly because initiatives of this kind have tended not to have been subjected to rigorous evaluation. Recent reviews of the relevant literature, however, suggest that the most effective programmes of primary and secondary prevention which aim to strengthen protective factors tend to be school or family focused (e.g. Farrington, 1996; Utting, 1996; Sherman et al., 1997; Asquith et al., 1998). As Asquith et al. (1998, p.52) have argued, 'crime prevention strategies should commence not as criminal justice reactions, but via a range of early-years health and education initiatives to counter the high-risk precursors of delinquent behaviour'. More specifically, there is some evidence that the following broad approaches – some of which are universal and, therefore, regarded as less stigmatising – may be effective in preventing delinquency and crime among young people:

- early intervention programmes aimed at improving parenting skills and providing support for parents;
- pre-school education programmes, particularly those which encourage parental involvement in their children's education;
- school-based anti-bullying strategies; and
- whole school initiatives aimed at modifying the school ethos, clarifying and communicating norms about behaviour and teaching and reinforcing social and cognitive skills.

With respect to young people who have begun offending, and especially persistent young offenders, there is a growing body of literature (e.g. Gendreau and Ross, 1987; McIvor, 1990; Lipsey, 1992, 1995; McGuire and Priestley, 1995; MacKenzie, 1997; Chapman and Hough, 1998; Underdown, 1998) which suggests that effective interventions:

- match the intensity of service provision with the level of offender risk;
- address criminogenic needs (that is, those characteristics and problems which contribute to offending behaviour at the individual level);
- are structured and focused;
- employ behavioural or cognitive-behavioural methods;
- are community-based; and
- have high levels of programme integrity.

Throughout the UK there is growing interest in the development of approaches to the supervision of offenders which are consistent with the above principles. Recent developments in this respect include the 'Getting Best Results' initiative in Scotland and the development of 'Pathfinder Projects' in England and Wales. The former consists of a Scottish Executive steering group with representatives from The Scottish Executive, the Scottish Prison Service, local authorities, the independent sector and the academic community which is developing a framework for the promotion of effective social work practice with offenders. The latter involves the identification of probation programmes which have been empirically informed by the effectiveness literature, which will be evaluated and accredited through a joint prison/probation accreditation system (Home Office, 1999).

CRIME AND SOCIAL INCLUSION

The significance of socio-economic factors such as unemployment, poverty and homelessness in the *aetiology* of criminal behaviour has been the subject of considerable debate. However research which has attempted to document the social circumstances of young offenders has consistently highlighted high levels of unemployment, family breakdown, homelessness, low educational achievement and poverty (e.g. Kennedy and McIvor, 1992; Stewart and Stewart, 1993; Stewart et al., 1994). That there is an *association* between adverse social circumstances and offending behaviour is difficult to deny; so too, however, is the relevance of other factors – such as environmental variables, personal characteristics and the role of formal criminal justice intervention – in understanding and responding to crime. What is less clear, however, is the relative significance of these factors to the choices made by young people concerning their participation in or resistance to offending behaviour.

The present study also explores the relevance of community re-integration and social inclusion to an understanding of offending among young people. Social inclusion – which includes access to material and cultural life experiences and opportunities which are consistent with notions of social justice (such as education, employment, housing and leisure) and which are underpinned by shared values emphasising choice, participation, inclusiveness and empowerment (Scottish Office, 1999b) – is now being invoked as a protective factor against crime (Scottish Office, 1999c). However, little is known about the subjective experience of social inclusion, its relationship, if any, to those factors which are assumed to promote it, and its relationship, if any, to criminal behaviour. The narrower – and more evidently functional – concept of community re-integration has similarly been invoked as impacting upon risk of offending behaviour (e.g. Haines, 1990). Yet re-integration into a community which shares values that are supportive of crime is likely to increase rather than decrease the risk of further criminal activity. Furthermore, re-integration into a community which is itself characterised by multiple disadvantage does not imply inclusion in wider society.

GENDER AND OFFENDING

In Scotland the issue of female offending has recently received increased policy attention following a series of suicides at Scotland's only female prison and a subsequent review by the Inspectorates of Social Work and Prisons into the use of community-based disposals and custody with women (Social Work and Prisons Inspectorates, 1998). Previous research which has focused upon the causes of offending or desistance from offending has concentrated almost exclusively upon males who at all ages are more likely than females to come into contact with the criminal justice system as a consequence of their offending. Moreover, the fact that females are significantly less likely than males to engage in offending behaviour has resulted in attempts to define and explain female delinquency and criminality with reference to constructs which are not usually invoked in similar attempts to understand offending by men. Asquith and Samuel (1994) identified a broadly similar relationship between the incidence of offending and age for men and women, even though the difference in the actual number of convictions between men and women was very large, leading them to argue that the gender difference in number of convictions tends to obscure an age-related pattern of offending among young women:

> The pattern which emerges from these data provides quite convincing evidence that for females, as with males, crime is very much a youth-related phenomenon in Scotland... To overlook and ignore this pattern...helps sustain the myth of female criminality as individualistic, pathological and essentially non-social.
>
> Asquith and Samuel (1994, p. 81)

More recent figures suggest, however, that although convictions are more common among both young men and young women in their late teens and early twenties, women's convictions tend to show a less marked age-related pattern than was previously said to be the case (Social Work and Prisons Inspectorates, 1998). A fuller understanding of the phenomenon of youth crime therefore demands that attention should also be focused upon the issue of offending by young women and girls – an area that has hitherto attracted little research interest and which, as a consequence, is ripe for empirical exploration.

THE PRESENT STUDY

In view of the broadly age-related nature of both male and female crime, an understanding of crime among young people in Scotland can be greatly enhanced by comparing the experiences and expectations of young men and women and by exploring how these may relate to their involvement or lack of involvement in delinquent or criminal behaviour. The present study builds upon previous studies and will further enhance our understanding of offending among young people:

- by focusing upon the crucial 'transitional' age group in which young people choose to refrain from, desist from or persist in criminal behaviour;
- by exploring the reasons for both starting and stopping offending;
- by embracing a sample of young people in two locations including those who have been subject to formal criminal justice intervention;
- by exploring the relationship and balance between the interventions of the criminal justice system and the other individual and social influences on young people;
- by identifying and exploring those factors which account for gender differences in offending among young people.

This study therefore explores the relationship between gender and the factors which prevent young people from becoming involved in offending; the reasons for young people's involvement in crime and delinquency and the forms that such behaviour takes; and the processes of desistance from offending.

CHAPTER TWO: METHODS

The study employed both quantitative and qualitative methods but the emphasis and focus was upon the latter. A qualitative approach was considered most appropriate because of the exploratory nature of the study and the need for flexibility and sensitivity. Furthermore, a qualitative approach allowed respondents to talk in their own 'frames of reference' which, in turn allowed the meanings and interpretations they attributed to events and relations, in respect of offending behaviour, to be understood (May, 1993).

In-depth interviews were conducted with young people in each of three inclusive age groups: 14-15 years, 18-19 years and 22-25 years. These age groups were selected on the basis that they may be assumed to represent significant points at which choices are made by young people with respect to offending behaviour. The first age group represents the peak age of recruitment into offending behaviour for boys (Scottish Office, 1997); the second the peak age of offending for young men and, though less markedly, young women (Scottish Office, 1999); and the third the age by which many young people will have 'grown out of crime' (Rutherford, 1985). Equal numbers of interviews were conducted with young women and men.

The sample consisted of young people of both sexes drawn from two geographical areas. Both are medium-sized Scottish towns located in areas which have crime rates close to the Scottish average. Westburgh is an established town which developed around heavy industry – and, in particular, shipbuilding – which is now in decline. Eastburgh is a new town the economy of which has developed around new technologies. In 1998 the male unemployment rate (based on the claimant count) in the local authority in which Westburgh is located was 9.4 per cent and in the authority in which Eastburgh is located was 7.0, which compares with a Scottish average of 8.2 per cent. The respective unemployment rates for women were 2.8 per cent, 2.3 per cent and 2.9 per cent. Male unemployment was, therefore, higher than the Scottish average in Westburgh while both male and female unemployment were lower than the national average in Eastburgh (Scottish Office, 1999d).

The majority of interviews were conducted in the young person's home, though alternative premises were available in which to conduct interviews if they preferred. The issues explored in the interviews included: education; employment; use of leisure and lifestyle; drug and alcohol use; offending; relationships with family, friends and partners; neighbourhood, community and society; values and beliefs; victimisation; identity; and aspirations. All interviews were tape-recorded and fully transcribed for analysis, using NUD.IST4[1]. The interview schedules varied slightly according to the 'offending status' of the young person (see system of categorisation below) and according to whether they had left or were still attending school.

An innovative element of the interview involved the use of a laptop computer on which young people completed a variety of questionnaires relating to drug use, risk-taking, self-esteem, attitudes towards offending and gender. The completion of

[1] A software package for qualitative data analysis.

questionnaires on the laptop was interspersed throughout the interview as a means of maintaining young people's interest in the interview process. Young people's views about the use of the laptop in the interview were sought via the subsequent completion of a brief questionnaire. The findings of this survey and copies of the schedules administered on the laptop are presented in the Appendix.

An initial questionnaire survey was undertaken to identify potential interviewees in the youngest age group. Six secondary schools in the two study areas participated in this initial phase of the research. Each distributed letters outlining the purposes of the research and the methods involved to the parents of pupils in S3 and S4. Pupils who did not want to participate in the study or whose parents did not want them to participate were able to indicate this by returning a consent refusal form to the school.

The questionnaire was administered by the researchers in the schools to groups of pupils. Care was taken to stress to young people that their responses would be completely confidential and that no information would be divulged to parents, teachers or any other authority figures such as the police. Since the completion of questionnaires was also a mechanism for recruiting a sample of young people to be interviewed, the researchers emphasised the opportunity the study provided for young people to express their views about an important social issue.

Young people who were willing to be interviewed were asked to provide their name, address and a contact telephone number. Questionnaires were otherwise completed anonymously, though all young people were asked to provide certain demographic information – sex, age, school year and school attended – to facilitate subsequent analysis.

The questionnaire consisted of 23 examples of a range of property offences and offences involving personal violence. The examples for the most part were identical to those employed by Graham and Bowling (1995) in their study of young people and offending in England and Wales, though there were some modifications. For instance, some of Graham and Bowling's examples related to the theft of items above a value of £5. We considered it inappropriate to assign an arbitrary monetary cut-off point for the purpose of defining an incident of theft as an 'offence', preferring to define all such incidents as illegal regardless of the value of the property involved. This clearly has implications for the spectrum of seriousness contained in particular offence categories.

In the questionnaires young people were asked to indicate how often they had committed each type of offence a) ever and b) in the last 12 months. A distinction was made between 'old' and 'recent' offending to enable the classification of young people into one of three groups, with, as far as possible, equal numbers of interviews being completed with young people in each category :

- **resisters:** young people who, on the basis of their questionnaire responses, had never offended;
- **desisters:** young people who had offended in the past but who had not done so in the previous 12 months;
- **persisters:** young people who had committed at least one serious offence or several less serious offences in the previous 12 months.

Interviews were conducted with 52 boys and 52 girls in the youngest age group. Among the boys there were 24 persisters, 14 resisters and 14 desisters. Among the girls there were 20 persisters, 12 desisters and 20 resisters. As discussed in subsequent chapters, the classification of young people sometimes had to be reviewed in the light of further information provided in interviews. For instance, some young people admitted to 'offences' which could not strictly be defined as such, with the behaviour being an omission rather than the deliberate commission of a delinquent or criminal act. The categories are, moreover, permeable and are appropriate only at a given point in time: resisters and desisters may become persisters and persisters may become desisters at different points in their lives.

The electoral registers in Eastburgh and Westburgh were accessed to identify young people aged 18 and 19 years in the study areas. A self-report questionnaire, covering letter and pre-paid reply envelope were sent to all young people who fell within the relevant age range, with this exercise repeated six months later to enable some young people who had not yet reached 18 years of age at the time of the first sweep to be included. This exercise resulted in a number of young people coming forward for interview but did not yield a sufficient sample size, nor did it provide access to young people in the oldest age group, whose recruitment into the study posed the greatest challenge.

Various strategies were adopted to augment the 18-19 year old sample and to identify young people aged 22-23 years. These included placing an advertisement in the local paper in Westburgh and enclosing flyers in the free weekly newspaper that was distributed to all homes in that area. A range of local organisations and businesses were contacted in both study areas. However, each of these strategies produced a disappointing response. A final attempt to recruit a sample by leafleting houses in the two study areas and offering young people a modest financial incentive (£15) to participate in the study proved more fruitful. This technique, combined with a decision to broaden the oldest age group to 22-25 years eventually produced the sample sizes required. In the middle age group (mostly 18 and 19 year olds but also including a small number of 17 and 20 years olds) interviews were conducted with 14 male resisters, 12 desisters and 17 persisters and with 19 female resisters, eight desisters and 18 persisters. In the oldest age group eight male resisters, 17 desisters and 18 persisters were interviewed as were 17 female resisters, 12 desisters and 12 persisters. Although self report questionnaires were used for the purposes of categorising young people in the older age group, these were not completed systematically and, given that they could not, in any case purport to relate to a representative sample of the population, have not been drawn upon in discussion of the findings.

Throughout the three groups of interviewees will be referred to as the youngest, middle and oldest age groups. Young people in the youngest age group will be referred to as boys and girls while those in the older two age groups will be referred to as young men and young women. Where reference is made to the 'older age groups' this refers to the middle and oldest age groups together and where reference is made to the 'younger age groups' this includes the middle and youngest age groups combined. Since self-report offending data were available only from the school based survey and since this survey included some 13 and 16 year olds, we will refer to this sample as the 3rd and 4th year secondary school sample to distinguish it clearly from the smaller sub sample of 14 and 15 year olds who were interviewed.

Interviews were also conducted with a range of professionals who are regularly in contact with young people who offend. This component of the research consisted of interviews with seven police officers (drawn from juvenile liaison and community involvement sections of the relevant forces); seven social workers or senior social workers (including three from criminal justice teams and four from children and families services); and five teachers (principal guidance teachers and assistant head teachers with responsibility for pupils in S3 and S4)[2]. These interviews explored the ways in which different professional groups perceive and respond to offending by young people to enable an assessment to be made of the extent to which professionals' understanding of offending among young people corresponds with the experiences and views of the young people themselves.

The interviews with young people form the primary source of data for discussion of the findings. Chapter Four focuses upon young people's attitudes towards and explanations of their own and other people's offending. Chapter Five explores the relationship between offending and the lifestyles adopted by young people. Chapter Six examines the significance of families, friends, partners and communities in relation to offending and desistance. Chapter Seven discusses young people's involvement with and attitudes towards various aspects of the criminal justice system and their experiences of victimisation. Chapter Eight explores the concepts of resistance, desistance and persistence while the conclusions and their implications for policy and practice are discussed in Chapter Nine. First, however, we begin in Chapter Three by considering the responses of the young people who participated in the school based survey of self-reported offending among 3rd and 4th year secondary pupils.

---

[2] All of the police officers and teachers were male while four of the social workers were female and three were male. Two other teachers were interviewed (one male and one female) but technical problems prevented transcription of the material.

CHAPTER THREE:
SELF-REPORTED OFFENDING BY BOYS AND GIRLS

INTRODUCTION

This chapter discusses the findings from the self-report survey of young people in six secondary schools in the two study areas[3]. The limitations of self-report data have been widely acknowledged, especially in the context of longitudinal studies of offending (e.g. Cernkovich et al., 1985; Loeber and Waller, 1988; Tarling, 1993; Klein, 1994) but they are also recognised as providing a useful approximation of delinquent and criminal behaviour (Rutter and Giller, 1983; Junger-Tas, 1994), especially in comparison with other sources such as official records of arrest or conviction. A further limitation of the data derives from the survey being undertaken primarily as a means of identifying potential interviewees for the main study proper. Since purposive rather than random sampling was employed to ensure that persisters, desisters and resisters were interviewed in sufficient numbers for meaningful analysis, there was no need to ensure the representativeness of the population from which interviewees were drawn. Only six of the nine secondary schools in the two study areas were involved in this stage of the research (4/5 in Westburgh and 2/4 in Eastburgh): the schools which did not participate served areas with differing socio-economic profiles from the other schools which did take part in the research[4]. This prevents any general conclusions from being drawn about the nature of offending by young people in the two towns (and this, as we shall see, impedes the interpretation of observed differences in offending across the two study areas). Nonetheless, despite these caveats, the self-report survey offers important insights into the nature and extent of offending amongst the sample of young people concerned and enables, in particular, gender differences in offending to be explored.

CHARACTERSTICS OF THE SAMPLE

Questionnaires were completed by 1274 young people, 725 of whom were from schools in Westburgh and 549 from schools in Eastburgh. Twenty-eight young people failed to indicate their sex on the questionnaire. Six hundred and ten respondents (49% of those whose sex was known) identified themselves as boys and 636 (51%) as girls. The proportion of boys and girls in each study area was broadly similar, with girls constituting 52 per cent of the sample in Westburgh and 50 per cent in Eastburgh. Six hundred and fifteen young people were in their 3rd year at secondary school and 659 in their 4th year. Administering the questionnaire to pupils by year meant that some young people who fell outside the designated age group were included in the sample, though, as Table 3.1 indicates, 85 per cent of

---

[3] This chapter considers self-report data for 3rd and 4th year pupils only. As already noted, similar data were not available in respect of young people in the two older age groups who were interviewed.

[4] For example, the school which did not participate in Westburgh had a catchment area covering the more affluent parts of the town. The two schools in Eastburgh covered areas which were characterised both by relative affluence and by poor social conditions.

both boys and girls were 14 or 15 years of age. The inclusion of a reasonable number of 13 year olds did, however, enable some age-related patterns of self-reported offending to be explored.

Table 3.1: Age of sample (years)

	No. of boys[5]	Percentage	No. of girls[6]	Percentage
13	86	14%	95	15%
14	256	42%	274	43%
15	261	43%	264	42%
16	4	1%	2	<1%
Total	607	100	635	100

INCIDENCE OF OFFENDING

In the self-report data – which, as will be discussed further, were not necessarily always reliable – 94 per cent of boys and 82 per cent of girls admitted that they had committed one or more offences in the past with 85 per cent of boys and 67 per cent of girls reporting having offended at least once during the previous 12 months. The proportions of boys and girls who fell into different categories with respect to their involvement or otherwise in offending are summarised in Table 3.2. The classification 'minor offender' was applied to young people who had committed one or two minor offences and whose offending was not sufficiently serious to warrant the label of 'desister' or 'persister'. For the purpose of analysis 'minor offenders' were grouped with young people who indicated that they had never offended to produce the category of 'resister' which will be used throughout the remainder of the book.

Table 3.2: Offending status of boys and girls

	Boys (n=607)	Girls (n=631)	Total (n=1264)[7]
Never offended	35 (6%)	111 (18%)	148 (12%)
Minor offender	17 (3%)	43 (7%)	61 (5%)
Desister	62 (10%)	73 (12%)	139 (11%)
Persister	493 (81%)	404 (64%)	916 (72%)

Consistent with previous research which has highlighted higher rates of offending among boys (e.g. Omedei, 1979; Canter, 1982; Elliot et al., 1989; Junger-Tas et al., 1994; Graham and Bowling, 1995) a higher proportion of boys than girls admitted to having offended at all and in the previous 12 months: while a quarter of girls could be classed as resisters, this was true of fewer than one in ten of the boys.

[5] Information missing in three cases.
[6] Information missing in one case.
[7] The number of young people who could be thus classified exceeds the combined total from the other columns since some young people did not indicate their sex on the questionnaire.

Furthermore, as Tables 3.3 and 3.4 demonstrate and consistent with previous research (Tripplett and Myers, 1995), boys were more likely than girls to have committed all but the least common offences for this age group.

Table 3.3: Offences committed by boys and girls

	Boys (n=610)	Girls (n=636)	
PROPERTY OFFENCES			
Damage property/vandalism***	421 *(69%)*	351 *(56%)*	
Shoplifting***	402 *(66%)*	336 *(53%)*	
Set fire to something***	357 *(59%)*	174 *(28%)*	
Handle stolen goods***	318 *(52%)*	248 *(39%)*	
Steal from school*	293 *(48%)*	264 *(42%)*	
Steal something else***	266 *(44%)*	149 *(24%)*	
Break into property***	192 *(32%)*	100 *(16%)*	
Steal from a machine***	162 *(27%)*	87 *(14%)*	
Steal a bicycle***	158 *(26%)*	61 *(10%)*	
Steal from a car***	129 *(21%)*	51 *(8%)*	
Pick someone's pocket***	118 *(19%)*	77 *(12%)*	
Steal from work***	89 *(15%)*	35 *(6%)*	
Steal a moped/motorcycle***	70 *(12%)*	15 *(2%)*	
Snatch a bag*	51 *(8%)*	32 *(5%)*	
Steal a car**	40 *(7%)*	16 *(2%)*	
Use a stole bank/credit card*	36 *(6%)*	18 *(3%)*	
Sell a stolen bank/credit card	23 *(4%)*	19 *(3%)*	
Make a false insurance/benefit claim	22 *(4%)*	11 *(2%)*	
VIOLENT OFFENCES			
Street fight***	413 *(68%)*	309 *(49%)*	
Beat someone up***	396 *(65%)*	221 *(35%)*	
Hurt someone using a weapon***	269 *(45%)*	121 *(19%)*	
Beat up family member***	189 *(31%)*	142 *(23%)*	
Mug someone***	114 *(19%)*	53 *(8%)*	

*p<.05; **p<.01; ***p<.001

Despite the marked differences in the rate of offending between boys and girls – which has been referred to as the gender ratio (see, for example, Triplett and Myers, 1995) – it is also important to note the striking *similarity* in the types of offences committed by them. For both boys and girls, for example, vandalism, fighting in the street and shoplifting were the three most widespread offences (Table 3.3), while stealing or using someone's bank or credit card and making false insurance or benefit claims were among the rarest types of offences for both sexes. The fact that these latter offences were uncommon no doubt reflects the fact that there are relatively few opportunities for young people under 16 years of age to commit offences of this kind.

Table 3.3 and 3.4 also suggest that the offences these young people had committed tended to be of a relatively minor nature, a conclusion which was supported in our subsequent interviews with a smaller sample of boys and girls. In other words, by the age of 15 most boys *and* girls will have committed an offence at least once in their lifetime, though in most cases the offence will have not have been particularly serious.

Table 3.4: Offences committed by boys and girls in the last 12 months

	Boys (n=610)	Girls (n=636)
PROPERTY OFFENCES		
Damage property/vandalism*	**286** *(47%)*	**260** *(41%)*
Shoplifting***	**205** *(34%)*	**151** *(24%)*
Handle stolen goods***	**205** *(34%)*	**154** *(24%)*
Set fire to something***	**203** *(34%)*	**102** *(16%)*
Steal from school	**179** *(30%)*	**170** *(27%)*
Steal something else***	**159** *(26%)*	**87** *(14%)*
Break into property***	**113** *(19%)*	**67** *(11%)*
Steal a bicycle***	**96** *(16%)*	**35** *(6%)*
Steal from a machine***	**88** *(15%)*	**48** *(8%)*
Steal from a car***	**81** *(13%)*	**34** *(5%)*
Pick someone's pocket**	**73** *(12%)*	**47** *(8%)*
Steal from work***	**61** *(10%)*	**21** *(3%)*
Steal a moped/motorcycle***	**40** *(7%)*	**11** *(2%)*
Snatch a bag	**28** *(5%)*	**26** *(4%)*
Steal a car**	**28** *(5%)*	**9** *(1%)*
Use a stole bank/credit card	**18** *(3%)*	**8** *(1%)*
Sell a stolen bank/credit card	**16** *(3%)*	**16** *(2%)*
Make a false insurance/benefit claim	**14** *(2%)*	**7** *(1%)*
VIOLENT OFFENCES		
Street fight***	**317** *(52%)*	**224** *(36%)*
Beat someone up***	**269** *(47%)*	**132** *(21%)*
Hurt someone using a weapon***	**171** *(28%)*	**69** *(11%)*
Beat up family member*	**134** *(22%)*	**108** *(17%)*
Mug someone***	**77** *(13%)*	**32** *(5%)*

*p<.05; **p<.01; ***p<.001

FREQUENCY OF OFFENDING

In addition to comparing the overall rate of offending among boys and girls the data permitted an analysis of the frequency of offending among those young people who admitted having committed different types of offence. It was not, however, possible to compute mean numbers of offences for comparative purposes since some young people, despite having been urged to be as precise as possible in their answers, had quantified their frequency of offending in rather vague terms. Even where a figure was provided rather than a general expression such as 'lots' or 'hundreds', it was not always clear to what extent the figure provided – for example 50, 100, 200 – was likely to be a precise or imprecise estimate of the actual frequency with which a young person engaged in a particular type of behaviour. For this reason, the frequency of offending was analysed by categorising the number of times that a young person admitted to having committed an offence, with the category '11 or more' including all references to a high but unspecified or imprecisely specified number of occasions.

As Tables 3.5 and 3.6 indicate, boys who had offended had committed a higher number of offences than girls, both in total and within the previous 12 months. In other words, girls were both less likely to offend and when they did offend were likely to commit fewer offences than boys.

Table 3.5: Number of offences committed by boys and girls

	Boys (n=574)	Girls (n=521)	Total (n=1095)
1-2	29 *(5%)*	66 *(13%)*	95 *(9%)*
3-5	56 *(10%)*	74 *(14%)*	130 *(12%)*
6-10	49 *(8%)*	94 *(18%)*	143 *(13%)*
11 or more	440 *(77%)*	287 *(55%)*	727 *(66%)*

p<.01

Table 3.6: Number of offences committed by boys and girls in the last twelve months

	Boys (n=503)	Girls (n=426)	Total (n=929)
1-2	83 *(16%)*	104 *(24%)*	187 *(20%)*
3-5	77 *(15%)*	77 *(18%)*	154 *(17%)*
6-10	87 *(17%)*	83 *(20%)*	170 *(18%)*
11 or more	256 *(51%)*	162 *(38%)*	418 *(45%)*

p<.01

Table 3.7 summarises gender differences in the frequency of commission of specific types of offence. The tables from which these data have been derived are presented in the Appendix (as Tables 3.7a-f). Table 3.7 indicates the percentage of young people who had committed an offence only once or twice out of all young people who had committed that type of offence, and presents the relevant data separately for boys and girls.

Table 3.7: Boys and girls committing offences who had done so on fewer than three occasions

	Boys	Girls	Total
Street fight***	145/413 *(35%)*	155/309 *(50%)*	300/722 *(42%)*
Set fire to something**	166/291 *(45%)*	106/256 *(60%)*	272/547 *(50%)*
Hurt someone with a weapon**	148/269 *(55%)*	91/121 *(75%)*	239/390 *(61%)*
Beat someone up***	120/396 *(30%)*	120/221 *(54%)*	240/617 *(39%)*
Stole from school**	112/293 *(38%)*	135/264 *(51%)*	247/557 *(44%)*
Stole something else*	148/266 *(56%)*	99/149 *(66%)*	247/415 *(60%)*

*p<.05; **p<.01; ***p<.001

As we can see, with each of these offences in respect of which gender differences were observed, boys were more likely to have committed the offence on a higher number of occasions. This is particularly true of violent offences where the clearest gender differences emerged. This finding is consistent with North American and British data which suggests that gender differences in offending are most pronounced in relation to offences involving personal force (Rutter et al., 1998) even though a perhaps surprising proportion of girls admitted to having been involved at least once in episodes where they used violence against another person.

AREA DIFFERENCES IN OFFENDING

The proportions of young people in the two study areas who were classified as persisters, desisters and resisters are presented in Table 3.8 and separately for boys and girls in Tables 3.9 and 3.10. Lest readers should be alarmed by the apparently high proportions of persistent young offenders in both areas, it should be recalled that a) many of the 'offences' included in the self-report questionnaire were of a relatively trivial nature and b) 'persistence' in the present context may have involved the commission of a small number of offences of this kind. There was a slightly higher proportion of resisters in Westburgh than in Eastburgh although this difference, statistically significant as it is, is not particularly marked and largely disappears – that is, is no longer statistically significant – when the data for boys and girls are considered separately.

Table 3.8: Offending status of young people in each study area

	Westburgh (n=717)	Eastburgh (n=547)	Total (n=1264)
Resister	103 *(14%)*	106 *(19%)*	209 *(16%)*
Desister	85 *(12%)*	54 *(10%)*	139 *(11%)*
Persister	529 *(74%)*	387 *(71%)*	916 *(73%)*

p<.05

Table 3.9: Offending status of boys in each study area

	Westburgh (n=333)	Eastburgh (n=274)	Total (n=607)
Resister	21 *(6%)*	31 *(11%)*	52 *(9%)*
Desister	35 *(11%)*	27 *(10%)*	62 *(10%)*
Persister	277 *(83%)*	216 *(79%)*	493 *(81%)*

Table 3.10: Offending status of girls in each study area

	Westburgh (n=363)	Eastburgh (n=268)	Total (n=631)
Resister	80 *(22%)*	74 *(28%)*	154 *(24%)*
Desister	47 *(13%)*	26 *(10%)*	74 *(12%)*
Persister	236 *(65%)*	168 *(63%)*	404 *(64%)*

Some other area differences in offending emerged, though these are, for reasons already alluded to earlier in this chapter, difficult to interpret. Although boys and girls in the two study areas were equally likely to have offended at some time, young people in Eastburgh were more likely than those in Westburgh to have stolen a bicycle (21% compared with 16%, p<.05), set fire to something (47% compared with 40%, p<.05), hurt someone with a weapon (37% compared with 28%, p<.01) or mugged someone (17% compared with 12%, p<.05). Young people in Westburgh, on the other hand, were more likely than those in Eastburgh to have handled stolen goods (50% compared with 40%, p<.001) or to have stolen from school (49% compared with 40%, p<.01).

These overall area differences, however, mask underlying area differences in offending among boys and girls. Boys in Westburgh were more likely than those in Eastburgh to have been involved in a street fight (74% compared with 61%, p<.01), to have beaten someone up (69% compared with 61%, p<.05), to have handled stolen goods (57% compared with 47%, p<.05) or to have stolen from school (55% compared with 39%, p<.001). Girls in Westburgh were more likely than those in Eastburgh to admit to having used a stolen bank or credit card (4% compared with 1%, p<.05) while girls in Eastburgh were more likely than those in Westburgh to have hurt someone with a weapon (25% compared with 15%, p<.01).

There were, as Tables 3.11 and 3.12 reveal, no area differences in the numbers of offences committed by young people overall and in the previous 12 months. However, as Table 3.13 indicates, young people in Eastburgh reported more frequent involvement in certain types of offences than did young people in Westburgh: that is, those who committed certain types of offences tended to do so more often.

Table 3.11: Number of offences that had been committed by young people who had offended in each study area

	Westburgh (n=647)	Eastburgh (n=472)	Total (n=1119)
1-2	52 *(8%)*	45 *(10%)*	97 *(9%)*
3-5	83 *(13%)*	49 *(10%)*	132 *(12%)*
6-10	92 *(14%)*	55 *(12%)*	147 *(13%)*
11 or more	420 *(65%)*	323 *(68%)*	743 *(66%)*

Table 3.12: Number of offences that had been committed in the last 12 months by young people who had offended in each study area

	Westburgh (n=541)	Eastburgh (n=408)	Total (n=949)
1-2	118 *(22%)*	73 *(18%)*	191 *(20%)*
3-5	82 *(15%)*	72 *(18%)*	154 *(16%)*
6-10	101 *(19%)*	72 *(18%)*	173 *(18%)*
11 or more	240 *(44%)*	191 *(47%)*	431 *(45%)*

Table 3.13: Young people committing offences in each study area who had done so six or more times

	Westburgh	Eastburgh	Total
Stole a bike**	8/113 *(7%)*	21/114 *(18%)*	29/227 *(13%)*
Damaged property***	130/457 *(28%)*	141/330 *(42%)*	271/787 *(34%)*
Street fight***	117/435 *(27%)*	111/302 *(37%)*	228/737 *(31%)*
Set fire to something***	60/291 *(21%)*	92/256 *(36%)*	152/547 *(28%)*
Hurt someone with a weapon*	30/199 *(16%)*	45/201 *(22%)*	75/400 *(19%)*
Beat someone up**	100/363 *(27%)*	108/268 *(40%)*	208/631 *(33%)*

*p<.05; **p<.01; ***p<.001

Area differences in the frequency of offending varied with gender. Boys in Eastburgh were more likely than boys in Westburgh to report having committed the following offences on six or more occasions: stealing a bicycle (22% compared with 8%, p<.05); breaking into property (34% compared with 27%, p<.05); vandalism (44% compared with 27%, p<.01); fighting in the street (46% compared with 29%, p<.001); setting fire to something (43% compared with 24%, p<.001); hurting somebody with a weapon (26% compared with 15%, p<.05); and beating someone up (52% compared with 31%, p<.001). Girls in Westburgh, on the other hand, were more likely than were girls in Eastburgh to have damaged property on six or more occasions (71% compared with 59%, p<.05).

These findings suggest that a higher proportion of boys in the Westburgh sample committed certain violent offences, such as fighting and beating people up, as well as certain offences involving dishonesty. At face value they might appear consistent with the 'tough' reputation associated with Westburgh – which was, as we shall see, alluded to frequently by different professionals who were interviewed from this area – and may reflect a heightened concern among boys in that town to conform to this stereotype. However, it also seems that boys in Eastburgh who became involved in certain types of behaviour tended to do so more frequently than their counterparts in Westburgh. This applied, moreover, to certain types of offences – fighting and beating people up – which were more prevalent in Westburgh.

Given the apparent relationship between unemployment and crime – albeit one which is varied, mediated and indirect rather than simple and direct (Downes, 1993) – it is worth recalling that Westburgh had higher male unemployment than Eastburgh. We would, however, be reluctant to draw any firm conclusions from these data alone since other factors (such as differences in the socio-economic profiles of the school catchment areas in the two towns) are likely to have had a bearing upon these results. Geographical considerations are also relevant: the sample in Eastburgh was drawn to a large extent from residential areas bordering woods where, as the interview data will subsequently show, the setting of fires was apparently a popular activity among teenage boys.

AGE DIFFERENCES IN OFFENDING

As we have already indicated, the inclusion of 13 year olds in the sample permitted an analysis of patterns of offending with age, albeit that the age range covered was only three years. As Table 3.14 demonstrates, 15 year olds were more likely than 13 or 14 year olds to have committed a range of offences (an exception being stealing from school which was most often reported by 14 year olds). Some of these offences became steadily more common with age (for example, fighting and shoplifting), some apparently became more common between the ages of 13 and 14 (for example, beating someone up) and others apparently became more common between the ages of 14 and 15 (for example, stealing from a car or stealing from work). In some respects an age related increase in offending is not surprising and need not indicate that 15 year olds are more likely to commit certain offences than are 13 or 14 year olds: an alternative explanation could be that the incidence of offending remains relatively constant over time but that 15 year olds are more likely to have offended in certain ways because, simply by virtue of being older, they have had more opportunity to do so.

Examination of self-reported offending in the previous 12 months enables these differing explanations to be explored. There were no significant differences in the proportions of young people of different ages who had shoplifted, handled stolen goods, stolen from school, broken into property, stolen a moped/motorbike, used a stolen bank or credit card or made a false insurance or benefit claim during the previous 12 months. This suggests that these offences did not become increasingly common with age (though the incidence of using stolen cards and making fraudulent claims was very low overall and age-related differences may not have been picked up).

Table 3.14: Offending by age (boys and girls)

	13 years (n=182)	14 years (n=532)	15 years (n=529)
Shoplifting*	97 (53%)	309 (58%)	333 (63%)
Street fight***	82 (45%)	300 (56%)	339 (64%)
Handle stolen goods**	70 (38%)	230 (43%)	266 (50%)
Beat someone up***	69 (38%)	269 (51%)	283 (53%)
Steal from school*	66 (36%)	255 (48%)	237 (45%)
Break into property*	33 (18%)	118 (22%)	144 (27%)
Steal from car**	18 (10%)	66 (12%)	98 (18%)
Steal from work**	12 (7%)	40 (8%)	71 (13%)
Steal a moped or motorbike*	10 (6%)	26 (5%)	49 (9%)
Use a stolen bank or credit card*	3 (2%)	19 (4%)	32 (6%)
Make a false insurance or benefit claim**	2 (1%)	7 (1%)	23 (4%)

* p<.05; **p<.01; ***p<.001

Fighting in public places and stealing from work, on the other hand, were progressively more likely with age to have been committed during the previous 12 months. In the case of stealing from work this might well reflect the fact that the likelihood of young people having part-time jobs such as paper rounds increased with age. As such, the opportunity to commit certain types of offences may increase with age because of age related experiences and responsibilities. Fifteen year olds were more likely than either 13 or 14 year olds to have stolen from a car, suggesting that this type of activity becomes more common at around 15 years of age. Fourteen and 15 year olds were equally likely to have beaten someone up during the previous 12 months and more likely to have done so than 13 year olds. This behaviour, it seems becomes more common at around 14 years of age.

Age-related patterns of offending also varied according to gender. As 3.15 shows, various types of offending were more likely to have been committed by boys the older they were.

Table 3.15: Offending by age (boys)

	13 years (n=86)	14 years (n=255)	15 years (n=261)
Beat someone up**	45 *(52%)*	164 *(65%)*	184 *(71%)*
Street fight***	43 *(50%)*	165 *(65%)*	200 *(77%)*
Handle stolen goods**	37 *(43%)*	121 *(48%)*	156 *(60%)*
Break into property***	20 *(23%)*	65 *(26%)*	104 *(40%)*
Steal from a car***	12 *(14%)*	38 *(15%)*	77 *(30%)*
Snatch a bag**	10 *(12%)*	10 *(4%)*	30 *(12%)*
Steal from work*	8 *(9%)*	28 *(11%)*	50 *(19%)*
Steal a moped/motorcycle**	7 *(8%)*	18 *(7%)*	44 *(15%)*
Make false insurance/benefit claim**	1 *(1%)*	4 *(2%)*	16 *(6%)*
Sell a stolen bank/credit card*	-	6 *(2%)*	16 *(6%)*

* p<.05; **p<.01; ***p<.001

The interesting feature of these data is that, apart from fighting or beating someone up, both of which are steadily more common with increasing age and snatching a bag, which was least likely to have been reported by 14 year olds, the incidence of most other types of offences appeared not to differ much between 13 and 14 year olds, but to differ significantly between the younger boys and the 15 year olds.

It also appeared that, with the exception of beating someone up – which boys of different ages were equally likely to have admitted to doing in the previous 12 months – all of these offences were more likely to have been committed by 15 year old boys than by younger boys within the last year. Furthermore, apart from fighting in public places, which seemed to become steadily more common with age, the other offences in Table 3.15 were equally likely to have been committed by 13 and 14 year olds. In other words, it would appear that certain types of offences become more common among boys at around 14-15 years of age.

There was less evidence of an age-related pattern of offending among girls. The only types of offences which were more often admitted by girls of particular ages were hurting someone with a weapon and stealing from school. The former was most often reported by 14 year olds (23%), was relatively common among 13 year olds (20%) and was least often reported by the 15 year olds (15%). Stealing from school was more likely to be reported by 14 year olds (48%) than by 13 year olds (35%) or by 15 year olds (38%). Such a finding is counterintuitive since the incidence of offending – given that it is a cumulative measure – cannot decrease with age. Instead it would seem that the 14 year old girls in this sample were unusually delinquent or that the 15 year olds were uncharacteristically well behaved.

The overall rates of offending by boys and girls and their rates of offending in the previous 12 months are summarised in Table 3.16. Similar proportions of 14 and 15 year old boys and girls admitted having committed at least one offence listed in the questionnaire, this being, in both cases, slightly higher than the reported incidence of offending by 13 year olds. When offending during the past 12 months is considered, however, a slightly different pattern of findings emerges for boys and for girls. Boys were slightly – though not significantly – more likely to have offended in the previous year the older they were. Fourteen year old girls, on the other hand, were most likely to have offended in the previous 12 months while 15 year olds were least likely to have done so.

Table 3.16: Offending by age and gender

	13 years	14 years	15 years
Ever offended			
Boys	**77/86** (90%)	**242/255**[8] (95%)	**249/261** (95%)
Girls	**74/94**[9] (79%)	**226/271**[10] (83%)	**218/264** (83%)
Offended in last 12 months			
Boys	**69/86** (80%)	**209/255** (82%)	**221/259** (85%)
Girls	**63/94** (67%)	**195/271** (72%)	**166/263** (63%)

It would appear that girls are most likely to offend at around 14 years and that their involvement in offending begins to decline thereafter, though this conclusion is highly tentative, especially in view of the earlier discussion about the typicality of girls of different ages in the sample.

Boys' offending, on the other hand, appears not to increase much with age: 15 year olds are not much more likely than younger boys to have offended in the last 12 months. Yet we have already seen that 15 year old boys are more likely than younger boys to report having committed a range of offences. It would therefore seem that the likelihood of a boy offending at all does not differ much between 13 and 15 years of age but that the repertoire of offences in which boys engage increases over that period of time.

SUMMARY

The present chapter has shown that most boys and girls will have offended by the time they reach 14-15 years of age but that the types of offences committed will not, in the main, have been of an especially serious nature. Age differences and area differences in offending were observed though these are difficult to interpret. The most striking findings concerned the relationship between gender and offending. Girls were less likely than boys to have committed all but the least common offences among this age group and girls who did engage in particular types of offence behaviour tended to do so less frequently than boys. Any theoretical explanations of gender differences in offending must, however, also

[8] Information missing in one case.
[9] Information missing in one case.
[10] Information missing in three cases.

be capable of accounting for the striking similarity in the types of offences committed by boys and girls (McIvor, forthcoming).

Overall 22 per cent of young people (284/1274) who participated in the self-report survey indicated that they would be willing to be interviewed. The proportions of boys (23%) and girls (22%) who agreed to be interviewed were broadly similar as were the proportions of resisters (22%), desisters (26%) and persisters (22%). It is to the interview data – which form the core of the ensuing chapters – that we now turn.

CHAPTER FOUR: OFFENDING – ATTITUDES AND EXPLANATIONS

INTRODUCTION

The primary focus of the interviews conducted with young people was their involvement or otherwise in offending and the explanations they invoked to account for their own behaviour and for the behaviour of other young people their age. This chapter discusses young people's attitudes towards offending and the reasons why they think others offend. In considering the explanations advanced by the young people we will also draw, where relevant, upon the views expressed by various professionals – teachers, police and social workers – to explore the correspondence between young people's views and the views of these different groups who come into regular contact on a professional basis with young people who offend.

ATTITUDES TOWARDS OFFENDING

One of the exercises undertaken on the laptop computers by young people who were interviewed sought to explore their views about the seriousness of various offences against property or against the person. The examples employed were identical to those included in the self-report questionnaire. Instead of indicating how often they had committed each type of offence, young people were asked to indicate, on a four-point scale, how serious they considered each type of offence to be: very serious, quite serious, not very serious or not serious at all. Since relatively few offences were considered not to be serious the latter two categories have been combined in Table 4.1.

Turning first to the data for the youngest age group of interviewees, there were no obvious gender differences in perceptions of offence seriousness, though girls less often than boys thought that beating another person up was very serious, with this view having been held by 50 per cent of the boys and only 29 per cent of girls. In general, however, there was a tendency for young people to ascribe greater seriousness to those offences in which they reported being rarely involved and less seriousness to those which were reportedly most common among the 14-15 year age group. The figures in parentheses in Table 4.1 indicate the rank order of each offence according to the proportions of young people who, in the self-report survey of 3rd and 4th year pupils, indicated that they had engaged in that behaviour. The most commonly reported offence – vandalism – has been assigned a ranking of one and the least commonly reported one – making a false insurance or benefit claim – has been assigned a ranking of 23. Three of the four least commonly reported offences were among the four offences most often considered very serious by young people. Conversely, the three most commonly reported offences among this age group were among the five offences least often considered very serious by the interviewees. What is less clear from these data, however, is the direction of the observed relationship. That is, do young people desist from becoming involved in certain types of offences precisely because they consider them to be so serious, or do they attempt to minimise their own behaviour by describing the types of offences they most commonly engage in as less serious than others? Matseuda (1989) has suggested that the impact of conventional moral beliefs upon offending is extremely small in comparison with the effects of delinquency upon belief, suggesting that involvement in minor offending may influence attitudes towards seriousness more than attitudes towards seriousness influence offending.

Table 4.1: Perceived seriousness of offences - youngest age group

	Very serious	Quite serious	Not serious
Steal a car (20)	96 (93%)	7 (7%)	-
Sell a stolen bank/credit card (22)	96 (93%)	5 (5%)	2 (2%)
Hurt someone using a weapon (8)	92 (89%)	10 (15%)	1 (1%)
Use a stolen bank/credit card (21)	91 (88%)	9 (9%)	3 (3%)
Mug someone (16)	86 (84%)	15 (15%)	2 (2%)
Handle stolen goods (6)	86 (84%)	11 (11%)	6 (6%)
Steal a moped/motorcycle (18)	77 (75%)	26 (25%)	-
Snatch a bag (19)	74 (72%)	26 (25%)	3 (3%)
Break into property (10)	69 (68%)	31 (30%)	2 (2%)
Beat up a family member (11)	64 (62%)	24 (23%)	15 (15%)
Set fire to something (5)	63 (61%)	37 (36%)	3 (3%)
Make a false insurance/ benefit claim (23)	61 (60%)	30 (29%)	11 (11%)
Steal from a car (14)	56 (55%)	42 (42%)	3 (3%)
Steal something else (9)	50 (49%)	45 (44%)	7 (7%)
Pick someone's pocket (15)	49 (48%)	46 (45%)	7 (7%)
Steal from work (17)	41 (40%)	54 (52%)	8 (8%)
Beat someone up (4)	41 (40%)	42 (41%)	20 (19%)
Steal a bicycle (13)	39 (38%)	54 (53%)	9 (9%)
Shoplifting (3)	30 (29%)	56 (54%)	17 (16%)
Street fight (2)	25 (24%)	53 (51%)	25 (24%)
Damage property/vandalism (1)	25 (24%)	50 (49%)	27 (27%)
Steal from school (7)	24 (23%)	37 (36%)	42 (41%)
Steal from a machine (12)	19 (19%)	54 (53%)	29 (28%)

Other observations may be made about the data presented in Table 4.1. For instance, offence seriousness appears to have been determined by young people with some regard to the value of goods appropriated in property offences. Stealing a bicycle, therefore, was considered less serious than stealing a motorbike which, in turn, was perceived as less serious than stealing a car. Perceptions of offence seriousness also appear to have been influenced in some respects by the existence or otherwise of identifiable victims. Although the least common offence among this age group – making a false insurance or benefit claim – was thought to be very serious by only 60 per cent of the sample, stealing from a machine was least often considered by young people to be a very serious offence.

The percentages of young people across the three age groups of interviewees who considered different types of offences to be very serious are shown in Table 4.2., from which several observations can be made. First, similar proportions of young people in each age group considered various offences involving actual or threatened personal violence to be serious (hurting someone with a weapon, mugging someone, snatching a bag and, beating someone up), suggesting that attitudes towards these types of offences are relatively invariant with age. Secondly, there appeared to be an increasing tolerance with age for property crimes of an essentially utilitarian nature (stealing a car, selling or using a stolen bank or credit card, handling stolen goods, making a false insurance or benefit claim, stealing from a car, stealing a moped or motorcycle, breaking into private or commercial property, stealing from work or school and stealing a bicycle) except where these involved a readily identifiable victim (mugging someone, snatching a bag or picking someone's pocket). Thirdly, there appeared to be a lower level of tolerance amongst the oldest age group for offences – such as street fights or vandalism – which tend to be associated with younger people.

Table 4.2: Young people in each age group who considered particular offences to be very serious

	Youngest (n=103)	Middle (n=88)	Oldest (n=77)
PROPERTY OFFENCES			
Steal a car	**96** *(93%)*	**62** *(70%)*	**42** *(55%)*
Sell a stolen bank/credit card	**96** *(93%)*	**61** *(69%)*	**38** *(49%)*
Use a stolen bank/credit card	**91** *(88%)*	**60** *(68%)*	**35** *(46%)*
Handle stolen goods	**86** *(84%)*	**24** *(27%)*	**9** *(12%)*
Steal a moped/motorcycle	**77** *(75%)*	**45** *(51%)*	**31** *(40%)*
Snatch a bag	**74** *(72%)*	**69** *(78%)*	**63** *(82%)*
Break into property	**69** *(68%)*	**49** *(56%)*	**42** *(55%)*
Set fire to something	**63** *(61%)*	**45** *(51%)*	**48** *(62%)*
Make a false insurance/benefit claim	**61** *(60%)*	**34** *(39%)*	**18** *(23%)*
Steal from a car	**56** *(55%)*	**37** *(42%)*	**24** *(31%)*
Steal something else	**50** *(49%)*	**37** *(42%)*	**20** *(26%)*
Pick someone's pocket	**49** *(48%)*	**47** *(53%)*	**37** *(48%)*
Steal from work	**41** *(40%)*	**26** *(30%)*	**19** *(25%)*
Steal a bicycle	**39** *(38%)*	**24** *(26%)*	**14** *(18%)*
Shoplifting	**30** *(29%)*	**22** *(25%)*	**7** *(9%)*
Damage property/vandalism	**25** *(24%)*	**20** *(23%)*	**25** *(32%)*
Steal from school	**24** *(23%)*	**9** *(10%)*	**10** *(13%)*
Steal from a machine	**19** *(19%)*	**18** *(20%)*	**11** *(14%)*
VIOLENT OFFENCES Hurt someone using a weapon	**92** *(89%)*	**74** *(84%)*	**69** *(90%)*
Mug someone	**86** (84%)	**66** *(75%)*	**64** *(83%)*
Beat up a family member	**64** *(62%)*	**49** *(56%)*	**49** *(64%)*
Beat someone up	**41** *(40%)*	**39** *(44%)*	**33** *(43%)*
Street fight	**25** *(24%)*	**23** *(26%)*	**29** *(38%)*

Attitudes towards offending also differed among young people categorised as persisters, desisters and resisters. As Table 4.3 shows, persisters tended to take a less serious view of certain types of offending than did desisters or resisters, with desisters occupying a position somewhere between resisters and persisters, having attitudes sometimes more similar to the former and sometimes more similar to the latter. Tables 4.3a-c in the Appendix demonstrate that this relationship between offender category and perceptions of offence seriousness was evident in each age group.

Table 4.3: Young people in each offender category who considered particular offences to be very serious – all age groups

	Register (n=93)	Desister (n=73)	Persister (n=102)
PROPERTY OFFENCES			
Steal a car	79 *(85%)*	57 *(78%)*	64 *(63%)*
Sell a stolen bank/credit card	81 *(87%)*	54 *(74%)*	60 *(59%)*
Use a stolen bank/credit card	75 *(81%)*	50 *(68%)*	61 *(60%)*
Handle stolen goods	56 *(60%)*	29 *(40%)*	34 *(33%)*
Steal a moped/motorcycle	58 *(62%)*	39 *(53%)*	56 *(55%)*
Snatch a bag	73 *(78%)*	56 *(77%)*	77 *(75%)*
Break into property	70 *(75%)*	43 *(59%)*	47 *(46%)*
Set fire to something	65 *(70%)*	43 *(59%)*	48 *(47%)*
Make a false insurance/benefit claim	48 *(52%)*	31 *(42%)*	34 *(33%)*
Steal from a car	53 *(57%)*	34 *(47%)*	30 *(29%)*
Steal something else	54 *(58%)*	27 *(37%)*	26 *(25%)*
Pick someone's pocket	57 *(61%)*	35 *(48%)*	41 *(40%)*
Steal from work	39 *(42%)*	19 *(26%)*	27 *(26%)*
Steal a bicycle	34 *(37%)*	15 *(21%)*	22 *(22%)*
Shoplifting	37 *(40%)*	8 *(11%)*	14 *(14%)*
Damage property/vandalism	27 *(29%)*	20 *(27%)*	18 *(18%)*
Steal from school	22 *(24%)*	11 *(15%)*	10 *(10%)*
Steal from a machine	25 *(27%)*	11 *(15%)*	12 *(12%)*
VIOLENT OFFENCES Hurt someone using a weapon	91 *(98%)*	67 *(92%)*	77 *(75%)*
Mug someone	86 (92%)	61 *(84%)*	77 *(75%)*
Beat up a family member	65 *(70%)*	46 *(63%)*	51 *(50%)*
Beat someone up	67 *(72%)*	27 *(37%)*	19 *(19%)*
Street fight	40 (43%)	21 *(29%)*	16 *(16%)*

There were no gender differences overall in perceptions of offence seriousness amongst the youngest age group. However, the types of offences in respect of which persisters' attitudes differed from those of desisters and resisters varied somewhat between boys and girls. Male persisters considered the following offences less serious than did other boys: beating someone up; setting fire to something; shoplifting; and stealing from a public or commercial building. Female persisters, on the other hand differed from other girls in terms of the lesser seriousness they attributed to the following offences: making a false insurance or benefit claim; damaging property; being involved in a street fight; stealing from a shop; and handling stolen goods.

Gender differences in perceptions of offence seriousness were, however, observed in the older age groups. For instance, young women in the middle age group were less likely than young men to consider vandalism (15% compared with 31%) or handling stolen goods (22% compared with 33%) to be very serious. Gender differences were more marked in the oldest age group, with young women tending to take a more serious view of offences than young men. In this age group young women were more likely than young men to consider the following offences to be very serious: beating someone up (59% compared with 26%); making a false insurance or benefit claim (28% compared with 18%); stealing from work (41% compared with 8%); hurting someone with a weapon (100% compared with 79%) and pickpocketing (61% compared with 40%). These gender differences – in particular those which point to young men's greater apparent tolerance for certain offences – may partly reflect the higher proportions of female resisters and male persisters in the oldest age group. However, the increasing gender difference in attitudes towards certain types of offences with age – especially the increasing tolerance of violent offences among young men – may also partly reflect the growing importance of gender socialisation over time, with young men increasingly identifying with a range of attributes traditionally associated with masculinity.

The data from the two older age groups were combined for the purpose of exploring gender differences in attitudes towards offending among persisters, resisters and desisters. Male persisters were less likely than male resisters (and usually also male desisters) to regard the following offences as very serious: beating someone up; making a false insurance or benefit claim; vandalism; street fighting; pickpocketing; selling a bank or credit card; stealing from a car; breaking into a private or commercial property; stealing from a machine; stealing something else; stealing from school; stealing from a shop; stealing from work and handling stolen goods. Female persisters, on the other hand, were more likely than female resisters (and, again, usually desisters) to be apparently more tolerant in their views towards the following offences: beating someone up; vandalism; selling a stolen bank or credit card; stealing from a car; stealing from a machine; stealing something else; stealing from school; stealing from a shop; handling stolen goods; stealing a car; mugging someone; or threatening someone with a weapon.

To an extent, therefore, the attitudes of female persisters were more similar to those of male persisters than they were to other young women of a similar age. Furthermore, female persisters differed from other young women in terms of their attitudes towards certain types of violent offences – mugging someone or hurting someone with a weapon – in respect of which there were less marked differences between male persisters and other categories of young men. We would speculate that these differences may reflect the greater identification of female persisters with more traditionally masculine attributes or values, which may be deemed necessary for survival in a culture of drug abuse, poverty and crime. This hypothesis would suggest that the association between attitudes towards offending and actual involvement in behaviour of this type may be partly in the direction of attitudes and values developing as a means of protecting individuals from the psychological consequences of engaging in socially unacceptable behaviour but that, equally, offending may be encouraged – or at least not discouraged – by broader identification with attitudes and values which may be supportive of crime.

SELF-REPORTED OFFENDING

Self-report data from the school-based survey were available for the 104 boys and girls in the youngest age group who were interviewed. The numbers admitting to having committed the various offences included in the self-report questionnaires are summarised in Table 4.4. Gender differences were apparent in relation to fewer offences than among the self-report sample as a whole, presumably because the smaller sample size made it less likely that differences would achieve statistical significance. Nonetheless, boys were still found to have been significantly more likely than girls to have beaten someone up, to have set fire to something or to have stolen a bicycle. However the number of young people who reported having offended on at least one occasion also differed between boys and girls – only 12 of the boys interviewed were classified as resisters compared with 20 of the girls – and this may have accounted for the differences observed. When the self-report data were examined for persisters alone no significant differences were found. The combination of purposive sampling and smaller numbers apparently has had the effect of masking the gender ratio which has been reported in Chapter Three and in other studies of offending among boys and girls (e.g. Steffensmeier and Allan, 1996 who also argue that the gender ratio may, in fact be smaller than was previously believed).

Table 4.4: Self-reported offending by boys and girls who were interviewed

	Boys (n=52)	Girls (n=52)	Total (n=104)
Shoplifting	34	28	62
Damage property/vandalism	32	23	55
Street fight	29	22	51
Steal from school	26	20	46
Beat someone up*	27	17	44
Set fire to something*	27	15	42
Handle stolen goods	22	17	39
Steal something else	20	12	32
Hurt someone using a weapon	15	8	23
Beat up family member	14	9	23
Steal a bicycle**	14	3	17
Steal from a machine	9	5	14
Break into property	8	5	13
Steal from a car	6	6	12
Pick someone's pocket	5	6	11
Mug someone	6	3	9
Steal a moped/motorcycle	4	1	5
Snatch a bag	3	1	4
Make a false insurance/benefit claim	2	1	3
Sell a stolen bank/credit card	-	3	3
Steal from work	-	3	3
Use a stole bank/credit card	1	2	2
Steal a car	-	1	1

* p<.05; **p<.01

FRAMING OF THEIR OWN OFFENDING

Through interviews with young people it became apparent that the accuracy and integrity of the information collected on the self-report questionnaire was largely intact, with a few exceptions. The wording of the self-report questionnaire did leave some degree of ambiguity. Consequently a few respondents had self reported themselves as offending when in fact the actual gravity of the act did not appear to warrant 'offence' status. This is probably best illustrated in reference to the self-report question about stealing a bicycle, which elicited the following responses: 'yeah I took it [the bicycle] and I gave it back, but they were still annoyed' (male desister, youngest age group). However, the 'borrowing' of a bicycle was not the only case in which the severity of the incident did not warrant 'offence' status.

In response to being asked about an incident of self reported stealing a male persister explained: 'I went into the kitchen and I wanted some orange juice and my mum told me I wasn't allowed some and I went in and took some anyway ... it's not serious because I've never stolen anything out of shops' (male persister, youngest age group). The advantage of the current study was that the researchers were able to explore persisters' and desisters' narrative accounts alongside their self reported offending so that these discrepancies could emerge. The remainder of the interview could then focus on the offending that persisters and desisters themselves acknowledged.

While most interviewees were forthcoming and frank *on the whole* in interview, many persisters and desisters offered a range of justifications and excuses for their actions. Maruna et al. (1997) identified the adoption of such 'narrative strategies' as follows: reports, concessions, excuses, justifications and refusals. A 'report' is 'an admission ... without admitting the negative aspects or offering any excuse/justification'. A 'concession' is 'any admission of guilt or offending behaviour in which the speaker takes full or partial responsibility for his or her behaviour and acknowledges it as a moral and social wrong' (Maruna et al., 1997). A minority of persisters and desisters in the current study made a 'report' or a 'concession' in respect of *all* their self-reported offending, unequivocally accepting their own self-report offending as this desister did:

Int:	And how would you describe your offending, if someone were to ask you, how would you describe -
Woman:	Well I think it's terrible. I'm disgusted by it.
Int:	Right.
Woman:	I'm disgusted by my criminal record ... I see everything I've done as offending (female persister, oldest age group).

However, interviewees' accounts more frequently contained Maruna et al.'s strategies: excuses, justifications and refusals. Each of these will be considered in turn, in relation to persisters' and desisters' descriptions of their offending.

Excuses

An excuse is a statement in which the speaker acknowledges some failure or offence, but pleads for acceptance by others on account of extenuating circumstances. Therefore, the person may recognise the behaviour as negative, but denies ultimate responsibility for the event (Maruna et al., 1997).

One of the commonest excuses, offered almost invariably by the older age groups rather than the younger age group, was that of drugs and alcohol (discussed in detail in Chapter Five). A typical example was: 'got to steal to get money if you have a drug habit. You got to feed your drug habit' and 'it was the drink made me do it' (male persisters, middle age group).

Another commonly used excuse was that of provocation, usually in the context of fighting, for example:

I think that was maybe – I'm not saying that I never done it or anything like that but I think it was more the violence and things that were getting shown towards me so I had to act that way back ... I've had to like learn to do these things, not because I just went out and done it. I would say it was more through circumstance than anything else (female desister, oldest age group).

A further excuse offered was loyalty to other people. Some spoke of 'helping' their friend: 'she was stealing and she sort of got a fair idea that somebody had seen her so she telt me to hold the bag for her ... I just wanted to so that she wouldn't get into trouble' (female desister, youngest age group). Loyalty was most often cited in relation to physical aggression. For example, a persister who had hit someone over the head with a bottle explained why:

I'm not ashamed of it either but – because most of the things that have happened are stupid or have been through – like when my pal got stabbed I thought that was just helping oot. I wasnae just going to stand and watch him getting stabbed with a bottle so I just went for it (male persister, middle age group).

Finally, persisters and desisters drew on what Maruna et al. (1997) refer to as 'situational factors' which are perceived to explain offending behaviour. One persister illustrates the point:

I used to do stupid things yeah, like the weekends when I was in town drinking – fight and get stopped by the police and done for breach of the peace and all that ... it's just because I stayed with my mum and I went away when I was about seven and I came back and moved to Westburgh ... I wish I'd never come up (female persister, middle age group).

Justifications

Although the word justification is often linked to excuses the two are actually opposites ... with an excuse, a person admits a failing, but denies responsibility. With a justification, the person admits responsibility, but rejects the idea that the behaviour is negative. To justify something is to make the behaviour legitimate (Maruna et al., 1997).

A common form of justification offered in interviews was to acknowledge that the incident took place, but to assert that it was a permissible act – either because no-one was injured by it or else because 'everyone does it'. As one desister explained: 'I wouldnae say I'd committed that much crime ... I wasnae doing anything that nobody else wasnae doing. I was just so damn unlucky that I didnae swallow mine [drugs] afore the police got here' (male desister, oldest age group). The most extreme illustration of justification in the form of claiming that no-one was hurt was provided by a persister who graphically described how his stabbing a relative had led to his death. Later in the interview he claimed: 'Even when I was offending I wouldn't say I've done anything bad to hurt anybody. As I say, I've got certain morals. There's things you do and things you don't do' (male persister, oldest age group).

Persisters and desisters frequently cited others who had committed worse crimes than they had as a justification for their behaviour, while others used their own actions as a yardstick by which to measure another more serious action, as the following excerpt from an interview illustrates:

Girl: We were – I think it was ice skating we were at and a lassie says 'hello' to me and I says to my mate 'you'll need to haud me back because I'm going to bounce her'. She's like that 'but she only says "hello" to you'. And I was like that 'I know but I don't like the look of her' and *I started flinging everything about and I put one of the ice skates through the window.*

Int: How old were you when you started committing offences, when you first sort of broke the law?

Girl: 11.

Int: And what happened?

Girl: Somebody ripped us there.

Int: Ripped you?

Girl: Uhu, but it was like with a credit card or something but it wasn't really sore.

Int: Down your cheek?

Girl: Uhu and I got them back except it -

Int: Except what?

Girl: It wasn't a credit card I used. It was a knife.

Int: Oh God, and where did you cut them?

Girl: On the face, right down there. So I got put into a home for about seven months.

Int: Right, and that was when you were 11, okay?

Girl: *And that's the only really bad thing I've ever done* (emphasis added, female persister, youngest age group).

This girl told the interviewer about two incidents. The first was not minor, being, by her own admission, an unprovoked attack on another girl resulting in ice skates going through the window at the ice rink. The second incident was of the girl cutting someone's cheek with a knife (albeit in response to a prior attack). She claims that the latter is 'the only bad thing I've ever done', which effectively negates the incident at the ice rink.

Refusals

In a refusal, a person denies either committing any offences at all or else evades questions regarding offending. This can involve outright refusals to describe or account for offending behaviour or else more subtle evasion tactics (Maruna et al., 1997).

Refusal was evident in some interviews, sometimes in the form of vagueness about the offending, for example 'I wouldn't say it was very heavy – daft stupid things' (male persister, middle age group). A desister who had been charged with breach of the peace explained it as 'just beer and drinking. When I was younger we used to like run about kicking bins and that over, just stupid behaviour' (male desister, middle age group). Offending behaviour was sometimes denied. For example, a young person begins an account of their self-reported offence by stating 'Oh, a youth club I was at I took a badminton racket. .. I got a life ban for that', but goes on to conclude 'it wasn't me that done anything' (male persister, youngest age group).

GENERAL VIEWS ABOUT OFFENDING

In response to a question about their general views of offending, most resisters and desisters emphasised two aspects of offending: the immorality and the futility of it. In respect of the first of these they did not elaborate, stating that it was wrong or that people should not offend. In respect of the futility of offending, it was said to be 'pointless', 'a waste of time', 'sad', 'stupid', 'silly', 'daft', 'petty' 'immature', 'a shame', 'not worth it' and 'unnecessary'. Victims of offending were also mentioned, particularly older women (victimisation is further discussed in Chapter Eight). Many expressed the view that if the offenders were caught it was their own fault; punishment was regarded as a legitimate response to offending.

In contrast to resisters and desisters, few persisters stated that offending was wrong *unconditionally* (although only a minority expressed total indifference or resignation). They suggested that it was contingent on a variety of factors, including the type or seriousness of the offence or the circumstances of the offender. The following excerpt illustrates the type of mitigating circumstances identified:

Woman: I don't suppose it can be justified, but I thought a lot of it could be explained – why people do offend and the reason behind it.

Int: Right, what sort of explanation would you be talking about?

Woman: Drugs, drink, madness, poverty (female persister, oldest age group).

When asked about their general view of offending, male interviewees frequently noted the negative consequences of offending for the offender, including detection, punishment, diminished life chances and feelings of guilt. In contrast, only two female interviewees mentioned the consequences for the offender.

EXPLANATIONS FOR OFFENDING

In Table 4.5 explanations offered by the young people for others' offending are presented. More resisters and desisters thought that young people's upbringing or their family were the reason for others' offending, while more persisters gave drug use as a reason. Further analysis by age revealed that drug use was also cited more by the older age groups than the youngest age group. The older persisters in particular, many of whom were drug users themselves, stressed the very strong link between others' offending and drug use, for example:

Int: So what about other people who maybe aren't addicts and they offend? Why do you think they offend?

Man: I don't know. I don't know one person that offends that isnae an addict to tell you the truth, do you? Honest to god I don't know one person that offends that's no a drug addict in this toon (male persister, oldest age group).

Table 4.5: Why young people think others offend

	Resisters (n=86)	Desisters (n=66)	Persisters (n=81)	Total (n=233)
Upbringing/family	35	24	19	78
Drug use	14	11	29	54
Friends/peer pressure	25	12	15	52
Shortage of money	14	18	15	47
For notoriety/attention	19	11	10	40
Boredom/nothing to do	17	9	9	35
Fun/thrill/buzz	8	8	12	28
Area live in	7	6	7	20
Alcohol use	2	6	5	13
Their nature/personality	5	2	2	9
Do not care/nothing to lose	5	2	2	9
Family has offended	1	2	4	7
Think they will get away with it	1	1	5	7
Mental health problems	2	4	1	7
Don't know	1	1	4	6
Not scared	-	1	4	5
To get it out of their system	4	-	-	4
Stupidity	1	1	2	4
No future	2	1	-	3
School problems	3	-	-	3
To get own back	2	1	-	3
For the sake of it	1	1	-	2
Want to	1	-	1	2
Bullied into it	-	2	-	
Class	1	-	1	2
Loneliness	2	-	-	2
Total number of responses	173	124	147	444*

*more than one response could be given by each respondent; factors mentioned less than twice are not included in the table.

ACCEPTABLE OFFENDING

Responses to the question as to whether or not any offending is acceptable are presented in Table 4.6a and 4.6b. More of those in the youngest age group (60%) than the older age groups (45% and 30%) were of the view that *no* offending (rather than *some* offending) was acceptable. More resisters (64%) than desisters (41%) and persisters (35%) thought that no offending was acceptable. Moreover, even some of the persisters who said that no offending was acceptable added caveats, for example: 'no, but people do anyway, so' and 'I suppose not really, not acceptable, but people do it; it still happens'.

Table 4.6a Whether offending is acceptable by age

	No offending is acceptable (n=123)	Some offending is acceptable (n=143)	Total (n=266)
Youngest age group	59 *(60%)*	39 *(40%)*	98 *(100%)*
Middle age group	39 *(45%)*	47 *(55%)*	86 *(100%)*
Oldest age group	25 *(30%)*	57 *(70%)*	82 *(100%)*

Table 4.6b Whether offending is acceptable by offence category

	No offending is acceptable (n=123)	Some offending is acceptable (n=143)	Total (n=266)
Resisters	56 *(64%)*	32 *(36%)*	88 *(100%)*
Desisters	30 *(41%)*	43 *(59%)*	73 *(100%)*
Persisters	37 *(35%)*	68 *(65%)*	105 *(100%)*

Table 4.7 indicates the offences that respondents considered to be acceptable[11]. Shoplifting, fighting and drug related offences were most often cited, apart from those offences which were said to be dependant on the circumstances. Further analysis revealed that there were differences across the age groups in respect of the types of acceptable offending identified. First, while drug related offences were considered to be acceptable by only one person in the youngest age group, 23 respondents in the older age groups found these to be acceptable. Secondly, more of those in the younger than older age groups were of the opinion that fighting was acceptable. Thirdly, more young people in the older age groups indicated that some offending was acceptable and many thought that this was dependant on the circumstances; for example, if people were experiencing poverty, theft was considered to be acceptable.

---

[11] Four respondents did not specify the type of offending that they considered to be acceptable.

Table 4.7: Offending identified as acceptable

	Resisters (n=31)	Desisters (n=43)	Persisters (n=65)	Total (n=139)
Dependant on circumstances	21	15	10	46
Shoplifting	6	6	21	33
Fighting[12]	8	7	14	29
Drug related	3	12	9	24
Vandalism/graffiti	-	5	8	13
Theft other than from shops	-	2	9	11
Underage drinking	-	-	4	4
Breach of the peace	-	-	4	4
Swearing at people	1	1	1	3
Buying stolen goods	-	-	2	2
Underage drinking	2	-	-	2
Road traffic offences	1	-	1	2
Rail fare avoidance	-	-	1	1
Breaking a curfew	-	-	1	1
Trespassing on private property	-	-	1	1
Fraud	-	-	1	1
Total number of responses	42	48	87	177*

*more than one response could be given by each respondent

Reasons were offered for why certain offences were deemed acceptable. First, many people offend: 'stealing. I wouldnae do it but a lot of people do it and it's no really a big thing' (female persister, youngest age group). Secondly, not getting caught or the police not being aware that an offence has been committed were also given as explanations for offending being acceptable. Thirdly, some crimes (such as shoplifting) were thought to be intrinsically 'less serious' than others and therefore acceptable. Fourthly, certain offences were rendered acceptable alongside clearly unacceptable crimes. For example, a desister stated that breaking into houses and stealing cars was unacceptable in comparison with stealing a '10 pence bag of crisps' or 'accidentally breaking a fence'. Fifthly, the view was expressed that individual problems and propensities provide mitigating factors in terms of the acceptability of offending, as was apparent in a male desister's comment that 'it might be acceptable in some cases because I've heard of people that are addicted to it and maybe they can't get help for it' and a male resister's view that 'if somebody is homeless, they've got to like steal something to survive'. Finally, self defence or people 'deserving' what happened to them was offered as an explanation , as one girl explained:

---

[12] Particularly if in self defence or as a result of provocation.

if it was like – just say somebody battered me for nothing and my cousin wanted to batter them, it's not really her fault because you shouldn't let people off with it, if you know what I mean. It's bad most of the time, but sometimes it's not really bad because some people deserve what they've got coming to them (female desister, youngest age group).

POLICE OFFICERS' PERSPECTIVES ON OFFENDING

The nature of offending by young people

The police officers who were interviewed found it difficult, for various reasons including the distinction between actual and detected offending, to estimate the prevalence of offending among young people. For example, one officer explained:

I would say that ...as far as young persons offending we're dealing with sort of 10 per cent of the young persons maybe 90 per cent of the time, which maybe only gives me a sort of warped view of how many kids are offending. It's probably a very, very small numbers of kids that are actually offending, but the same group are offending all the time.

Police were mostly of the view that offending among young people was not particularly common, though distinctions were made between 'criminal transgressions' and 'misbehaviour', with the latter said to be fairly prevalent:

I think it depends on what your view of offending is and when it starts to fall off the bottom of the scale into 'misbehaviour' and 'just being one of the lads' or, you know, 'it's what young people do when they get into a group'.

Amongst younger people the most common offences which came to the police's attention were said to be vandalism, public order offences, shoplifting and 'violence towards their own age group', with only a 'small hard core' of young people committing more serious crimes such as housebreakings or thefts of or from cars. Public order offences were thought to become more common at around 13-15 years when 'they first get a wee taste for alcohol or maybe something slightly stronger'. Offending among slightly older people was said often to be drug-related, involving, for instance, shoplifting and other property offences to obtain money to buy drugs:

[shoplifting] normally comes thereafter when they've gone from drink onto drugs, so they've got to feed their habit. They're not stealing clothes to *wear,* they're stealing clothes, razor blades to *sell.*

The incidence of offending was acknowledged to be higher among boys than girls and there were said by police officers to be differences in the types of offences committed, with shoplifting relatively common among girls and public order offences and other types of property offences relatively rare. That said, there was unanimous agreement that girls were becoming increasingly involved in a wide range of offences, with the increase in violence among girls being said to be particularly marked. As one officer explained:

We've always certainly been arresting them for stealing things but there seems to be less and less of a gender difference between crimes of violence of any kind.

He was, however, keen not to over-exaggerate or sensationalise the issue:

I'm aware of the situation in the States about girl gangs and things like that. We're not really into that stage yet. The female offenders, the under 16s, they're into violence and everything but it's not serious just yet.

'Hanging about' in groups was said to be increasingly popular among girls, with one officer suggesting that the gender composition of these groups had become more evenly balanced and offering an explanation as to why this was the case:

Police: ...when I was sort of 14, 15, 16 you'd hang about in a big group of guys, maybe about 8, 9, 10 of us, there'd be three or four girls, but now it's right down the middle, it's 50-50.
Int: Have you any idea why that's the case?
Police: Girlpower!

The concept of girlpower was evoked by another officer to account for girls' increasing involvement in forms of anti-social or illegal behaviour which were formerly considered mainly to be the province of boys:

I mean, I'm not an expert in the field, but the media and the culture that the girls are now being encouraged to live in is this girlpower thing. It's OK to swear, it's OK to be like a boy and it's OK to dress like one. Femininity seems to be becoming a sort of old-fashioned, unattractive thing and now they want it to be macho, you know, macho, swearing, drinking, fighting.

The notion that girls' attitudes and behaviour were becoming more 'masculine' and that this accounted for their greater willingness to engage in anti-social behaviour was expanded upon by a third officer in the following exchange:

Police: They're, girls aren't girlie any more, they're not. Certainly not the ones that we meet... the guys that are fighting up the schemes, the girls are as vicious, girl gangs, maybe more so, but I don't know. It's maybe just progress, you know more than anything else, girls aren't keen to be girlies any more, they're just macho like everybody, like the rest of the gang.
Int: Equality!
Police: Absolutely! Equal opportunity gang warfare!

Reasons for offending

Police officers drew upon a range of factors as providing reasons for offending among young people. These included lack of effective parental supervision and discipline, alcohol and drug misuse, peer pressure, bravado, excitement, consumerism and lack of personal direction. The notion of offending arising from boredom – as opposed to the desire to get a 'buzz' – was strongly rejected by one officer on the grounds that young people failed to make use of recreational facilities, even if they were available:

A lot of them say boredom, but when we actually look at what's actually available in their area – sports stadiums, community centres, that sort of thing – there's something out there if they want to do it. It's an old argument, you know, 'we've got nothing to do', you know, 'we need this and we need that'. But when you actually supply these places, these kids are the people who are not going to go to these places anyway.

Although some of the factors invoked to explain offending among young people in general would apply equally to boys and girls, others were thought to apply more to one sex than to the other. Boys, it was suggested, were more likely than girls to succumb to peer pressure, while offending among young women was, it was proposed, often linked to drug dependency or relationships with male partners who were involved in crime:

A lot of the lassies end up pregnant with these guys and a lot of the guys are in prison and then the girls have ended up in prison as well. A lot of them have had their kids taken off them. It's quite sad, it really is.

The phenomenon of youth crime was thought by officers to be universal, with none considering that their own area was different from others in this respect. All could, however, readily identify places *within* their own area which were associated with greater or lesser levels of crime. High risk areas tended to be council housing schemes which were 'deprived' and had high levels of unemployment, while low risk areas were described as 'affluent' and characterised by relatively high levels of private ownership. Town centres or shopping centres were also said to be a focus for property crime (primarily shoplifting) and for vandalism and street fights. Tolerance for crime among residents of an area was thought to have an impact upon the locations selected by young people for 'hanging about'. For instance groups of young people in Eastburgh were perceived as being more likely to assemble in locations within or close to the council estates because people who lived in these areas were more tolerant of anti-social behaviour.

The areas in which young people congregated were also said to be influenced strongly by territoriality, with territorial behaviour featuring significantly among young people in both areas and being said to be more prominent than factions based upon religion or school. Territoriality was said to be 'all over the place', with its effects being to restrict the movements of young people to their own locality and impede their ability to make use of resources such as youth clubs or sports facilities in other areas. One officer explained that 'in the [housing] schemes it's territorial areas and they don't venture into each other's territory unless they're looking for a fight... I think Westburgh's always been like that – there's always been gangs, every area has a gang name'. The extent of gang culture and territoriality was such that one area in Westburgh was said to be routinely referred to by the police by its gang name.

Various factors were identified by police officers as putting young people at risk of offending, though reference to family factors was most common: lack of parental supervision; the absence of pro-social role models; lack of parental interest in their children; and parental involvement in crime:

> If parents took more responsibility for their kids and were aware where their kids were at night and what they were doing. And asking them what they were doing – that would make a difference. They're put at risk by their own parents quite a bit.

Other factors identified included associating with friends who were involved in delinquent activity and the misuse of drugs and alcohol. Environmental factors were also thought to play a part, with one officer in particular referring to the 'ghetto-isation' of vulnerable people in high risk areas characterised by poor housing a lack of community facilities and a 'cycle of decline'.

Self-esteem was considered to be a protective factor against involvement in crime, though parental influence and attitudes were most often considered to be crucial. Offending was considered less likely among young people whose parents were caring, taught their children the difference between right and wrong and exercised appropriate control. Concern was expressed on several occasions about young people 'wandering the streets' late at night, leading to speculation that they sometimes did so because 'maybe they're not welcome at home'.

Offending among young people was also widely acknowledged to be related to a range of other problems including unemployment, a 'breakdown in family life', truancy (which, in turn, was said sometimes to be a response to bullying at school) and various forms of child abuse and neglect. Some offending, it was suggested, was a 'cry for help' by young people in an attempt to draw attention to their personal distress.

Links between drug use – which was said to be ubiquitous in both study areas, but especially so in Westburgh – and offending were also clearly drawn:

> When they do turn to drugs, you probably find the crime that they commit is to feed their habit. It's not a case of they're criminals and they commit crime so they turn to drugs – it's the other way round;

> I've spoken to people who're maybe taking – they're not heavy drug addicts by any means – but they're maybe taking four, five, six bags of heroin a day... So that's £60 worth of heroin a day. They're getting £72 per fortnight, they're spending £60 a day on heroin so, yeah, they've got to go out and offend.

Just as the interviews with young people suggested, serious drug use was said to be relatively uncommon amongst those under 16 years. Whilst the use of cannabis was acknowledged to be relatively widespread among 14 and 15 year olds, the use of class A drugs – and, in particular, opiates and opioids – was thought to start at around 16-17 years and escalate fairly rapidly thereafter.

Officers were also keen to point out, however, that although they perceived a relationship between crime and other social problems, young people who were relatively well protected from social disadvantage were not necessarily exempt from involvement in crime. Those from more affluent backgrounds, it was suggested, tended to have more disposable income and, consequently, greater purchasing power with respect to alcohol which was, in turn, associated with public order offences and violence.

TEACHERS' PERSPECTIVES ON OFFENDING

The nature of offending by young people

The teachers who were interviewed did not consider offending to be particularly prevalent among young people of school age, although they also acknowledged that they only tended to become aware of a pupil offending if a report was requested for a children's hearing. It was suggested that the public perception of young people did not necessarily accord with the reality:

> There's a perception of young people because of the way they're hanging about in bigger groups, because of the way they're dressed and because of the publicity they're getting, but I still believe that the vast majority of them are good kids.

The incidence of offending by pupils was believed likely to vary from school to school, depending upon the catchment area. However, it was suggested that young people who were offending outside the school tended not to create problems within the school:

> I would say that in my experience the real offenders don't give a great deal of problem in the school. The real offenders, it tends to be that they have enough street sense to know that it's just more hassle for them.

Whilst second and third year pupils were said to present more discipline problems in school, third and fourth year pupils – 14 and 15 year olds – were said to most often be the subject of reports to the children's hearings system on offence grounds and were said most often to be excluded from school:

> Kids from 13 up to 15 tend to kick over the traces. They're trying to establish themselves as adults in their own right. They're testing their parents, they're testing the values that they have been brought up with, they're testing the values of society...Peer group pressure at that time of life is more acute than at any other time and until they've got themselves fixed they can't relate...to society.

The main offences that teachers considered young people to become involved in were vandalism, assaults, breaches of the peace (often alcohol-related) and, less commonly 'car related offences, breaking into cars, and occasionally breaking into houses'. Panel reports for children referred on offence grounds were more often requested for boys than for girls, with girls being thought more likely to be referred to the reporter for ... cy. Shoplifting was associated more with girls than with boys – ... re likely to be involved in vandalism, violent offences and drugs u... a perception that girls' were becoming more involved in a range ... at those who did offend tended to be more troublesome – and trou... ling boys.

Reasons...

Teach... offending among young people was attributable to a range of f... eer group pressure, social and economic deprivation, a lack of po... ; a lack of coping and life skills, poor parenting, poor parental su... ck of parental interest in their children. The media – through its ... down' and promotion of consumerism – was thought by some te... responsible for an increase in youth crime linked to alienation a... exclusion.

> The less ... people don't have any clear perception of their place in s... society as out there and they see themselves as 'well, I do... any of that so stuff them'.

Offending amongst boys was attributed by some teachers to their desire to be 'macho' while it was suggested that girls' offending may be more often rooted in family problems, including sexual abuse. Consistent with some current thinking that the gender ratio in offending might be accounted for by the greater degree of supervision exercised over girls, girls were thought more likely to stay at home and do 'girlish things' while boys were more likely to socialise outdoors which according to, the 'routine activities' theory of crime (Felson and Cohen, 1980; Felson, 1997) would place them at greater risk of both offending and victimisation. That said, the view was expressed that some girls – especially those who were under-achieving – were increasingly inclined to compete with boys by, in a sense, 'outdoing them at their own game':

> One of the things we noticed were 14 to 15 year old girls quite deliberately aping boys in the way they spoke, in the way they spoke about sex, the way they spoke about sport, the way they walked and sometimes even the way they dressed. And it was quite a deliberate policy of 'I'm going to hammer you – just because I'm a girl doesn't mean I can't hit you' and all that sort of thing. And I would imagine that it has its effects on their attitude to thieving as well – sort of horrible thought! – girls trying to trap a guy by saying 'look, you know I can break into that shop just as good as you can and doesn't that make me fanciable'.

Teachers thought that it was relatively easy to identify those young people who might become involved in offending, whether as the 'leaders' or the 'hangers on'. The factors which were believed to predispose young people towards offending included parenting problems, poverty, lack of success at school, lack of motivation, truancy, risk-taking personalities, exposure to drugs and offending in the family:

> I think if you idolise your big brother and he goes out knocking things off there is a good chance you will as well.

Teachers tended to make a link between truancy and shoplifting, though they thought that young people did not necessarily truant in order that they might offend ('When they truant it tends to be not to go off and do something, but it's to be not in school'). If anything, the relationship was perceived as being in the opposite direction – that is, offending occurred because when they were absent from school young people were in places where opportunities for it existed – or truancy and offending were viewed as being part of a broader repertoire of non-conforming behaviour which also included, for instance, under-age drinking, drug use and under-age sex.

Geographical location was also considered relevant, with the risk of offending thought to be higher in more disadvantaged communities where drugs were also more widely available. However it was suggested that more intensive policing in certain areas (with, for example, young people being more likely to be stopped and questioned by the police) could create a false impression of higher crime rates in these areas and that offending among young people was likely to occur in any location where large groups of young people tended to hang about.

The factors which were thought to protect young people against offending included parental care and support, personal motivation, aspirations, a sense of direction and purpose and self esteem ('kids who feel good about themselves').

SOCIAL WORKERS' PERSPECTIVES ON OFFENDING

The nature of offending by young people

The social workers who were interviewed suggested that most young people would offend at some time but that only a relatively small proportion would actually get caught. Those who did come into contact with the social work department as a result of their offending were, however, said to be responsible for both a high number and wide range of offences, though there was a perception among children and families workers that young people were increasingly coming to their attention for reasons other than offending. Various types of thefts – but especially shoplifting – and vandalism were thought most common among younger people with offending among older people often linked to alcohol or drug misuse and involving, for example, violence, housebreaking and shoplifting on a larger scale.

Although there was thought to be an increase in girls' involvement in offending compared with a few years ago, relatively few girls were said to be placed on supervision as a consequence of offending. However criminal justice workers in Westburgh, where the use of drugs was widespread, reported a significant increase in the proportion of women on social workers' caseloads which was said to have increased from 'probably under five per cent till a few years ago' and was 'running at something like 20 per cent now'. This increase was attributed directly to an increased level of drug addiction among young women:

> Of all the females we've had on probation, probably a large number are addicted in some way or another and have often fairly rapidly re-offended.

Reasons for offending

Offending among young people was said to result from a variety of factors, such as 'dysfunctional families' (including offending by other family members), lack of parental supervision, low school achievement, truancy ('If kids are not at school they've got huge amounts of time on their hands so the shopping centre becomes a kind of magnet to them'), poverty, unemployment and social exclusion. Consumerism was also believed to play a part through the increased pressure upon young people to have expensive designer trainers and clothes. As one worker commented:

> They also know that their parents are unemployed, but they still want. So one of the ways to get it is through crime.

Views were divided over whether boredom was a contributory factor, with the suggestion, on the one hand, that young people often attributed their offending to having nothing to and the alternative position, on the other, that 'there are things to do...but they don't want to pursue any activities that might be around':

> I mean, young people will say that it is sort of lack of amenities but really I think it's to do with really young people hanging around the streets drinking...It's a culture.

There was more general agreement, however, that peer pressure was associated with offending among younger people, whether it be young people egging each other on or a desire to uphold a 'macho' identity:

> There's a lot of peer pressure around and I think too, in this area, it's very much the kind of macho thing, you know – running around in large groups. And certainly in some areas – well, one area in particular has been having lots of problems with, you know, large groups of youngsters running around at night and causing terrible damage. And in fact someone was quite seriously assaulted recently by these youngsters.

The significance of the 'macho culture' was emphasised in particular in Westburgh, which was described as having a long tradition of 'low pay, heavy industry, heavy drinking' and which more recently had developed a 'virulent drug scene'. Offending among young women was considered often to be influenced by 'who their partners are', with young men introducing young women to drugs. As one social worker explained:

I think it would be very unusual to have a young female heroin abuser whose partner was not in the same kind of lifestyle...I think often it might be the case that he introduced her to it...I couldn't recall a case where she was abusing and he was absolutely straight.

Young people were thought to be more at risk of offending if they failed to develop an interest in education, if their parents did not exercise effective supervision, if there were other problems within the family (such as parental offending or substance misuse), if they lived in an area characterised by poverty and high levels of unemployment and if they became involved in the misuse of alcohol or drugs. Substance misuse itself was thought often to be a response to other problems in young people's lives, with one social worker suggesting that 'it may be that they're using that to hide being physically abused as a child or sexually abused as child' and that once a pattern of offending and substance misuse had developed it 'keeps perpetuating'.

Parental expectations and values and an appropriate degree of structure in the home were, it was suggested, protective factors with respect to offending. Social workers in Westburgh echoed the views of teachers there (see Chapter Five) in suggesting that many young people had limited academic and vocational aspirations and little interest or hope in the future. Yet having interests and having something positive in their lives was said to increase young people's self esteem and help protect them against the risk of becoming involved in offending, leading one social worker to advocate the greater involvement of community education staff in endeavours to re-integrate children who have been banned because of their offending into local organisations and amenities:

I would like to see community education maybe try and do something more with people who are presenting difficult behaviour, to help them come back into the organisations for children rather than rejecting them.

The need for policies aimed at promoting social inclusion was, it was suggested, all the greater because members of extended families no longer lived close to each other, greatly reducing their potential to provide additional structure and support

SUMMARY

There was a tendency for those in the youngest age group to ascribe greater seriousness to offences in which they were rarely involved and less seriousness to those which were most common to them. There appeared to be an increasing tolerance with age for property crimes of an essentially utilitarian nature (except where these involved a readily identifiable victim) and a lower level of tolerance for offences (such as street fights or vandalism) which tend to be associated with younger people.

Persisters tended to take a less serious view of certain types of offending than did desisters or resisters, with desisters occupying a position somewhere between the two. Gender differences were found in the older age groups and included a greater tolerance of violent offences among young men. To an extent female persisters were more similar to male persisters than they were to other young women of a similar age, including their attitudes towards certain types of violent offences (there were less marked differences between male persisters and other categories of young men).

While most interviewees were forthcoming and frank in interview, many persisters and desisters also offered justifications and excuses for their offending.

In response to a question about their general views of offending, most resisters and desisters emphasised two aspects of offending: the immorality and the futility of it. In contrast, few persisters stated that offending was wrong unconditionally, often suggesting that it was contingent on a variety of factors, such as the type or seriousness of the offence. Young men and boys more frequently noted the negative consequences of offending for the offender (including detection, punishment, diminished life chances and feelings of guilt) than their female counterparts.

More resisters and desisters (particularly females) suggested that young people's upbringing or their family was a reason for others' offending compared with persisters (particularly males), more of whom suggested that drug use was a reason.

More of those in the youngest age group (60%) were of the view that no offending (rather than some offending) was acceptable compared with those in the two older age groups (45% and 30%). More resisters (64%) than desisters (41%) and persisters (35%) thought that no offending (rather than some offending) was acceptable.

Differences across the age groups emerged in respect of which offences, if any, were thought to be acceptable. The older age groups were more likely to think that drug related offences were acceptable or that whether it was acceptable was dependant on circumstances, whereas more of those in the youngest age group thought that fighting was acceptable.

Professionals believed that relatively few young people were involved in serious offending but that there was an increase in young women and girls' involvement in delinquency and crime, with this being attributed to an increase in drug misuse among young women and to contemporary cultural influences which encouraged girls' identification with attitudes and behaviour traditionally associated with boys. Professionals were generally agreed that offending among young people was linked to family factors, peer influences, drug misuse, school failure and social exclusion while supportive families, self-esteem, education and employment could help protect young people from becoming involved in crime.

CHAPTER FIVE: OFFENDING AND LIFESTYLE

INTRODUCTION

Drawing on quantitative and qualitative interview data this chapter will discuss various aspects of young people's lifestyles and how they relate to offending. In particular it will concentrate on drug and alcohol use; young people's propensity to risk taking and impulsiveness; their use of leisure time; and education, employment and aspirations.

PATTERNS OF DRUG AND ALCOHOL USE

The nature and frequency of substance use among young people was explored via the completion of a checklist on the laptop computer. Young people were asked to indicate whether, when and how often they had used a range of substances. The list consisted of alcohol; amphetamines; cannabis; cocaine; crack; ecstasy; heroin; LSD; magic mushrooms; methadone; solvents; temgesic; temazepam; and tranquillisers. Young people could also indicate if they had used other illegal substances not included in the list.

The number of young people in the youngest age group who reported having used each of these substances is summarised in Table 5.1. Tables 5.1a and 5.1b (in the Appendix) present the relevant data separately for boys and girls. Cocaine, crack cocaine and temgesic have been excluded from these analyses because none of the youngest age group reported using them.

Table 5.1: Drug and alcohol use – youngest age group

	Resisters (n=34)	Desisters (n=26)	Persisters (n=44)	Total (n=104)
Alcohol	**18** *(53%)*	**23** *(88%)*	**38** *(86%)*	**79** *(76%)*
Amphetamines	-	-	**2** *(5%)*	**2** *(2%)*
Cannabis	**3** *(9%)*	**3** *(11%)*	**25** *(57%)*	**31** *(30%)*
Ecstasy	-	-	**2** *(5%)*	**2** *(2%)*
Glue/gas	-	**1** *(4%)*	**6** *(14%)*	**7** *(7%)*
Heroin	-	-	**1** *(2%)*	**1** *(1%)*
LSD	-	-	**6** *(14%)*	**6** *(5%)*
Magic mushrooms	-	-	**4** *(9%)*	**4** *(4%)*
Methadone	-	-	**1** *(2%)*	**1** *(1%)*
Temazepam	-	-	**5** *(11%)*	**5** *(5%)*
Tranquillisers	-	-	**1** *(2%)*	**1** *(1%)*
Other substance	**1** *(3%)*	-	**3** *(7%)*	**4** *(4%)*

Almost four-fifths of young people reported that they had consumed alcohol, with most of the persisters and desisters falling into this category. By contrast, just over half of the young people who had never offended indicated that they had consumed alcohol. Apart from alcohol, cannabis was the substance that had most commonly been used by young people (c.f., MVA, 1998), with three in ten young people admitting that they had done so. Table 5.1 also reveals that drug-taking was almost exclusively the province of young people classified as persisters. The relationship between drug use and offending category held true for both boys and girls. Whilst the numbers are low overall, it appeared that more girls were involved in the use of a wider range of drugs than were boys. More girls, in particular, admitted to current or previous use of cannabis and solvent abuse, with six girls indicating that they had engaged in the latter behaviour compared with only one boy.

Overall 34 young people (33%) had used substances other than alcohol. This was true of 15 boys (29%) and 19 girls (36%). Almost all of those who had used illicit drugs admitted to having used cannabis (all but three of the boys and all but one of the girls). The incidence of drug use (including solvents) was highest among persisters, 27/44 of whom (61%) admitted to having used drugs on at least one occasion. This compares with 4/26 desisters (15%) and 3/34 resisters (9 percent). There was also an apparent gender difference in drug use among persisters: 12/24 male persisters (50%) admitted having used drugs in comparison with 15/20 (75%) of offending girls.

It would appear that, with the exception of magic mushrooms, the majority of drug use by young people was either current or recent (that is within the previous 12 months). In most instances the use of alcohol or drugs was relatively infrequent though three of the seven young people who were abusing solvents were doing so on an almost daily basis. Information about when and how frequently boys and girls used different drugs is presented in Tables 5.1c and 5.1d in the Appendix.

Table 5.2: Drug and alcohol use – middle age group

	Resisters (n=35)	Desisters (n=19)	Persisters (n=35)	Total (n=89)
Alcohol	35 *(100%)*	18 *(95%)*	34 *(97%)*	87 *(98%)*
Amphetamines	4 *(11%)*	7 *(37%)*	21 *(60%)*	32 *(36%)*
Cannabis	16 *(46%)*	16 *(84%)*	29 *(83%)*	61 *(69%)*
Cocaine	-	2 *(10%)*	6 *(17%)*	11 *(12%)*
Crack	-	1 *(5%)*	3 *(9%)*	4 *(5%)*
Ecstasy	3 *(9%)*	6 *(32%)*	22 *(63%)*	31 *(35%)*
Glue/gas	-	2 *(10%)*	9 *(26%)*	11 *(12%)*
Heroin	-	3 *(16 %)*	17 *(49%)*	20 *(57%)*
LSD	5 *(14%)*	8 *(42%)*	23 *(66%)*	36 *(40%)*
Magic mushrooms	-	2 *(10%)*	5 *(14%)*	7 *(8%)*
Methadone	-	2 *(10%)*	10 *(29%)*	12 *(13%)*
Temgesic	-	-	8 *(23%)*	8 *(9%)*
Temazepam	-	5 *(26%)*	19 *(54%)*	24 *(27%)*
Tranquillisers	1 *(3%)*	3 *(16%)*	14 *(40%)*	18 *(20%)*
Other substance	2 *(6%)*	-	4 *(11%)*	6 *(7%)*

The pattern of drug use is shown for the middle age group in Table 5.2 and separately by gender in Tables 5.2a and 5.2b (in the Appendix). In comparison with the youngest age group there was amongst this group of young people an increase in the prevalence of drug use in each offending category, though the incidence of drug use among both young men and young women was still highest among persisters and lowest among resisters. Alcohol was the substance most commonly used by young people in their late teens, followed by cannabis, LSD, amphetamines and ecstasy. The pattern of use amongst young men and young women was broadly similar, though female interviewees were more likely to report having used tranquillisers.

The majority of persisters (33/35) reported having used a substance other than alcohol while this was also true of the majority of desisters (16/19) but just under half of the resisters (17/35). Drug use among resisters was confined largely to cannabis and, to a lesser extent, to other 'recreational' drugs. Although similar proportions of desisters and persisters had used illegal substances, the latter were distinguishable from the former by their more widespread use of a range of drugs, including opiates. Young women were slightly less likely than young men to have used substances other than alcohol, with 33/47 having done so in comparison with 33/42 young men.

As with the youngest age group, much of the substance misuse reported was relatively recent, with the exception of cocaine, crack, ecstasy, solvents, LSD and magic mushrooms, which young people were more likely to report having last used more than 12 months previously. The frequency of drug use varied according to the type of substance concerned. Certain substances were reported in most instances as having been used relatively infrequently – amphetamines, cocaine, crack, ecstasy, solvents, LSD and magic mushrooms. The frequency of use of others – methadone, temazepam and tranquillisers – varied across the sample. Alcohol, cannabis and heroin tended to be used on a more regular basis, though the pattern of cannabis use suggests a degree of bifurcation, with some young people apparently using it on an occasional, perhaps experimental, basis and others admitting to its use on a fairly regular, and in several cases daily, basis. (see Tables 5.2c and 5.2d in the Appendix).

Table 5.3: Drug and alcohol use – oldest age group

	Resisters (n=35)	Desisters (n=19)	Persisters (n=35)	Total (n=89)
Alcohol	23 *(96%)*	27 *(93%)*	25 *(89%)*	75 *(93%)*
Amphetamines	9 *(38%)*	17 *(57%)*	23 *(82%)*	49 *(60%)*
Cannabis	15 *(62%)*	26 *(90%)*	26 *(93%)*	67 *(83%)*
Cocaine	3 *(12%)*	10 *(34%)*	17 *(61%)*	30 *(37%)*
Crack	1 *(4%)*	4 *(14%)*	10 *(36%)*	15 *(18%)*
Ecstasy	6 *(25%)*	18 *(62%)*	24 *(86%)*	38 *(47%)*
Glue/gas	3 *(12%)*	7 *(24%)*	15 *(54%)*	25 *(31%)*
Heroin	1 *(4%)*	12 *(41%)*	25 *(89%)*	38 *(47%)*
LSD	8 *(33%)*	18 *(62%)*	22 *(79%)*	48 *(59%)*
Magic mushrooms	2 *(8%)*	10 *(34%)*	19 *(68%)*	31 *(35%)*
Methadone	1 *(4%)*	11 *(40%)*	25 *(89%)*	37 *(46%)*
Temgesic	1 *(4%)*	10 *(34%)*	20 *(71%)*	31 *(35%)*
Temazepam	5 *(21%)*	15 *(52%)*	24 *(86%)*	44 *(54%)*
Tranquillisers	2 *(8%)*	6 *(21%)*	21 *(75%)*	29 *(36%)*
Other substance	1 *(4%)*	1 *(3%)*	3 *(11%)*	5 *(6%)*

As Table 5.3 shows (and Tables 5.3a and 5.3b in the Appendix), the highest level of drug use was reported by the oldest age group, though this to some extent will reflect the fact that some respondents, especially those in the oldest age group, were located via a local drug misuse project in one of the study areas. Again, however, a clear difference emerges between resisters, desisters and persisters with respect to drug use, with the resisters least often reporting that they have used illegal substances and the persisters most often reporting having done so. Among the young men there were comparable levels of usage of what might be termed 'recreational' drugs – amphetamines, cannabis, cocaine, ecstasy and LSD – among desisters and persisters, but persisters were characterised by a greater use of tranquillisers and opiates. All of the female persisters in the oldest age group reported having used heroin and methadone, with most also indicating that they had used a wide range of other substances.

Overall, 27/28 persisters, 27/29 desisters and 16/24 resisters admitted to having used a substance other than alcohol. There was relatively little difference in the proportions of young men and young women who reported having used illegal substances at 38/42 and 32/39 respectively. As with the youngest age groups much of the drug taking was relatively recent, though solvents, LSD and magic mushrooms tended to have been last used more that 12 months previously. Alcohol, cannabis, heroin, methadone, temazepam and tranquillisers were, by contrast, more likely to have been used within the last 12 months.

The frequency of drug use again differed according to the type of substance concerned, with amphetamines, cocaine, crack, ecstasy, solvents, LSD and magic mushrooms having most often been used on only an occasional basis. Alcohol, cannabis, heroin, temazepam and tranquillisers were most likely to be used on a more frequent, and often daily basis. For instance, all of the female persisters in this oldest age group reported daily use of heroin. Clearly, then, within the present sample there was an escalation in both the seriousness and frequency of drug use with age. As before, information about how recently young people had used alcohol and drugs and the frequency of their use is presented in Tables 5.3c and 5.3d in the Appendix.

DRUG USE

Tables 5.4 to 5.6[13] illustrate that when interviewed persisters were most likely to report current and past use of drugs and the majority of persisters in the older age groups reported that they were currently using drugs.

There were a number of explanations for drug use which were common to users in all age and offender categories and these included: friend/peer pressure, 'for a laugh', opportunity, curiosity, to relax, enjoyment, recreation and boredom. A few interviewees viewed drug use as a substitute for alcohol or as a means of coping with depression. Use of cannabis, in particular, was identified as a means to enhance confidence, to stimulate creativity and to reduce propensity to get into 'trouble'. Two male persisters in the oldest age group explained their use of drugs in terms of it being a part of their upbringing, whereby both had been introduced to heroin by their fathers, though they emphasised that this was in terms of smoking rather than injecting (both were intravenous heroin addicts).

---

[13] This information was not available for all cases.

Table 5.4: Drug use by Resisters

	Youngest age group		Middle age group		Oldest age group	
	Male	Female	Male	Female	Male	Female
No drug use	14 *(100%)*	18 *(90%)*	7 *(50%)*	10 *(67%)*	2 *(25%)*	6 *(38%)*
Current drug use	-	-	5 *(36%)*	2 *(13%)*	3 *(37%)*	5 *(31%)*
Past drug use	-	2 *(10%)*	2 *(14%)*	3 *(20%)*	3 *(37%)*	5 *(31%)*
Total	14	20	14	15	8	16

Table 5.5: Drug use by Desisters

	Youngest age group		Middle age group		Oldest age group	
	Male	Female	Male	Female	Male	Female
No drug use	12 *(86%)*	12 *(100%)*	3 *(25%)*	1 *(14%)*	-	2 *(17%)*
Current drug use	1 *(7%)*	-	6 *(50%)*	2 *(29%)*	11 *(69%)*	4 *(33%)*
Past drug use	1 *(7%)*	-	3 *(25%)*	4 *(57%)*	5 *(31%)*	6 *(50%)*
Total	14	12	12	7	16	12

Table 5.6: Drug use by Persisters

	Youngest age group		Middle age group		Oldest age group	
	Male	Female	Male	Female	Male	Female
No drug use	14 *(61%)*	5 *(25%)*	1 *(6%)*	1 *(6%)*	-	-
Current drug use	6 *(26%)*	10 *(50%)*	13 *(76%)*	13 *(81%)*	16 *(94%)*	9 *(75%)*
Past drug use	3 *(13%)*	5 *(25%)*	3 *(18%)*	2 *(13%)*	1 *(6%)*	3 *(25%)*
Total	23	20	17	16	17	12

The most striking difference in terms of explanations for drug use between the youngest and the two older age groups was the prevalence of addiction. None of the boys or girls in the youngest age group attributed their drug use to addiction. However, by eighteen years the potential for addiction had obviously increased. Addiction (largely to heroin) was the explanation offered for drug use by three female persisters and two male persisters in the middle age group and by eight male persisters, seven female persisters, two male desisters and one male resister in the oldest age group. One male persister (oldest age group) commented: 'All you're interested in is that fucking pin-head going in your arm. It sounds horrible but it's the truth'. Furthermore, a male desister (oldest age group) noted how difficult it was to come off heroin despite voluntarily going to a rehabilitation centre and then attending a local drug centre. As he explained:

> I came back from the rehab and one of these guys I knew came up [in drug centre]. And he was like that ... 'how are you doing? What are you up for?' I was like that ... 'what's that supposed to mean?' He was talking about needles. I was like that ... 'no I'm clean and off it. I haven't touched it in weeks'. He was like that... 'bullshit man what are you talking about you're back in Westburgh.' [...] So it must have been about a week and a half after I came back from there, just started taking it again.

The reasons given for not taking drugs (mostly by resisters and desisters) included: the perceived expense associated with using drugs; the risk/danger to life and health; the fact they did not want to/need to take drugs; the fact they were scared to take them; the witnessed effects of drugs on others; the fact that drugs are illegal and that taking drugs was 'stupid'. A male resister (in the middle age group) explained his non drug use in the following terms:

> I don't want to get to a stage where I don't know what I'm doing. Well if you ask any serious drug addict and it all started with cannabis. It just sort of progressed from that because the kind of high they were getting on that doesn't really do much for you any more so you are getting onto stronger drugs and they are stealing to feed the habit and you get to a stage where you don't know what you are doing.

Of those who reported past drug use common explanations for discontinued use among all age groups were not having liked the effects of drugs or being fearful of the effects; feeling sick; not being in control and being scared of hurting themselves. For example:

> I did smoke some [cannabis] once at a party but I didn't like them and so I decided not to do it anymore. (female resister)

> Just didn't like it when I took the jellies [temezepam]. After about 9 o'clock, well from 9 o'clock onwards I couldn't remember what I'd done and I could have done anything in that space of time. So I didn't like the fact of not knowing what I'd done. (male resister)

The effects of drugs on others also appeared an important factor in discontinued drug use. Girls in the youngest age group related cautionary tales of how a member of their family or a friend had died because they had taken drugs. Young people in the older age groups noted the impact of friends' use and experience of drugs as influential in their decisions to stop. Others in all age groups were concerned with the financial costs of continued drug use and in the case of the older two age groups discontinued drug use was also explained in terms of having 'grown up' or no longer feeling any need to repeat the experience because they had experimented in the past. Young women in the older two age groups noted the importance of pregnancy (two cases) and having a child (one case) in their decisions to stop using. One young man had made a conscious decision to stop using drugs in order to commit himself more fully to his work and part-time study.

A number of persisters in the older age groups who were currently using drugs (largely heroin) talked of their desire to stop using, for example:

> I've always had money to support my habit and it was just pure getting to me and I decided I'd had enough and I wanted a lot more things from life. I wanted to go and do something at college and like do qualifications so I don't need to work in factories anymore, in fact I'm totally fed up with Westburgh. I want to get out of Westburgh. (female persister)

Man: I had tried a few times over the last two and a half years to come off it [heroin] but I never managed.

Int: So what's different about this time? [he had stopped using for a few days]

Man: I've got more will power I think. I want to get my life back together and start going out and enjoying myself and doing things I should be doing instead of just sitting about wasted all day doing nothing.

It was apparent that use of drugs was viewed by interviewees (all categories) as a common practice, for example 'everybody's doing it', 'we're the 'E' generation' and 'there's one in every family that does get involved with drugs'. In keeping with previous research findings (Asquith et al., 1998) it seemed that use of cannabis was not viewed by the interviewees as taking drugs in the same way that other drugs were. For example, several girls in the youngest age group felt able to say that they did not take drugs but that they did use cannabis. By contrast, boys in the youngest age group and young people in the older age groups appeared aware of the illegality in their use of cannabis but emphasised that they 'only' used cannabis rather than anything 'heavy'. It was also apparent that cannabis was relatively freely available to the youngest age group and that most drugs were available to the older age groups. Young people got access to drugs through peers, friends, dealers (often based within their own neighbourhoods) and some young people in the youngest age group reported that they were able to get drugs at school. The seeming significance of age with respect to the availability of drugs is emphasised in the experience of one boy categorised as a persister:

To start off with I first tried to get it when I was about 13 or something like that – 'no chance, get away home to your mummy' and that, but then I started to get a bit older and got to know people I could just get it easy and then I started to be able to get it for myself and other people (male persister, youngest age group).

The perceived severity of drug use was unsurprisingly relative to the type of drug being used. Cannabis and use of cannabis was rarely viewed as serious in any way and several young people were of the opinion that cannabis was comparable to or less harmful than alcohol. As one young woman explained:

If you go in a place and everybody is drinking then definitely by the end of the night someone is going to fall out with someone, whether it's their husband or their wife or a guy with another guy. I mean it's much better I think, a better atmosphere when people are taking drugs, and as long as you're sensible and you know what to do, I mean it's okay. I don't see a problem with hash. I think it should be legalised (female desister, middle age group).

Heroin use and addiction were identified as serious and problematic to young people. The majority of young people who were addicted reported heroin habits which required two to three 'bags' a day each costing £10. This obviously had financial repercussions for the majority of users who were either unemployed or claiming sickness benefit. Others reported how they had progressed from smoking heroin to injecting it, with all of those who reported themselves as being addicted to heroin commenting that they injected it. A desister in the middle age group who had got on a methadone programme commented: 'I started off jagging into my arm, then my legs and then my groin. I was pretty bad with that'. Several addicts also related instances of when they had overdosed (often they had overdosed on more than one occasion). One persister in the oldest age group explained why this had not deterred him from using heroin:

Man: I can't remember nothing, know what I mean. So if somebody was to sit and take a picture of me or film me or something like that in an o/d [overdose], in a proper o/d, pure blue lips and all that, know what I mean, hey man, wait a minute.

Int: Would you stop?

Man: It wouldn't make me stop but it'd probably give me a fright.

Int: He's [friend] just told you you've done it.

Man: I know that but I'd need to see it for myself. I've been in fucking comas and all that, life support machines, talking about chopping my arm off, massive heart attacks and everything. I've had the works done to me. I'm still fucking here.

At the personal level, drug use and offending were not thought to be related by either the girls or the boys in the youngest age group or by the majority of desisters in the older two age groups. Three boy persisters in the youngest age group did, however, comment that they often did not know what they were doing while under the influence of drugs (or for that case alcohol) and therefore could have offended and not known about it:

Like LSD you are really, you don't have a clue what you're doing at that time and ecstasy as well, you are just pure hyper as anything, you don't have a clue what you're doing and stuff. So you never know what you've done. It's just really the drugs in general. (male persister, youngest age group)

While the majority of desisters did not view their drug use as being in any way connected to their offending the few who did noted that drug use had led to shoplifting, theft and housebreaking in order to get money to buy drugs (largely heroin). One male desister in the middle age group noted that he had sold drugs in order to support his heroin addiction. Persisters also commented that funding their drug use was directly connected to much of their current offending. Shoplifting, theft and housebreaking were again common means of raising money. Two female persisters reported being involved in credit card and cheque fraud and two male persisters admitted that they had used weapons to demand money from people (usually other drug users). The illegality of drug use had also resulted in possession charges for one male desister in the middle age group and for two male persisters in the oldest age group. Violent crimes and fighting were most often associated with the use temezepam among male (three cases) and female (one case) persisters.

When asked whether they thought their drug use would change in the future, most of the young men and women interviewed did not expect their drug use (or lack of it) to change in six months time. The reasons for continuing not to use drugs included the associated danger; the fact that their peer group did not take drugs; the need to concentrate on school and career; 'settling down' and being 'too busy'. In the two older age groups, in which heroin use was more prevalent, the majority of those who thought their drug use would be different in six months time explained that they hoped to reduce or stop using drugs. This anticipated outcome was attributed by male persisters in the oldest age group to awaited access to a drug rehabilitation centre (3 cases) or methadone programme (2 cases) and in one case to actually using methadone. A female persister in the middle age group hoped to stop using drugs because she was pregnant and another hoped to stop using when she moved out of the area. One male persister in the oldest age group explained that his drug use was likely to get less as he was 'getting more into drink'.

ALCOHOL USE

Tables 5.7 to 5.9[14] illustrate young people's use of alcohol by offending category. The majority of young people reported that they had begun to drink alcohol at the age of 12, 13 or 14 years. In the youngest age group use of alcohol, like drugs, was more common among those girls and boys categorised as persisters and desisters. However, in speaking about their alcohol use it was apparent that for desisters and resisters this was largely confined to special occasions, such as new year or birthday celebrations and that furthermore, use of alcohol by these two groups was largely supervised by adults. By contrast persisters were more likely to recount incidences of unsupervised and public drinking with friends which often occurred on a regular basis. It could be that these persisters would be 'hanging about' outside anyway and while there they drink. On the other hand they might be 'hanging about' because they are in search of a place to take part in this illegal activity without being caught. The following response to a question about where the girl drinks, suggests that the latter might be the case: 'there's fines. If you get caught with an open bottle of alcohol you get fined so we usually just – there's a car park, a disused car park and it has got hundreds of trees, just behind the trees'.

[14] This information was not available for all cases.

Table 5.7: Alcohol use by Resisters

	Youngest age group		Middle age group		Oldest age group	
	Male	Female	Male	Female	Male	Female
No alcohol use	8 *(57%)*	10 *(50%)*	-	-	1 *(12%)*	-
Current alcohol use	6 *(43%)*	10 *(50%)*	14 *(100%)*	18 *(100%)*	7 *(88%)*	12 *(100%)*
Total	14	20	14	18	8	12

Table 5.8: Alcohol use by Desisters

	Youngest age group		Middle age group		Oldest age group	
	Male	Female	Male	Female	Male	Female
No alcohol use	3 *(21%)*	2 *(17%)*	1 *(8%)*	-	3 *(18%)*	1 *(8%)*
Current alcohol use	11 *(79%)*	10 *(83%)*	11 *(92%)*	8 *(100%)*	14 *(82%)*	11 *(92%)*
Total	14	12	12	8	17	12

Table 5.9: Alcohol use by Persisters

	Youngest age group		Middle age group		Oldest age group	
	Male	Female	Male	Female	Male	Female
No alcohol use	3 *(13%)*	-	4 *(24%)*	1 *(6%)*	4 *(22%)*	8 *(67%)*
Current alcohol use	20 *(87%)*	20 *(100%)*	13 *(76%)*	17 *(94%)*	14 *(78%)*	4 *(33%)*
Total	23	20	17	18	18	12

Despite being under the legal age to buy alcohol getting access to alcohol does not appear to present a problem for the 14-15 year olds. For those whose parents do not allow them to drink at home older friends, boyfriends (in the case of girls) and siblings purchase it, while others said they looked old enough to be served themselves in off licences, 'pubs', clubs or for ordering home delivery services. Some young people relied on strangers, for example 'if there's somebody walking past, I ask somebody to buy it ... there's a lot of people hang around and they are old enough to get served for it' (female persister) and 'usually – see one of the wee alcies [alcoholics] that stand outside the shop – usually buy them a can of beer and they'll get you [alcohol]'. The reasons given for drinking alcohol included: 'for fun', 'to relax', 'to try it', 'to unwind', 'to have a laugh', 'everybody does it', 'hanging about with an older group of people', 'there's nothing else to do' and 'to feel lively'. Those who did not drink alcohol explained this in terms of 'choice', the potential for being caught by parents, the 'bad side effects', or viewing it as 'pointless'.

For all boy resisters and the majority of boy desisters unsupervised drinking was uncommon and thus the extent of their alcohol use was limited to a bottle of beer or a glass of wine. However, girl resisters and desisters reported consciously limiting their drinking: 'we're all sensible', 'I didn't overstep the limit' and 'I wouldn't want ever to be took home to my mum or anything like that, you know, anything happening, because that would just be silly'. An interesting comment was made by one girl resister about parental attitudes to drinking: 'my mum and dad let me and my other friends come in the house so we're not like out in the streets drinking, hiding from people... [my friends] are not allowed to drink, so they end up doing it behind their [parents'] back'. Other girls believed their parents knew they drank alcohol even though they did not approve. For example, one girl explained: 'well, my mum knows that I drink and that but she wouldn't go out and get me a carry out, but she knows I do it' (female persister, youngest age group).

Several persisters in the youngest age group talked about getting drunk: 'at the weekend I go out and get absolutely blootered [drunk] basically ... I drink about every Friday and Saturday' (girl, persister) and:

> ...my mum cracks up at me all the time. I walked in one night pure right out of it [drunk] and my mum was like 'you're grounded' and then the next day she was like that 'you ever come in in that state again I'm going to put your face through that wall'. I was lucky that night that [my dad] wasn't in because he would have had my blood over the walls (female persister, youngest age group).

In the older two age groups alcohol use was a common practice for the majority of young people, with the exception of female persisters in the oldest age group. On the whole alcohol use appeared to be an integral part of young people's social lives usually taking place at pubs, clubs, parties, or at their own or others' homes. It was largely undertaken in the company of friends and to a lesser extent families. Young men were more likely to say that they drank on a regular basis, usually at weekends, while a greater number of young women commented that their alcohol use was limited to special occasions and social outings. All those who did not use alcohol in the two older age groups related their non use of alcohol to the fact they were drug users (the majority were heroin addicts). A few of the young male persisters who used drugs and alcohol noted that they were trying to reduce their drug use and subsequently used alcohol more frequently. However, many male drug users reported themselves as regularly using alcohol albeit to a very limited extent. Two young men noted that their alcohol use was a source of some concern. A desister in the middle age group reported that as a condition of his probation order he had to attend 'Alcoholics Anonymous' meetings and yet continued to drink 50-55 units of alcohol a week. A desister in the oldest age group reported that he was reducing his alcohol intake because of a violent incident he had perpetrated on his brother and girlfriend when drunk.

Many of the interviewees in the youngest age group equated drinking alcohol with breaking the law, although in fact only the activities around it, such as underage purchasing of alcohol or drinking alcohol in public, are illegal. When asked whether consuming alcohol had led them to committing other offences half the girl persisters, but no girl desisters, said it had, while only two boy persisters thought that alcohol use had led them to offend. Several girls and one boy related alcohol use with fighting, usually initiated by them. The other boy commented that alcohol had resulted in his involvement in vandalism and theft 'but nothing too serious' while some girls commented that drinking alcohol had led to them using drugs, for example:

> There was this group of guys we used to hang out with and his big brother was dealing it at the time and he got hundreds off him, you know, for nothing and he says to me 'do you want a couple?' and because we were steaming

[drunk] we were like 'aye' and that was it (female persister, youngest age group).

Another girl described the relationship between offending and alcohol as cumulative. She had needed money to pay for alcohol which led to her offending and then because she drank too much that led to more offending:

I was stealing to get money for drink. When I was drunk I was fighting, fighting with everybody, vandalising, breaking into places, basically pretty much everything, but I was stealing a lot to get money for drink. It had – in fact I think most of my charges are through, are alcohol related ... breaking into houses – that was for drink money (female persister, youngest age group).

Apart from the persisters who said that drinking alcohol had led to offending, both girl persisters and girl desisters noted other alcohol related incidents, which while not constituting offending served to raise their profile in relation to the police, may have led to charges and might have increased their chances of being charged in the future. For example, a girl persister said of the police 'they pour your drink out in front of you' and a girl desister related:

Well we did get accused – well a friend got accused of breaking and entering of some sort, but there were other groups hanging around – it could've been them ... she wasn't drinking, but we were drinking and so we didn't know what was going on. I think she got the biggest fright. It gave us a fright as well. We didn't drink for at least a year. It was really scary. Police are scary people.

In the older two age groups alcohol was not generally associated with criminal activity. Those who did report offending which was associated with alcohol use did not on the whole perceive this offending to be particularly serious. Alcohol was thought to have been a contributing factor to young people becoming involved in:

- fights
- disorderly behaviour or breaches of the peace
- vandalism

The majority of this offending had not elicited any statutory intervention. However, one female persister reported that she had spent a night in police cells as a result of an assault on a police officer, a male persister had to attend alcohol counselling as part of his sentence for an assault and a male desister was fined and lost his driving license as a result of driving while drunk.

When asked whether they thought their alcohol use would change in the future the majority of young people stated that they did not expect their consumption to change six months hence. However, several of the girl persisters who drank thought they might drink less for the following reasons: they needed to 'calm down'; study for exams was to take priority; they would be bored with alcohol; and taking drugs reduced the urge for alcohol. In the older two age groups young men identified a partner having a child; working abroad for a year; and having to train to participate in competitive sports as influential in their being likely to reduce their alcohol consumption. The few young people who thought their alcohol consumption would increase in the next six months attributed this to reducing or stopping their drug use, having more free time, being able to go out more and the fact that the weather would be warmer.

RISK-TAKING AND IMPULSIVENESS

Previous studies have suggested an association between risk-taking and impulsiveness among young people and their involvement in delinquent or criminal behaviour (Pulkkinen, 1986; White et al., 1994). The observed association between offending and drug use in the present study would suggest that some young people are more likely than others to engage in a range of risk-taking behaviours.

The concepts of risk and impulsiveness were further explored by means of a questionnaire administered on the laptop computer. A series of 10 scenarios were presented and young people were invited to indicate how likely they would be to adopt the course of action indicated in the scenario. The examples employed were drawn from McGuire and Priestley (1985)[15]. In each case young people were asked to indicate whether they were absolutely certain, very likely, quite likely, not very likely or not at all likely to behave in that particular way. Each item was scored from one to five, with a lower score indicating a more impulsive response. A total risk-taking score was derived by summing the score achieved on each individual item. The scenarios are presented in full in the Appendix.

[15] This book discusses the relationship between offending and a range of personal/social factors, provides examples of exercises that can be used by social workers or probation officers to address these factors and discusses how the impact of these interventions can be assessed.

Table 5.10: Percentage of young people who would engage in risk taking behaviours

	Youngest (n=102)[16]	Middle (n=88)[17]	Oldest (n=80)[18]
Buy on impulse	77 *(76%)*	70 *(80%)*	63 *(79%)*
Spend windfall	73 *(72%)*	74 *(85%)*	74 *(94%)*
Say what you think	59 *(58%)*	55 *(65%)*	50 *(64%)*
Go to see commotion	59 *(58%)*	42 *(48%)*	42 *(52%)*
Go clubbing with friends	53 *(52%)*	52 *(60%)*	35 *(45%)*
Buy second hand goods	40 *(40%)*	46 *(52%)*	41 *(51%)*
Go for a spin with friends	29 *(29%)*	38 *(44%)*	31 *(39%)*
Do something dangerous	15 *(15%)*	11 *(12%)*	11 *(14%)*
Associate with known criminal	9 *(9%)*	15 *(17%)*	26 *(32%)*
Climb in a pub window	6 *(6%)*	11 *(12%)*	16 *(20%)*

The responses of young people to each of the examples are summarised in Table 5.10 which shows the percentage of young people in each age group who indicated that they were likely to engage in the behaviour described (that is, those who said they were certain, very likely or quite likely to do so). It would appear that young people in the middle and oldest age groups were more likely than those in the youngest age group to engage in a range of risky behaviours which were, or verged on, the illegal: climbing in a pub window that has been left open late at night; borrowing money from someone who, in return, might call upon you to 'do a job' for him some time; going for a spin in a car which you suspect to be stolen; or buying second hand goods.

There were no significant differences between boys and girls in terms of their responses to the individual scenarios and few gender differences among the older age groups in this respect: in the middle age group men were more likely than women to go to explore the cause of a commotion outside in the street, while in the oldest age group men were more likely than women to buy second hand goods or climb in an open pub window.

Persisters, desisters and resisters did, however, differ in terms of apparent propensity towards risk taking. As Table 5.11 indicates, across all age groups persisters were significantly more likely to say that they would engage in a range of risk taking or impulsive behaviours. Furthermore, among the middle and oldest age groups especially (though this also applies to going for a spin in the youngest age group) the largest differences were observed with respect to those scenarios most closely associated with illegal behaviour.

---

[16] Data are missing in a small number of cases. Percentages are based upon the number of young people providing a response to the example.

[17] Data are missing in a small number of cases. Percentages are based upon the number of young people providing a response to the example.

[18] Data are missing in a small number of cases. Percentages are based upon the number of young people providing a response to the example.

Table 5.11: Percentage of young people who would engage in risk-taking behaviour

	Resisters	Desisters	Persisters	Total
YOUNGEST AGE GROUP (N=102)[19]				
Say what you think*	**16** *(47%)*	**12** *(46%)*	**31** *(74%)*	**59** *(58%)*
Go to see commotion**	**21** *(38%)*	**13** *(50%)*	**33** *(79%)*	**59** *(58%)*
Go clubbing with friends*	**12** *(35%)*	**14** *(54%)*	**27** *(64%)*	**53** *(52%)*
Go for a spin with friends***	**4** *(12%)*	**4** *(15%)*	**21** *(51%)*	**29** *(29%)*
Do something dangerous**	**2** *(6%)*	**1** *(4%)*	**12** *(29%)*	**15** *(15%)*
MIDDLE AGE GROUP (N=88)[20]				
Say what you think**	**16** *(46%)*	**12** *(71%)*	**27** *(82%)*	**55** *(65%)*
Go clubbing with friends*	**15** *(44%)*	**11** *(58%)*	**26** *(76%)*	**52** *(60%)*
Buy second hand goods*	**13** *(37%)*	**10** *(53%)*	**23** *(67%)*	**46** *(53%)*
Go for a spin with friends***	**9** *(26%)*	**7** *(37%)*	**22** *(65%)*	**38** *(43%)*
Associate with known criminal***	**2** *(6%)*	-	**13** *(38%)*	**15** *(17%)*
Climb in a pub window***	-	**1** *(5%)*	**10** *(29%)*	**11** *(12%)*
OLDEST AGE GROUP (N=80)[21]				
Say what you think**	**10** *(42%)*	**18** *(64%)*	**22** *(85%)*	**50** *(64%)*
Go to see commotion**	**7** *(29%)*	**15** *(52%)*	**20** *(74%)*	**42** *(52%)*
Go for a spin with friends***	**4** *(17%)*	**7** *(24%)*	**20** *(77%)*	**31** *(39%)*
Associate with known criminal***	**2** *(8%)*	**2** *(5%)*	**22** *(82%)*	**26** *(32%)*
Climb in a pub window***	-	**5** *(17%)*	**11** *(42%)*	**16** *(20%)*

* p<.05; **p<.01; ***p<.001

Table 5.12 indicates there were no significant differences in mean composite risk taking scores by gender. However, across each age group and for both male and female respondents the lowest risk scores (indicating a greater propensity towards risky or impulsive behaviour) were found among persisters and the highest scores (indicating a lesser propensity towards risk-taking) among resisters. Desisters, on the other hand, occupied a middle position, suggesting that they were more likely to take risks than resisters but less likely to do so than young people who were actively involved in offending at the point of interview.

[19] Data are missing in a small number of cases. Percentages are based upon the number of young people providing a response to the example.
[20] Data are missing in a small number of cases. Percentages are based upon the number of young people providing a response to the example.
[21] Data are missing in a small number of cases. Percentages are based upon the number of young people providing a response to the example.

Table 5.12 Risk-taking by age, gender and offending category

	Resisters	Desisters	Persisters
YOUNGEST AGE GROUP **Male (n=49)**	39.6	38.2	33.0
Female (n=47)	38.8	36.5	31.4
MIDDLE AGE GROUP **Male (n=40)**	36.0	35.8	29.5
Female (n=41)	38.5	33.5	30.2
OLDEST AGE GROUP **Male (n=40)**	36.8	34.9	25.8
Female (n=33)	38.1	37.1	26.8

USE OF LEISURE TIME

The young people were asked what they did in their spare time and the hobbies they engaged in were classified as formal[22] or informal[23], alone or social. Tables 5.13- 5.15[24] indicate the types of hobbies in which young people, in each of the offender categories, were involved.

Table 5.13: Types of hobbies engaged in by resisters

Resisters	Formal and social	Formal and alone	Informal and social	Informal and alone
YOUNGEST AGE GROUP **Girls (n=20)**	**15** *(75%)*	**1** *(5%)*	**14** *(70%)*	**7** *(35%)*
Boys (n=13)	**7** *(54%)*	**1** *(8%)*	**10** *(77%)*	**7** *(54%)*
MIDDLE AGE GROUP **Women (n=18)**	**7** *(39%)*	-	**10** *(55%)*	**4** *(22%)*
Men (n=14)	**6** *(43%)*	-	**14** *(100%)*	**6** *(43%)*
OLDEST AGE GROUP **Women (n=12)**	**3** *(25%)*	**1** *(8%)*	**3** *(25%)*	**4** *(33%)*
Men (n=8)	**3** *(37%)*	-	**5** *(62%)*	**2** *(25%)*

[22] 'Formal and social' pursuits included playing in an orchestra, singing in a choir, drama, debating, the scouts, cadets, a variety of classes and a variety of sports, such as athletics, gymnastics, hockey, badminton, rugby, horse riding, football, golf, karate and bowling. 'Formal and alone' pursuits included music classes and tuition.

[23] 'Informal and social' pursuits included going to the cinema, dancing, music, walking, cycling, computer games (boys) and several sports (bowling, swimming, ice skating, football and tennis). 'Informal and alone' pursuits included walking, cycling, weight training and computers.

[24] The total adds up to more than the number of resisters, desisters and persisters as some reported having more than one hobby.

Table 5.14: Types of hobbies engaged in by desisters

Desisters	Formal and social	Formal and alone	Informal and social	Informal and alone
YOUNGEST AGE GROUP **Girls (n=12)**	7 *(58%)*	1 *(8%)*	7 *(58%)*	4 *(33%)*
Boys (n=14)	1 *(7%)*	-	12 *(86%)*	4 *(29%)*
MIDDLE AGE GROUP **Women (n=8)**	7 *(87%)*	-	2 *(25%)*	4 *(50%)*
Men (n=12)	6 *(50%)*	-	8 *(67%)*	6 *(50%)*
OLDEST AGE GROUP **Women (n=12)**	2 *(17%)*	-	3 *(25%)*	7 *(58%)*
Men (n=17)	2 *(11%)*	-	13 *(76%)*	1 *(6%)*

It is perhaps not surprising that the youngest age group was most likely to participate in hobbies of all kinds. It was apparent that a wide range of activities were available to this age group from a diverse range of sources including schools, youth clubs, cadets, leisure facilities and private classes. The older two age groups were more likely to comment on the fact that their participation in hobbies was limited by time, money and commitments, such as work and study. It was also apparent that young men in the middle and oldest age groups were more likely than young women of a similar age to participate in hobbies. To a large extent this was accounted for by playing football either in organised tournaments, such as pub leagues or five-a sides, or just 'kicking a ball about' with a crowd of friends. It also appeared that young men (of all ages) were more likely to regularly use or play games on computers. Some young women who did not participate in hobbies attributed this to having children and only a few attributed it to lack of interest.

Table 5.15: Types of hobbies engaged in by persisters

Persisters	Formal and social	Formal and alone	Informal and social	Informal and alone
YOUNGEST AGE GROUP **Girls (n=20)**	7 *(35%)*	-	13 *(65%)*	7 *(35%)*
Boys (n=23)	11 *(48%)*	-	12 *(52%)*	4 *(17%)*
MIDDLE AGE GROUP **Women (n=18)**	1 *(5%)*	-	4 *(22%)*	5 *(28%)*
Men (n=17)	3 *(18%)*	-	15 *(88%)*	5 *(29%)*
OLDEST AGE GROUP **Women (n=12)**	-	-	-	2 *(17%)*
Men (n=18)	-	-	8 *(44%)*	4 *(22%)*

The above tables also demonstrate that for resisters and desisters in all age groups there was some degree of involvement in hobbies while for persisters in the oldest age group participation in hobbies involving some kind of social interaction was particularly limited. In part this is probably explained by the fact that this particular offender category and age group was the one most heavily using drugs. Indeed, six young male and female persisters attributed their lack of involvement in any hobbies to the fact they were using drugs, with one young woman explaining: 'I've not really been doing anything 'cause it was just ... You've no energy through drugs ... you're just interested in going and getting a bag and getting squared up'.

'HANGING ABOUT'

'Hanging about' was an issue which was of most concern to the youngest age group. This is consistent with Hendry's (1993) finding that 'hanging about' peaked at ages 13-16 years and decreased thereafter[25]. Most persisters and desisters in the youngest age group reported 'hanging about' in public spaces whereas no resisters said they did so. Indeed some resisters consciously decided not to hang about, for example:

> ... they end up doing stupid things just out of having nothing to do and end up getting into trouble ... I don't even hang about with my friends at the weekend because they do go out and just kind of get up to nothing. I'd rather stay in than walk about the streets so I'm not involved in it. (female resister, youngest age group)

There were certain common characteristics of the 'hanging about' engaged in by persisters and desisters:

- the places they hang about include: the streets, outside tenements, around shops, in parks, at train stations, in an old church, a disused car park, old sheds and a quarry
- hanging about often involved the consumption of alcohol and, less frequently, the use of drugs
- the groups which gathered could be large (10, 20, 50 and over 100 were some of the estimates of how many young people congregated in one park)
- the groups were frequently the source of police intervention, particularly to move them on
- police intervention led to interactions with the police which could become the source of friction.

---

[25] Several young people in the middle age group noted of instances of walking about the streets and town centre and a few reported that they consumed alcohol on the streets with friends.

EDUCATION

It might be expected that young people not strongly committed to school would be more likely to offend (see Braithwaite, 1997; Graham and Bowling, 1995). Tables 5.16 and 5.17 illustrate when young people left school and whether they were suspended or excluded. These data may be assumed to serve as indicators of the extent to which the young people were committed to their education.

Table 5.16: When young people left or planned to leave school[26]

	Resisters		Desisters		Persisters	
	Male	Female	Male	Female	Male	Female
4th year	3 (10%)	6 (13%)	14 (41%)	10 (32%)	24 (51%)	19 (40%)
5th year	5 (17%)	9 (20%)	6 (18%)	9 (29%)	9 (19%)	16 (34%)
6th year	21 (72%)	30 (67%)	14 (41%)	12 (39%)	14 (30%)	12 (25%)
Total	29	45	34	31	47	47

Resisters of all ages were more likely to plan to stay on or to have stayed on at school until sixth year. By contrast persisters, especially young men, seemed to have left school at the earliest opportunity.

Table 5.17: Whether young people were suspended or excluded from school[27]

	Resisters		Desisters		Persisters	
	Male	Female	Male	Female	Male	Female
Suspended or excluded	5 (17%)	1 (2%)	10 (31%)	8 (27%)	33 (60%)	22 (51%)
Not suspended or excluded	25 (83%)	48 (98%)	22 (69%)	21 (72%)	22 (40%)	21 (49%)
Total	30	49	32	29	55	43

Persisters were most likely to have been suspended or excluded from school. The majority of young people reported that they had been suspended rather than excluded and the types of incident that had resulted in this outcome included fighting with other pupils, vandalism of school property, disruptive behaviour in the classroom, verbal abuse to teachers, theft and assault of a teacher. Many of the persisters commented that they had been suspended on more than one occasion and the length of suspension had generally ranged from a few days to two weeks.

TEACHERS' PERSPECTIVES ON EDUCATION AND OFFENDING

The role of teachers in relation to offending by young people

As already mentioned in Chapter Four, teachers would generally become aware that a pupil was involved in offending if the reporter to the children's panel

[26] This information was not available for all cases.
[27] This information was not available for all cases.

requested a report from the school. However, such requests were treated confidentially and the guidance teacher – who would compile the report – would not disclose the grounds of referral to other teachers 'unless there was a specific reason which might affect the child in school and child protection issues and things like that'. Other sources of information about young people's offending would be parents – although that was said to occur rarely – and the community involvement police, who may visit the school to enquire about a particular young person.

Whilst it was suggested that all teachers should endeavour to help young people if they become aware of problems such as offending, guidance staff – by virtue of having access to information about pupils that would not normally be divulged to other teachers – were the most common source of advice and support, although their ability to provide such support was said to be dependent upon the willingness of pupils and parents to accept it:

> Our mission statement would refer to the importance of individual support for pupil, teacher and family, so any pupil that was in any sort of trouble, we would hope to be there as a support for them. That really depends on whether or not the pupil and/or the family want that support. It's an understandable reaction that some families will deny any sort of offending as far as the school is concerned because they would rather it wasn't happening.

In each of the schools the guidance teacher was the formal point of contact for young people if they had problems, though each of the teachers who were interviewed emphasised that pupils were encouraged to approach any teacher they felt comfortable talking to about difficulties they were experiencing inside or outside the school. Other sources of help included school chaplains and educational psychologists. Although confidentiality would be maintained where possible, child protection policies meant that 'guidance staff or any teacher is no longer in a position to guarantee confidentiality in advance of disclosure of anything'. Furthermore, teachers were said to have a responsibility to report serious offending, such as the use of drugs in the school.

The issue of offending would be raised in a general way within schools via the social education programme, which included 'talking about acceptable and non-acceptable behaviour', sessions on crime and punishment and drug use and inputs from the local police. Teachers from Roman Catholic schools also emphasised the importance of the moral ethos within the school:

> We have got a fairly clear moral code and values so our line would be not just that you don't break the law but that you show respect to each other and to each individual as you would expect it to be shown to you. And virtually every form of offending is infringing on somebody else's rights, or whatever. So it would be within the school's ethos.

The approach adopted by schools to instances of offending within the school varied according to the nature and circumstances of the offence. Assaults against fellow pupils – the types of offences that were said to be most common – would usually result in the young person being suspended for up to three days, with the parents being asked to attend the school to discuss the situation. In more serious cases the police would become involved, either through being contacted by the school or by the victim of the offence or his/her parents. Teachers emphasised that while exclusion could be an effective strategy with many pupils – children were, it was suggested, often 'grounded' by their parents while the suspension was in effect and this could serve as a deterrent against further anti-social behaviour – it was used as sparingly as possible.

Multi-agency approaches to young people in difficulty were in existence in both study areas. In Westburgh this took the form of school based assessment teams consisting of social workers, psychologists, guidance teachers and learning support staff which would meet on a regular basis to discuss young people at risk or in need of help and support. In Eastburgh a slightly more formalised arrangement had been put into place wherein monthly external meetings were held between representatives of all of the agencies involved in 'supporting young people'.

Offending and school-related problems

Teachers identified an association between offending among young people and other social problems such as unemployment, poverty, family breakdown and drugs. One teacher also suggested that boys' offending might be partly a response to the increasing academic achievements of girls and their increased involvement in activities that were formerly associated primarily with boys:

> The thing that started to really concern us in schools as you know is boys opting out of competing with girls academically and therefore having to find other ways of making a name for themselves...One of my feelings on the drug situation was now that you can get girls down there smoking as freely as boys, they have to go one step further to preserve their kind of self esteem and I think maybe offending is something to do with that as well.

There was also said to be a link between truancy and offending, with young people who truanted being more likely to become involved in shoplifting, drinking, drug taking and under-age sex. Although not all young people who truanted were thought likely to offend – and for many, it was suggested, truancy was more about not being at school than about deliberately becoming involved in anti-social or delinquent acts – truancy was thought in some cases to be associated with other risk factors for offending:

> I think that a pupil who can truant and get away with it probably has less parental control than you would want and therefore is in a situation for under age drinking or drug taking or joy riding or whatever.

Partly because of the perceived link between truancy and offending and partly because of the established relationship between high levels of non-attendance and school achievement, truancy was said not to be tolerated and each of the schools adopted vigorous approaches towards it. Truancy was, however, thought sometimes to be related to problems at home and sometimes to be condoned by parents. Bullying was another issue that the police officers who were interviewed suggested may be a cause of truancy. All of the teachers acknowledged that bullying occurred in their school, though they were keen to differentiate between the existence of bullying and the existence of a bullying problem. Bullying – which was evident both among girls and among boys, though with the former was said more often to take the form of threats rather than actual violence – was considered to be linked to other forms of violence among pupils and each of the schools reported having policies to deal with this type of behaviour.

Teachers identified clear links between parental interest and support, truancy and school achievement and, therefore, albeit indirectly, between school achievement and crime. However, even 'high achievers' could, it was suggested, become involved in offending and related behaviours if they ran with 'a crowd of boys who have no great aspirations' or if they had more money to buy alcohol and drugs. The schools consequently attached considerable importance to encouraging parental involvement in their children's education:

In this school we're trying to take steps to try and make sure that the parents get much more information and that we are doing what we can to break down the barrier to try and get them involved.

Strategies to involve parents included parents' nights, open door policies in which parents can arrange to see a guidance teacher or assistant head teacher by appointment, regular bulletins and correspondence by letter, telephone or in person about pupils' progress and specific concerns. In one school the latter took the form of 'cause for concern reports' if pupils were thought to be under-achieving or otherwise giving cause for concern, and 'praise postcards' which would be sent to parents if their child had done particularly well. More generally teachers pointed to the importance of communicating positive news to parents rather than simply focusing on the problems which had tended to be the practice in the past.

Young people's attitudes towards education were said to be mixed, with particular concern expressed for those who failed to make an effort to achieve their full potential. Reference was made to 'a lack of spark, a lack of enthusiasm, a lack of expectation' among some pupils which was reflected in limited aspirations. Teachers in Westburgh also alluded specifically to limited aspirations among young people with respect to further education: even if they were capable of achieving in higher education, young people would often prefer, instead, to find a job. This was attributed partly to their narrow vistas and reluctance to move from their own area, no matter how disadvantaged that may be.

Education was considered by teachers to be a crucial factor in preventing offending among young people both through the ethos promoted by the school and through the opportunities that education afforded young people in the future. It was also recognised, however, that schools could not fully compensate for the disadvantaged family background that many young people experienced:

An awful lot of it comes back to giving them a sense of purpose, a sense of direction, improving their self esteem and confidence and all the rest of it... For a lot of these kids...we are the only chance they've got and we've got to be doing what we can to take them all on to give them an idea...to give them aspirations.

The broader strategies identified by teachers as offering some promise with respect to the reduction of youth crime included teaching parenting skills to families with 'no role models of how to cope with school, how to cope with society, appropriate life skills or anything', creating organisations that would 'involve kids in sport, in culture, in music and art' and listening to young people to learn what they would like to see provided in their local communities.

EMPLOYMENT

Commitment to employment may also be an important factor in whether young people offend. Employment may serve to give young people a 'stake in society' and, as a consequence, a recognition that they have too much to lose by becoming involved in offending behaviour. Table 5.18 illustrates young people's current employment status at the time of the interviews.

Table 5.18: Employment status of young people[28]?

	Resisters		Desisters		Persisters	
	Female	Male	Female	Male	Female	Male
YOUNGEST AGE GROUP 'Saturday' job	3 *(17%)*	2 *(14%)*	1 *(10%)*	1 *(7%)*	1 *(5%)*	-
Part-time job	5 *(28%)*	2 *(14%)*	3 *(30%)*	1 *(7%)*	3 *(15%)*	4 *(19%)*
Casual job	-	1 *(7%)*	-	1 *(7%)*	-	-
No job	10 *(55%)*	9 *(64%)*	6 *(60%)*	11 *(79%)*	16 *(80%)*	17 *(81%)*
Total	18	14	10	14	20	21
MIDDLE AGE GROUP Further education	11 *(73%)*	4 *(28%)*	4 *(57%)*	2 *(18%)*	1 *(6%)*	2 *(12%)*
Employed	4 *(36%)*	6 *(43%)*	1 *(14%)*	6 *(55%)*	3 *(19%)*	3 *(18%)*
Unemployed	-	4 *(28%)*	2 *(29%)*	3 *(27%)*	12 *(75%)*	12 *(70%)*
Total	15	14	7	11	16	17
OLDEST AGE GROUP Further education	1 *(6%)*	1 *(12%)*	1 *(8%)*	-	-	-
Employed	9 *(56%)*	4 *(50%)*	3 *(25%)*	5 *(31%)*	1 *(8%)*	3 *(17%)*
Unemployed	6 *(38%)*	3 *(38%)*	8 *(67%)*	11 *(69%)*	11 *(92%)*	15 *(83%)*
Total	16	8	12	16	12	18

[28] This information was not available for all cases.

In the youngest age group girls, resisters and desisters were generally most likely to have a job. In the older two age groups a striking feature is the extent of unemployment among persisters. This situation may reflect the fact that quite a high proportion had described themselves as regular drug users and many had experience of the criminal justice system. A criminal record was recognised by the young people themselves as constituting a barrier to gaining employment.

ASPIRATIONS AND EXPECTATIONS OF YOUNG PEOPLE

Generally the young people's aspirations were notable by their conservatism. Almost all mentioned study, secure employment, marriage or children (or a combination of these), while very few mentioned the possibility of travel, promotion, alternative lifestyles or personal ambitions (for example, achievement in sport or music). Tables 5.19-5.21 illustrate young people's aspirations in four years time.

In four years time

Table 5.19: What resisters want to be doing in four years time

Aspirations	Youngest age group		Middle age group		Oldest age group	
	Male (n=14)	Female (n=19)	Male (n=14)	Female (n=19)	Male (n=6)	Female (n=15)
Job/career	11 *(78%)*	2 *(10%)*	7 *(50%)*	15 *(79%)*	2 *(33%)*	6 *(40%)*
University/college	10 *(71%)*	16 *(84%)*	3 *(21%)*	3 *(16%)*	1 *(17%)*	1 *(7%)*
Progressing in job	3 *(21%)*	-	2 *(14%)*	2 *(10%)*	2 *(33%)*	3 *(20%)*
Own or better home	6 *(43%)*	2 *(10%)*	6 *(43%)*	6 *(31%)*	-	2 *(13%)*
Partner/marriage	3 *(21%)*	-	3 *(21%)*	1 *(5%)*	3 *(50%)*	3 *(20%)*
Children	-	-	-	1 *(5%)*	-	2 *(13%)*
Work abroad	1 *(7%)*	-	1 *(7%)*	1 *(5%)*	1 *(17%)*	-
Travel	-	-	-	-	-	-
Move outwith area	-	-	-	1 *(5%)*	-	1 *(13%)*
Don't know	1 *(7%)*	-	-	-	-	-

Table 5.20: What desisters want to be doing in four years time

Aspirations	Youngest age group		Middle age group		Oldest age group	
	Male (n=14)	Female (n=11)	Male (n=10)	Female (n=8)	Male (n=14)	Female (n=12)
Job/career	8 (57%)	7 (64%)	6 (60%)	4 (50%)	7 (50%)	7 (58%)
University/college	8 (57%)	3 (27%)	1 (10%)	1 (12%)	-	-
Progressing in job	-	1 (9%)	-	2 (25%)	3 (21%)	-
Own or better home	-	-	3 (30%)	-	3 (21%)	5 (42%)
Partner/marriage	-	1 (9%)	4 (40%)	1 (12%)	5 (36%)	3 (25%)
Children	-	-	-	-	2 (14%)	3 (25%)
Work abroad	-	-	2 (20%)	-	-	-
Travel	-	-	-	-	1 (7%)	-
Move outwith area	-	-	-	-	-	3 (25%)
Don't know	-	-	1 (10%)	-	-	2 (17%)

Table 5.21: What persisters want to be doing in four years time

Aspirations	Youngest age group		Middle age group		Oldest age group	
	Male (n=22)	Female (n=20)	Male (n=16)	Female (n=18)	Male (n=15)	Female (n=12)
Job/career	15 (68%)	9 (45%)	10 (62%)	12 (67%)	9 (60%)	9 (75%)
University/college	8 (36%)	9 (45%)	-	2 (11%)	-	1 (8%)
Progressing in job	-	-	2 (12%)	1 (5%)	1 (7%)	-
Own or better home	1 (4%)	4 (20%)	3 (19%)	4 (22%)	3 (20%)	3 (25%)
Partner/marriage	1 (4%)	-	2 (12%)	2 (11%)	4 (27%)	-
Children	-	-	1 (6%)	1 (5%)	2 (13%)	1 (8%)
Work abroad	2 (9%)	-	1 (6%)	-	-	-
Travel	-	1 (5%)	-	1 (5%)	-	-
Move outwith area	-	-	1 (6%)	-	1 (7%)	-
Off drugs	-	-	1 (6%)	4 (22%)	6 (40%)	2 (17%)
Don't know	-	-	1 (6%)	-	-	-

On the whole young people, in all offender categories, tended to have fairly similar aspirations in terms of what they wanted to be doing in four years time. Within the youngest age group resisters were more likely to say they wanted to attend university or college while desisters and persisters were more likely to say they wanted a job. However, in addition to the information illustrated in the tables many of the young people emphasised that ultimately they wanted to be employed in jobs that gave them some satisfaction. Many of the young people wanted to gain a degree of independence in the next four years, often noting their desire to settle down with partners and have children.

When young people were asked what they expected to be doing in four years time, the majority re-iterated their desires – that is they expected to be doing what they wanted to do. Many young people also noted that they were ultimately responsible for whether or not they achieved what they wanted to in the next four years. For example, a female resister in the middle age group explained: 'I think if you are determined enough and have got the drive and ambition, I think you will do what you want to do'. In similar terms a male desister in the oldest age group commented: ' I don't expect anything. If something is going to happen to me it will be through my own doing. I don't expect things just to come to me'.

A few resisters commented that if they had not attained what they hoped to they would be satisfied as long as they were 'happy', 'content' and doing something they 'wanted' to do. Three resisters were more pessimistic about their chances of achieving what they wanted to within four years, with two expecting to be in 'crappy' or 'brain dead' factory jobs and the third – who had sustained multiple injuries in an accident – expecting a substantial deterioration in his health which would undermine his ability to work. Female desisters in the older age groups who were uncertain whether they would achieve what they wanted within four years largely attributed this to the likelihood of assuming caring responsibilities either for children or for parents. Male desisters in the middle age group who had doubts about their ability to achieve what they wanted within four years thought they were likely to be in exactly the same position as currently or would be inhibited because they had a criminal record. A few persisters in the older age groups commented that they were unlikely to achieve what they wanted because they would probably get sentenced to custody or because they would still be using drugs. In contrast to the generally optimistic and high expectations of the youngest age group it is interesting that it is only within the persister category that doubts about the ability to achieve their four year aspirations were raised. For example, several persisters commented that they would probably end up in unskilled, 'dead end, or 'crappy' jobs.

In eight years time

Tables 5.22 to 5.24 illustrate that young people's projected eight year aspirations were not substantially different to those they identified at four years.

Table 5.22: What resisters want to be doing in eight years time

Aspirations	Youngest age group		Middle age group		Oldest age group	
	Male (n=14)	Female (n=19)	Male (n=14)	Female (n=19)	Male (n=6)	Female (n=15)
Job/career	14 *(100%)*	15 *(79%)*	7 *(50%)*	9 *(47%)*	2 *(33%)*	7 *(47%)*
University/college	-	1 *(5%)*	1 *(7%)*	-	-	2 *(13%)*
Progressing in job	-	-	2 *(14%)*	1 *(5%)*	1 *(17%)*	1 *(7%)*
Own or better home	2 *(14%)*	3 *(16%)*	-	3 *(16%)*	2 *(33%)*	2 *(13%)*
Partner/marriage	3 *(21%)*	7 *(37%)*	5 *(36%)*	7 *(37%)*	3 *(50%)*	7 *(47%)*
Children	1 *(7%)*	3 *(16%)*	3 *(21%)*	4 *(21%)*	2 *(33%)*	6 *(40%)*
Work abroad	2 *(14%)*	1 *(5%)*	1 *(7%)*	-	-	1 *(7%)*
Travel	1 *(7%)*	-	-	1 *(5%)*	-	-
Move outwith area	-	-	2 *(14%)*	-	1 *(17%)*	2 *(13%)*
Don't know	-	1 *(5%)*	2 *(14%)*	-	-	1 *(7%)*

Table 5.23: What desisters want to be doing in eight years time

Aspirations	Youngest age group		Middle age group		Oldest age group	
	Male (n=14)	Female (n=10)	Male (n=10)	Female (n=8)	Male (n=13)	Female (n=12)
Job/career	12 *(86%)*	8 *(80%)*	2 *(20%)*	5 *(62%)*	3 *(23%)*	2 *(17%)*
University/college	-	-	-	-	-	-
Progressing in job	-	-	1 *(10%)*	-	3 *(23%)*	1 *(8%)*
Own or better home	5 *(36%)*	1 *(10%)*	3 *(30%)*	4 *(50%)*	5 *(38%)*	2 *(17%)*
Partner/marriage	3 *(21%)*	2 *(20%)*	4 *(40%)*	3 *(37%)*	3 *(23%)*	-
Children	2 *(14%)*	1 *(10%)*	3 *(30%)*	3 *(37%)*	1 *(8%)*	1 *(8%)*
Work abroad	-	-	1 *(10%)*	-	-	-
Travel	-	-	-	-	-	-
Move outwith area	-	-	-	1 *(12%)*	1 *(8%)*	-
Financial security	-	-	-	-	-	2 *(17%)*
Don't know	1 *(7%)*	1 *(10%)*	3 *(30%)*	1 *(12%)*	1 *(8%)*	4 *(33%)*

Table 5.24: What persisters want to be doing in eight years time

Aspirations	Youngest age group		Middle age group		Oldest age group	
	Male (n=21)	Female (n=19)	Male (n=15)	Female (n=17)	Male (n=13)	Female (n=11)
Job/career	15 (71%)	17 (89%)	7 (47%)	11 (65%)	2 (15%)	6 (54%)
University/college	3 (14%)	1 (5%)	-	-	-	-
Progressing in job	-	-	3 (20%)	-	-	-
Own or better home	8 (38%)	4 (21%)	3 (20%)	4 (23%)	1 (8%)	3 (27%)
Partner/marriage	3 (14%)	3 (16%)	7 (47%)	1 (6%)	2 (15%)	1 (9%)
Children	-	4 (21%)	4 (27%)	2 (12%)	2 (15%)	3 (27%)
Work abroad	2 (9%)	1 (5%)	-	-	-	-
Travel	-	1 (5%)	-	-	-	-
Move outwith area	1 (5%)	-	1 (7%)	1 (6%)	-	3 (27%)
Off drugs	-	-	-	-	3 (23%)	-
Don't know	-	1 (5%)	1 (7%)	-	4 (31%)	-

Eight years into the future the majority of young people reported their desire to have a job or to be continuing in their chosen career and not surprisingly many more were concerned to be making or progressing adult transitions such as getting married and having children. Overall, resisters and desisters were fairly confident that they would be able to achieve what they wanted to within this eight year time frame. A male resister explained: 'I think the further into the future the more likely it is to become'. A female desister in the oldest age group commented that she was uncertain whether she would be able to work as she wished because of the responsibilities of motherhood and a male desister in the oldest age group explained that he was unlikely to gain his desired employment given that 'the number of people in jobs they like is minimal ... there's not that many'. Persisters in the older age groups who noted their uncertainty of achieving what they wanted to in eight years time explained this in terms of drug use or the likelihood of being sentenced to custody.

SUMMARY

Overall, almost four fifths (76%) of young people in the youngest age group reported that they had consumed alcohol and 3 in 10 admitted to using cannabis. Resisters were least likely to have consumed alcohol and drug use was almost exclusively undertaken by persisters. Girls (75%) were more likely than boys (50%) to admit to using drugs on at least one occasion. Reported drug use for all in the youngest age category was relatively infrequent and the majority of this drug use had been relatively recent.

There was an escalation in the severity and frequency of substance use by age. In the older two age groups resisters were least likely and persisters most likely to report use of illegal substances and the experiences of young men and young women were broadly similar. The frequency of use differed according to the substance with alcohol, cannabis, and heroin often used regularly, or in some cases daily, while amphetamines, cocaine, crack, ecstasy, solvents, LSD and magic mushrooms were more often used on an occasional basis.

Common explanations forwarded to account for drug use included peer pressure, enjoyment, opportunity, curiosity, relaxation, recreation and to counteract boredom. Addiction was only an issue for 23 (14%) of the young people in the two older age groups and was most prevalent among persisters in the oldest age group with almost half (47%) of the young men and almost three-fifths (58%) of the young women in this group attributing their drug use to (usually heroin) addiction.

Common explanations for non use of drugs included the associated expense, the perceived danger, the illegality of drugs, choice, fear and the effects drugs had on others. Discontinued use of drugs was also accounted for in terms of expense and the effects of drugs on others but was also informed by the young people's own experience, particularly their dislike and fear of the effects of drugs, and the fact that they had matured or were responsible for children.

It appeared that drugs were relatively easy to access and that young people considered drug use to be a relatively common practice among their peers. Cannabis was generally perceived as less serious than other illegal substances while heroin use and addiction was recognised as serious and problematic. Persisters in the two older age groups were mostly likely to identify a link between their use of drugs and offending, generally in terms of offending to get money to fund their drug use.

Young people reported initial alcohol use between 12-14 years. Alcohol use was generally supervised by adults for resisters and desisters in the youngest age group while persisters were most likely to report unsupervised and public use of alcohol. Use of alcohol was common among young people in the middle and oldest age groups and was often described as an integral part of their social lives. Young men were more likely to report regular use of alcohol and older young women were more likely to comment that their use of alcohol was limited to special occasions and social outings. Non use of alcohol among young people in the older age groups was generally associated with drug use and, in particular, heroin addiction. Half of the girl persisters and two boy persisters commented that alcohol use had led them to offend – generally fighting – while older young people on the whole did not associate alcohol use with criminal activity.

In response to a range of risk taking scenarios young people in the middle and oldest age groups were more likely than those in the youngest age group to say they would engage in a range of risky behaviours which were, or verged on, the illegal. There were no significant differences between boys and girls in terms of their responses to individual scenarios and few gender differences among the older age groups in this respect. Persisters were significantly more likely to say they would engage in a range of risk taking or impulsive behaviours.

Boys and girls in the youngest age group were most likely to participate in a range of hobbies. In the older age groups young men were more likely than young women to engage in hobbies largely as a result of their participation in organised and informal football games. Resisters and desisters of all ages were more likely than persisters to be involved in hobbies which were both formal and social.

Resisters of all ages were most likely to plan to stay on or to have stayed on at school until sixth year. By contrast persisters, especially young men in the oldest age group, seemed to have left school at the earliest opportunity. Persisters were most likely to have been suspended or excluded from school.

Education was considered by teachers to be a crucial factor in preventing offending among young people both through the ethos promoted by the school and through opportunities that education afforded young people in the future. It was also recognised that schools could not fully compensate for the disadvantaged family background that many young people experienced.

Persisters of all ages were least likely to have a job and the majority of older persisters were unemployed. Young people's aspirations generally focused upon employment and making adult transitions, such as getting their own home, forming relationships with partners and having children. The majority expected to achieve what they wanted, though persisters were slightly less optimistic in this respect.

CHAPTER SIX: OFFENDING: RELATIONSHIPS AND SOCIAL NETWORKS

INTRODUCTION

Informal social control exerted by families, communities and friendship networks is often considered an effective form of social control. Control theory (Hirschi, 1969) suggests that the stronger young people's attachments are to others, particularly parents and school teachers, the stronger the control exerted and the less likely it will be that the young person will offend. Furthermore it is suggested that the extent to which individuals believe in particular values, for example the importance of not breaking the law, or of not bringing disgrace upon one's family, will also effect propensity to offend. This chapter will explore these issues by examining young people's views on the importance and impact of their relationships and social networks and how these relate to their decisions regarding involvement in offending.

FAMILY AND OFFENDING

Table 6.1: Whether family members are known to have offended[29]

	Family had offended (n=82)	Family had not offended (n=106)	Total (n=188)
Resisters	**13** *(18%)*	**58** *(82%)*	**71** *(100%)*
Desisters	**24** *(53%)*	**21** *(47%)*	**45** *(100%)*
Persisters	**45** *(63%)*	**27** *(38%)*	**72** *(101%)*

Prior research has confirmed the links between parental and child offending patterns (Farrington, Barnes and Lambert, 1996). In the current study, the respondents were asked whether they knew if any of their family had offended. Table 6.1 indicates that the majority of resisters (82%) reported that their families had not offended and that the majority of persisters (63%) reported that their families had offended. Desisters were closer to persisters in this respect, with just over half (53%) reporting that a member of their family had offended. A variety of offences were reported to have been committed by families, including: shoplifting, fraud, breach of the peace, drug use, vandalism, robbery, arson and murder. The family members identified as having offended were: fathers, step-fathers, brothers, cousins, uncles, mothers, sisters and a grandmother and there were notably more male than female offending family members. Interestingly, more girls and women reported greater numbers of female than male family members having offended. Persisters more frequently referred to relatives having been in prison, for example 'my dad's side of the family end up in jail like every six months or something'; 'my cousin is in jail for attempted murder' and 'my auntie's husband, he has just got out of prison ... I think he shot somebody'.

[29] This question was not directly asked in many of the interviews with 14-15 year old boys as the main concern was to explore family's views and attitudes and their impact on the young people.

When asked what their families' general views about offending were, almost all resisters reported that their families were 'against it', 'do not approve', 'don't like it' or 'think it's wrong'. The converse was not the case – that is the majority of persisters and desisters did *not* say that their family approved of or were indifferent to offending.

OFFENDING AND FAMILIES: THE EFFECT ON YOUNG PEOPLE

Table 6.2 illustrates whether or not families' views on offending were thought to make any difference to the young people interviewed[30].

Table 6.2: Whether or not families' views on offending made any difference

	Resisters		Desisters		Persisters	
	Male	**Female**	**Male**	**Female**	**Male**	**Female**
YOUNGEST AGE GROUP Families' views made a difference	13 *(100%)*	11 *(73%)*	7 *(70%)*	6 *(75%)*	12 *(63%)*	10 *(53%)*
Families' views made no difference	-	4 *(27%)*	3 *(30%)*	2 *(25%)*	7 *(37%)*	9 *(47%)*
Total	13	15	10	8	19	19
MIDDLE AGE GROUP Families' views made a difference	12 *(92%)*	16 *(89%)*	8 *(73%)*	4 *(67%)*	7 *(44%)*	3 *(21%)*
Families' views made no difference	1 *(8%)*	2 *(11%)*	3 *(27%)*	2 *(33%)*	9 *(56%)*	11 *(79%)*
Total	13	18	11	6	16	14
OLDEST AGE GROUP Families' views made a difference	8 *(100%)*	11 *(69%)*	9 *(56%)*	4 *(40%)*	2 *(12%)*	1 *(20%)*
Families' views made no difference	-	5 *(31%)*	7 *(44%)*	6 *(60%)*	15 *(88%)*	4 *(80%)*
Total	8	16	16	10	17	5

Young people's perceptions of the effect of their families' views on them differed most clearly according to gender and offender category but to a lesser extent by age. It appears that young women on the whole were less inclined to indicate that their families' views made a difference to them and persisters in the middle and oldest age groups were more likely to indicate that their families' views about offending made no difference to them.

Those young women, male resisters and male desisters who commented that their families' views on offending made no difference to them explained this in

[30] Data was not available for all interviewees.

terms of their independence and the fact that they held and acted upon their own views and principles, which for many were similar to those held by their families. As one female resister in the middle age group commented:

> If you look at me and my sister, we are two totally different people but we were brought up in the same household. Well she has tried some drugs and she drinks quite a lot and we're totally different in that way... It just kind of depends on how strong a person you are. Before I would have said it was to do with upbringing and I still do to an extent, but then you look at my sister, I mean she doesn't go out and murder people or mug people and things like that, but we are different ... but we both came from the same household.

A few young people noted that in respect of drugs and drug use (largely cannabis) their views were more liberal than those held by their parents. Desisters commented that their families' views had limited impact on their previous offending as they had often offended despite knowing it was wrong, or attributed their involvement in offending to the area in which they lived and/or to peer pressure.

The majority of resisters and desisters who perceived their families' views on offending to have made a difference to them attributed this to sharing and respecting their families' views, to having been brought up not to offend or to viewing offending as wrong. A few desisters noted that their families' views had stopped them from committing more serious offences. A female resister in the middle age group explained why her upbringing had made a difference as follows:

> I was taught that you shouldn't do that [offend] and judging by what I saw, there was no hypocrisy in how I was brought up. I wasn't told not to do something and then my parents went and did it. I suppose if I wanted to offend I would and then a lot of my parenting would go out the window. But I think it must have made a difference, because I am who I am because of my parenting and I don't offend.

Other explanations of why families' views on offending made a difference to young people and their reluctance to offend or re-offend included: the shame, upset and hurt that involvement in offending would cause or had caused to their families; guilt; fear of their families' reaction; the desire not to lose or break their families' trust or pride in them; and the fact they had witnessed the negative effects of offending on their family or more generally through involvement in offending by a relative. For example:

> I just don't want to be like what my brother is. I don't want to be in jail at all. Maybe it would be different if my brother hadn't been inside. Maybe I'd be inside now. But going through the experiences with him, I just don't want to go there. I've been to visit him and they are bad places. I couldn't handle the jail (male resister, oldest age group).

In explaining why their families' views on offending had made no difference to them many persisters attributed this to the fact that they held and acted upon their own views and principles: 'I'm my own person'; 'I go by my own rules' and 'I look out for myself'. Many others explained that their families' views made no difference to them because of their drug use and addiction. A young women who stole from her family to support her use of heroin commented: 'I hate the thought of them all [family] talking about us and knowing what I'm doing because it hurts my mam and that but at the time I'm no caring'. Others attributed their involvement in offending to peer pressure or living in an area where offending was rife and acceptable, while a few identified the lack of a 'father-figure' in their upbringing as influential in their offending. A male persister in the oldest age group, whose father and mother were separated, explained:

I don't know why my father never came to that police station and says 'listen you' and gave me a slap on the fucking face and says 'come on I'll fucking help you'. Not once did he come and say that to me. If that was a daughter of mine, if I knew my daughter was doing drugs or using drugs I'd go and fucking skelp her arse, you know. That's what I'd do as a father you know. I'm not the best father in the world you know but there's fucking things that I would do that he didn't do.

Persisters in the youngest age group who thought that their families' views on offending had made a difference to them largely explained this in terms of their families punishing them or discussing their offending with them. A few persisters in the middle and oldest groups commented that they were concerned not to hurt or upset their families and that while in the past they had not taken their families' views into consideration they were more inclined to do so now. Some commented that overall their families had been a positive influence on them, by preventing them from becoming involved in more serious offences such as armed robbery, while others expressed their gratitude for support received from their families. A female persister in the middle age group who had received support and help from her mother commented:

More or less I've done what she's [mother] done. It's mad. It's me living her life over again, because everything she's told me she's done, I've done it, know what I mean, and now my Mum's doing good, so, if she can do it I suppose I can do it. [...] She's no very happy with me at the moment, know, according to the way I am and that, but there's nothing she can do, the only person that can do something about it is me.

FRIENDS AND OFFENDING

Most of the offences discussed in the interviews were said to have been carried out in the company of others. Previous research has found a strong association between young people offending and their having delinquent friends (for example, Reiss, 1988; Rouse and Eve, 1991). It therefore comes as no surprise that the majority of persisters reported having friends who had offended[31], as Table 6.3 illustrates. The relationship between peer group and offending is arguably bi-directional – that is, partly a result of young people who are predisposed towards offending choosing to associate with each other in the first place and partly because delinquent peer groups actively promote offending among members (Menard and Elliot, 1994; Thornberry et al., 1994).

Table 6.3: Whether friends are known to have offended

	Some/all friends had offended (n=174)	No friends had offended (n=80)	Total (n=254)
Resisters	**34** *(40%)*	**52** *(60%)*	**86** *(100%)*
Desisters	**46** *(74%)*	**16** *(26%)*	**62** *(100%)*
Persisters	**94** *(89%)*	**12** *(12%)*	**106** *(101%)*

Table 6.3 is interesting in two respects. First, it indicates that a significant minority of resisters (40%) also have friends who have offended. It could be argued that 'resister' is a more appropriate term for this sub group (than for the 60% of resisters who report no friends who have offended) as they are more likely to have been subject to negative peer influence in relation to offending, which they have indeed resisted. Secondly, it is notable that desisters resemble persisters more closely than resisters in being more likely to report having friends who offend.

Some of those interviewed were ambivalent about naming their friends' behaviours as offending – drug use being the most often cited example in this context – and quite subtle distinctions were made. For example, one persister who had been involved in shoplifting and vandalism described a friend as:

> more like respectable. She's been brought up – like plays the piano and everything and she's really – she's into music and – but she does offend as well, but not like, not actually – well it is a criminal offence – she smokes hash and she does drugs right, but she doesn't actually offend as in shoplifting (female persister, youngest age group).

Asked what their friends' general views of offending were, most resisters reported them to be the same as their own, namely: 'they don't approve', 'they think it's wrong as well' or 'don't agree with it'. A few resisters, who had friends who had offended, said there was a difference between their views and those of their friends. More desisters and persisters reported that their friends were not opposed to offending: 'she isn't really bothered about it' (desister), 'one of them comes in and boasts about it' (desister) 'some of my friends think that offending is great' (persister), 'they think it's up to them what they do' (persister), 'they don't care' (persister) and 'other ones think it's funny' (persister).

[31] A few resisters and desisters had past friends who had offended.

OFFENDING AND FRIENDS: THE EFFECT ON YOUNG PEOPLE

Table 6.4 summarises whether or not young people thought that their friends' views on offending made any difference to them[32]. It demonstrates that the majority of young people did not think that their friends' views about offending directly affected them or how they behaved. There was some difference in terms of gender, with certain groups of young men being more likely to believe that they were affected by their friends' views. When explaining why friends' views made no difference to them many young people claimed that they had their own opinions and were ultimately responsible for their own decisions. For example:

I think I'm sort of responsible and sensible enough to say well if they're going to be doing something like that then I'll make sure I'm no there. You know I'll not get involved. I'd like to think I'm strong enough as a person to say that (male resister, oldest age group);

I wouldn't force my opinion down any of my friends' throats, so because of that fact alone I wouldn't listen to any of my friends' opinions (male resister, oldest age group);

I would do what I wanted to anyway regardless of what they thought or what they said (male persister, middle age group).

[32] Data was not available for all interviewees.

Table 6.4: Whether or not friends' views on offending made any difference

	Resisters		Desisters		Persisters	
	Male	Female	Male	Female	Male	Female
YOUNGEST AGE GROUP						
Families' views made a difference	6 (46%)	-	7 (64%)	-	17 (74%)	1 (13%)
Families' views made no difference	7 (54%)	9 (100%)	4 (36%)	6 (100%)	6 (26%)	7 (87%)
Total	13	9	11	6	23	8
MIDDLE AGE GROUP						
Families' views made a difference	4 (36%)	3 (27%)	1 (10%)	5 (83%)	5 (39%)	9 (50%)
Families' views made no difference	7 (64%)	8 (73%)	9 (90%)	1 (17%)	8 (61%)	9 (50%)
Total	11	11	10	6	13	18
OLDEST AGE GROUP						
Families' views made a difference	4 (57%)	5 (36%)	5 (36%)	2 (20%)	4 (24%)	1 (14%)
Families' views made no difference	3 (43%)	9 (64%)	9 (64%)	8 (80%)	13 (76%)	6 (86%)
Total	7	14	14	10	17	7

Resisters and desisters noted that in many respects their views were very similar to their friends. For some this was thought to have reinforced their views and discouraged them from offending. A female desister (oldest age group) who thought she was influenced by her friends' views commented: 'Their views would probably be the same as mine, you don't think it's right, you probably would stay away from people that had offended as well, but if they wanted to be pals I'd be like that, no sorry I'm not into that'. In discussing their own involvement in offending desisters thought that their friends' views had been influential at the time, especially since many had only offended in the company of others and never alone. A few commented that, like them, their friends had subsequently 'grown out of offending' while two young men in the oldest age group explained that they now had a different circle of friends and would be embarrassed and ashamed if their current friends found out about their past offending.

Older persisters (three young men and two young women) made reference to their drug use when explaining why their friends' views made no difference to them: 'The only person I care about is myself – when you are on drugs you don't want to care about your friends. They just stab you in the back' and 'They hate coming with me, hate me like shoplifting. They hate it but I've got to do it just to keep the habit going.' (female persisters). In explaining why friends' views did have some impact on them, persisters – especially those in the youngest age group – said that they offended with friends or that their friends were involved in the same types of things as themselves (c.f: Farrington, 1996; Loeber et al., 1991). A few persisters commented on the fact that friends' views had a positive impact upon them in terms of offending. As one male persister explained: 'it makes me go through a wee bit of growing up as well. Well they can do it [stop offending], surely I can do it. And if they're no doing it, I'm no going to get involved in it with them'.

PARTNERS AND OFFENDING

Previous research has demonstrated that for young women forming relationships, getting married and having children are all strong predictors of desistance but that the same is not true for young men (Graham and Bowling, 1995). Table 6.5 summarises whether or not the young people's boyfriends or girlfriends had offended. Girls and young women were on the whole more likely to have partners who had offended, which is not particularly surprising given that boys and young men are more likely to offend than girls and young women. However, there also appeared to be a relationship between the offending categories and whether or not a young person's partner had offended, especially in the middle and oldest age groups. This is reinforced by the finding that when talking about their partner's offending the majority of desisters commented that this was something that had happened in the past and in most cases had not been particularly serious (involving, for instance, shoplifting or fighting) although some desisters also reported that their partners had been involved in fraud, housebreaking, and drug dealing. The partners of female persisters appeared to be involved in relatively serious offending including housebreaking, drug dealing, reset and armed robbery. Furthermore, three of the female persisters observed that their partners were currently serving custodial sentences.

Table 6.5: Whether or not partners had offended

	Resisters		Desisters		Persisters	
	Male	Female	Male	Female	Male	Female
YOUNGEST AGE GROUP **Partner had offended**	-	1 *(33%)*	-	-	-	7 *(87%)*
Partner hadn't offended	-	2 *(67%)*	2 *(100%)*	-	2 *(100%)*	1 *(13%)*
Total	-	3	2	-	2	8
MIDDLE AGE GROUP **Partner had offended**	-	1 *(17%)*	3 *(100%)*	5 *(83%)*	-	6 *(67%)*
Partner hadn't offended	4 *(100%)*	5 *(83%)*	-	1 *(17%)*	1 *(100%)*	3 *(33%)*
Total	4	6	3	6	1	9
OLDEST AGE GROUP **Partner had offended**	-	1 *(17%)*	5 *(71%)*	7 *(88%)*	3 *(75%)*	7 *(88%)*
Partner hadn't offended	2 *(100%)*	5 *(83%)*	2 *(29%)*	1 *(12%)*	1 *(25%)*	1 *(12%)*
Total	2	6	7	8	4	8

When asked about their partners' views of offending the majority of resisters and desisters commented that either their partners were against offending or that they shared similar views about offending to their own. A few were of the opinion that their partners did not feel strongly about offending unless it affected them personally or someone who was close to them. A few desisters suggested that their partners, like themselves, had 'changed', 'calmed down', or 'grown out of offending'. Many persisters (slightly more young men than young women) also commented that their partners believed all offending to be unacceptable. However, other persisters explained that their partners were accepting of their offending, often because they offended themselves. One young man in the middle age group, whose partner did not offend, believed his own involvement in offending was 'part of the attraction'.

All the female resisters and one male resister were of the opinion that their partner's views of offending made no difference to them because they had their own independent views and opinions. Others indicated that their partners' views were essentially the same as their own or that their families' views were taken more seriously. The majority of male resisters, however, were of the opinion that their partner's views on offending did make a difference to them either because they and their partners shared similar views or because their relationship could come under threat if they did offend.

On the whole male desisters thought their partners' views on offending made a difference to them and that their partners had a positive influence on them in terms of offending. This was largely attributed to the threat that the relationship might end or be adversely affected by further offending or simply because they respected and accepted their partners' views and opinions. Female desisters were more likely to think that their partners' views about offending did not affect them because they valued their own opinions, they viewed themselves as a positive role model, or because they had slightly different views about offending than their partners. The few female desisters who did think that their partners' views affected them attributed this to wanting to achieve and build good lives for them both and to avoid causing their partners any hurt or embarrassment.

The majority of male persisters thought that their partners' views on offending did not make any difference to them and the majority of female persisters thought the opposite. All of the male and a few of the female persisters who thought they were affected by their partners' views on offending believed this was a positive influence. In explaining this a few commented that they appreciated the advice and support their partners offered. Others explained that they respected their partners and therefore did not want to upset them, while one young man was concerned to protect his relationship with his partner and child. Several female persisters commented that their partners' views and actions in relation to offending had resulted in their becoming involved in offending and/or drug use. Male persisters who thought that their partners' views on offending had no effect on them explained this in terms of their own drug use, that they did not value their relationships, that their partners were unaware of the extent or severity of their offending or, conversely, the fact that their offending wasn't serious enough to elicit their partners' concern.

COMMUNITY AND OFFENDING

The majority of young people identified their community in geographic terms as the street, neighbourhood or town in which they lived. A few also recognised that geographic limitations did not adequately include all those whom they perceived as being part of their community. Therefore, for some young people their community was also identified as a network of friends and relationships. Overall, the majority of young people (66% of resisters, 65% of desisters and 67% of persisters) felt 'part' of their community and this was aided by being well known, knowing others, being involved in community activities, being brought up in a particular area or working in a particular area. Those who did not feel part of their communities attributed this to apathy, to choice, to not being involved in community activities, to there not being anything for them to be involved in, to being an offender or to the desire to avoid associating with offenders.

When asked if there was a community view on offending the majority of young people thought that their community would be 'against' offending and consider it 'wrong'. Some young people thought that there were likely to be different views within the community as to the acceptability or otherwise of offending. Attitudes were thought to vary according to whether or not individuals offended themselves, to whether or not families had children who were involved in offending or general nuisance and according to age. For instance, one male desister explained:

Well the old ones about here they're like that – it depends on how old you're talking about. Some of them go 'oh that's sick' and all the rest of it, but as they get younger they're like that 'yeah do it, that's one over the police' and all that.

Others also commented that offending, particularly drug related offending, was common in the areas in which they lived and that because many residents were involved in some offending – largely described as 'minor' offending – it was viewed as acceptable or at least understandable.

Table 6.6 shows whether or not young people thought that their communities' views on offending made any difference to them.

Table 6.6: Whether or not communities' views on offending made any difference

	Resisters		Desisters		Persisters	
	Male	Female	Male	Female	Male	Female
YOUNGEST AGE GROUP						
Communities' views made a difference	2 (22%)	1 (14%)	4 (67%)	1 (20%)	5 (50%)	2 (50%)
Communities' views made no difference	7 (78%)	6 (86%)	2 (33%)	4 (80%)	5 (50%)	2 (50%)
Total	9	7	6	5	10	4
MIDDLE AGE GROUP						
Communities' views made a difference	5 (55%)	12 (86%)	7 (87%)	1 (20%)	2 (15%)	2 (18%)
Communities' views made no difference	4 (44%)	2 (14%)	1 (13%)	4 (80%)	11 (85%)	9 (82%)
Total	9	14	8	5	13	11
OLDEST AGE GROUP						
Communities' views made a difference	3 (100%)	2 (20%)	5 (62%)	1 (20%)	1 (11%)	1 (14%)
Communities' views made no difference	-	8 (80%)	3 (38%)	4 (80%)	8 (89%)	6 (86%)
Total	3	10	8	5	9	7

Overall it appears that their communities' views on offending were not considered to be particularly important by many of the young people interviewed, with the exception of male desisters. In accounting for this young people in all categories identified the importance of their own views and opinions, the fact that they were not actively involved in community life and that they were not interested in and/or didn't care about the views of the community. One young woman in the middle age group commented that although she did not like the thought of people in her community talking about her, this was not enough in itself to make her stop offending or using drugs, while a male persister in the same age group explained: 'I don't care about anybody but myself'. Two young men explained that they were not affected by the community view because members of the community had perpetrated more serious offences themselves (a male desister) and because members of the community were willing to buy goods he had stolen (a male persister). Those young people who did think they were affected by the communities' view of offending largely attributed this to sharing the same views on offending or the concern to 'fit in' and not to be isolated within the community.

SUMMARY

More resisters reported that their families had not offended than desisters and persisters, with desisters being more similar to persisters in this respect. Girls and young women reported more female family members as having offended. When asked what their families' general views about offending were, almost all resisters reported that their families were against offending. The converse was not the case – that is the majority of persisters and desisters did *not* say that their family approved of or were indifferent to offending.

Persisters and young women in the middle and oldest age groups were more likely to indicate that their families' views of offending made no difference to them. Persisters often attributed this to holding and acting upon their own views or to drug use/addiction. The young women also explained that their own views were often similar to those held by their families. Resisters and desisters who thought that their families' views made a difference to them in respect of offending explained that they shared their families' views or that they had been brought up not to offend.

The majority of persisters reported that their friends had offended, as did a substantial minority of resisters, while desisters resembled persisters more closely than resisters. Most resisters reported their friends' views of offending to be the same as their own (that is disapproving). More desisters and persisters reported that their friends were not against offending. The majority of young people did not, however, think that their friends' views of offending directly effected them or how they behaved.

Girls and young women were more likely than boys and young men to have partners who offended. Generally resisters' partners were non offenders, desisters' partners were thought to have stopped offending and persisters' partners were identified as offenders. The majority of resisters and desisters thought their partners were against offending and therefore shared similar views to their own. Many persisters also thought their partners were against offending though others explained that their partners were generally accepting of their offending because they were often offenders themselves.

All female resisters and the majority of female desisters did not believe their partners' views made any difference to them or their behaviour because they held and valued their own views. By contrast the majority of male resisters and desisters believed their partners' views did make a difference because they did not want to jeopardise their relationships. Female persisters thought their partners' views made a difference to them, usually in a positive direction. By contrast, the majority of male persisters did not think their partners' views of offending made any difference to them.

The majority of young people felt 'part' of their communities which were generally identified as the street, neighbourhood or town in which they lived. Communities were, on the whole, thought to be against offending but the community view was not considered very important by many young people, with the exception of male desisters. In explaining the lack of community influence young people identified the value of their own views, the fact they were not involved in community life and that they lacked interest in or respect for the views of the community.

CHAPTER SEVEN:
YOUNG PEOPLE AND THE CRIMINAL JUSTICE SYSTEM

INTRODUCTION

So far we have explored young people's attitudes towards and explanations of offending and the interaction of their resistance, desistance or persistance with their lifestyles, family and friends. In this chapter the focus moves from these informal influences towards the formal systems of criminal and juvenile justice. Young people's attitudes towards the police, courts, social workers and prisons and young offenders institutions will be explored, with a particular emphasis on the extent to which they act as a deterrent. Although not part of the criminal justice system, the children's hearings system will also be included because of its role in dealing with young offenders.

(i) POLICE

The most obvious manifestation of the concerns and surveillance of young people in relation to crime is in the contact they have with the police. The Milton youth survey (1997) found that 47 per cent of young people had been in trouble with the police, a figure which is slightly higher than national self-report figures, which indicate that 43 per cent reported police contact at some time in one of the following forms: being told off or asked to move on (a third); being stopped and asked questions (a quarter); being searched (5%); being warned (5%); being taken to a children's hearing[33] (2%) or being charged and taken to court (1%) (MVA, 1998). Dobash et al. (1987) concluded that the majority of contacts between young people and the police did not result in serious actions or consequences. Indeed, they found that the most likely police response was to warn the young people or attempt to place unofficial restrictions on their movements, for example in the form of curfews or advising them to stay in their own area. The Scottish Crime Survey figures (SCS) add support to this view, since only three per cent of contacts resulted in a children's hearing or a court appearance. However, the SCS also revealed that 61 per cent of young people who reported some kind of police contact said they had offended at some time and 43 per cent admitted offending in the last 12 months, suggesting that this group were significantly more likely to offend than those who had never had police involvement.

It is against this background that the young people's experience of the police in the current study will be considered.

Police involvement with police in relation to their behaviour

Involvement with the police in relation to their behaviour ranged from those who reported no contact at all to one male persister who claimed to have had over

---

[33] The majority of children referred to the children's hearing system are dealt with by the reporter by measures other than a referral to a hearing (only 23% were referred to a hearing in 1997-8).

100 convictions by the age of 16. Tables 7.1a and 7.1b give reported police involvement across offender type and include not only those who have been charged, but also those who have had their details taken by the police, been moved on or have been stopped and searched[34].

Table 7.1a: Reported involvement with the police by offender category: boys and men

	No involvement (n=55)	Some involvement (n=82)	Total (n=137)
Resisters	23 (64%)	13 (36%)	36 (100%)
Desisters	15 (35%)	28 (65%)	43 (100%)
Persisters	17 (29%)	41 (71%)	58 (100%)

Table 7.1b: Reported involvement with the police by offender category: girls and women

	No involvement (n=72)	Some involvement (n=66)	Total (n=138)
Resisters	51 (91%)	5 (9%)	56 (100%)
Desisters	13 (41%)	19 (59%)	32 (100%)
Persisters	8 (16%)	42 (84%)	50 (100%)

Tables 7.1a and 7.1b indicate that the majority of persisters and desisters reported involvement with the police. Far fewer female resisters (9%) reported involvement with the police than male resisters (36%).

How well the police do their job

Young people identified three general aspects of the work of the police. First, their role was to 'stop crime', 'keep the peace' and 'keep law and order'. Secondly, once crimes had been committed, their role was to catch criminals. Thirdly, they were to 'help' with a range of matters, including: 'if you have got lost', 'if someone dies', the retrieval of stolen goods and to 'protect' the public – largely from criminals and in particular those involved in drugs, violent crime or housebreaking. Although these identified roles were fairly predictable, there were interesting differences between offender categories. The greatest contrast was between female resisters and male persisters, with 50 per cent (28) of the former identifying the role of the police as providing protection and/or help compared with 12 per cent (6) of the latter, with other categories falling somewhere between these two extremes.

Dobash et al. (1987) found that over half the young people they interviewed thought that the relationships between youth and police were 'fairly bad' or 'very bad'. Anderson et al. (1994) note the vicious circle that is created as more crimes go undetected because young people will not disclose information to the police, which leads to a position in which 'the police are left to resort to the very

[34] Other police involvement, for example calling the police because a crime has been committed against them, is not included in these tables.

adversarial methods that contributed to this lack of information in the first place' (p158). The Scottish Crime Survey (MVA, 1998) concluded that young people's views about the police depended on police contact; those with either recent or past police contact were consistently more negative about the police than those who had never had police contact. The views of the current sample support this finding, as Tables 7.1a and 7.1b indicate.

Table 7.1a: How well boys/young men think the police do their job

	Resisters (n=36)	Desisters (n=42)	Persisters (n=56)	Total (n=134)
Positive response	15 *(42%)*	13 *(31%)*	7 *(12%)*	35 *(26%)*
Mixed response	13 *(36%)*	10 *(24%)*	15 *(27%)*	38 *(28%)*
Negative response	8 *(22%)*	19 *(45%)*	34 *(61%)*	61 *(46%)*

Table 7.1b: How well girls/young women think the police do their job

	Resisters (n=54)	Desisters (n=31)	Persisters (n=49)	Total (n=134)
Positive response	30 *(56%)*	10 *(32%)*	15 *(31%)*	55 *(41%)*
Mixed response	12 *(22%)*	8 *(26%)*	9 *(18%)*	29 *(22%)*
Negative response	12 *(22%)*	13 *(42%)*	25 *(51%)*	50 *(37%)*

Tables 7.1a and 7.1b indicate that resisters (more than desisters and persisters) gave a positive response to the question as to how well the police did their job, particularly female resisters (56%). More persisters gave a negative response, particularly male persisters (61%). [Further analysis also indicates that those in the older age groups were more negative about the police than those in the youngest age group]. Given that 'there is some evidence that males are more likely to be picked up by police than females indulging in the same behaviour' (Coote, 1994:5), it could be argued that a more lenient approach by police to girls and women is reflected in the latter's response: equally it may be that the more positive female response in turn evokes a more favourable police approach. There is some evidence to suggest that the degree to which the police are shown respect does influence their subsequent actions (McConville et al., 1991; Maguire and Norris, 1992).

Positive comments made by resisters related to specific situations in which the police were helpful, for example 'if you are burgled or something they're always there' or 'I mean my brother had his bike stolen and if it wasn't for them [the police] he wouldn't have got it back'. Others cited particular initiatives which they thought were effective, such as an operation which entailed weapons being voluntarily handed into the police and fines being imposed on people for consuming alcohol in the streets. The danger the police faced evoked admiration: 'they do a good job. Westburgh's a nightmare to live in. It's very dangerous at night time'. Their visibility also evoked praise, for example:

For quite a while you didn't really see a policeman and then they started to come round in cars and stuff at night and kind of patrol the area and a lot of the offences around the place kind of stopped – all the fights and things that were going on all sort of died down a bit (male desister, youngest age group)

However, lack of visibility was also a source of criticism:

You don't see them walking up and down the street you know. What happens if there's two policemen walking up the street if they see a couple of kids carrying on they can chase them. They're in their cars. They cannae catch folk in these cars, no in a built up area like this. They need to be on foot round here (female resister, oldest age group).

Lack of resources, mainly manpower, was raised by many as a reason why police were unable to do their work as effectively as they might otherwise do.

One main negative aspect identified was that the police were not concentrating on those who were 'really offending', namely muggers, rapists, 'nutters', murderers, drug dealers, car thieves and housebreakers, rather than purportedly focusing on less serious crime (such as vandalism, shoplifting and speeding). Relatedly, many of those interviewed – across the categories – suggested that the police knew who the drug dealers were, but took no action, for example:

They're pulling the wrong people. Like they know – see in this scheme alone there's quite a lot of drug dealers. They know where they are, who they are, yet they're getting away with it ... they know what's happening, but they're just turning a blind eye to it (male persister, oldest age group).

The police were also judged by their response to incidents and were criticised if they failed to take immediate or no action, for example:

Woman: I'm not impressed. I mean I phone them one night. There was guys sitting out there. They were smoking joints. They were standing in the middle of the road, standing, drinking beer cans. Phoned the police -'we'll send somebody up'[they said].
Int: And that took a while?
Woman: Never showed up (female desister, oldest age group).

Persisters drew on their own experience or that of their friends in formulating their opinions about the police. Claims were made that the police charged them wrongly (when they had not committed a crime) or unnecessarily (for example, with breach of the peace for 'harmless drunkenness') and stopped and searched them without cause. Others complained of the way the police treated them 'as if you were the scum of the earth' or 'like a bit of shit'. Even more serious were allegations, particularly from the older age groups, of mistreatment or violence from the police and of corruption within the police force (the language used by many of the older persisters about the police being particularly abusive). Anderson et al. (1994) employ the concept of 'cautionary tales' to explain the existence of such allegations. A further concern, expressed largely by the youngest age group across the three categories, was police surveillance of them by the police in public places, usually at night time. As this evoked such extensive comment it will be discussed in more detail.

Police taking names and moving young people on: the youngest age group

It is not surprising that the youngest age group were particularly verbal about the police, given their propensity for exposure to them. The SCS (1998) found that 51 per cent of 12-15 year olds had ever had contact with the police at some stage and that 39 per cent had been approached by the police recently. The main issue for young people in the current study, which they raised spontaneously, was that of their names being taken and of their being moved on. The majority found this police response annoying, puzzling or irrelevant. A persister explains what frequently happens to her and her friends:

Girl: Aye, every night they [the police] write your name down.

Int: So what happens then, I mean once they write your name down?

Girl: They come into the park and the cars pull up beside us. They say 'get into a line', but they don't need to say that any more because we just get into a line for them coming. Then they say 'name, address, age, school, move, disappear, don't come back' and then everybody all goes away to the shops and then comes back and then they come again and do the same thing. They take your name down about four times a night.

Int: And is it the same police?

Girl: Aye most of the time. They don't take your name and that all again. They just put a wee line beside it, how many times you've been into trouble.

Int: And then what happens? Like have they ever come to the house here?

Girl: No.

Another girl recounted what happens if young people refuse to do what the police tell them to do: 'see if they tell you to move and you don't move, they say 'last warning'. If you don't move they take you home'. Explanations as to why the police might record their names down were offered by the young people, for example:

I think they just like the fact that they take people's names. I think that's classed as their job. Like say they go – they've got a wee black book they go in to their Sergeant or whoever is the top man and they say 'I've took such and such a name' or 'I've charged such and such a person. I've lifted such and such a person' and that means I think they feel higher. They feel good about themselves (female persister, youngest age group).

Explanations as to why the police might move them on were also offered by young people:

There's a church down near the park as well and a couple of weeks ago we all got found in it – took my name and they said if I was ever found in the church again they were going to report me to a children's panel. They said they were going to phone my parents because I was in the church and I shouldn't have been there. But it's an old church, there's nothing in it, it's broken down and I take it they're only concerned for our safety, but if we weren't concerned for our safety, I don't know. I don't think we really care about our safety when we're in the church and that but it's somewhere to go (female persister, youngest age group).

One desister said that she and her parents asked the police why the young people get moved on: 'I've asked them before and they just said 'people are complaining in case there's trouble between all of you, in case you smash windows', but there's no trouble at all, so I don't know why and they realise that because they come down every single weekend' Another said:

There's like 50 of us down the X Park. They don't know what's happening. They don't understand we're all friends together, do you know what I mean? Even though we don't hang around together we're all friends together and I think it's just because there's hundreds of us they think we're going to start trouble. That's the main purpose they think we're going out for – trouble – but we're not (female desister, youngest age group).

Others spoke of neighbours having phoned the police to complain about them:

And there was a guy who thought these stairs were his so we used to go up just to annoy him. He used to always say 'beat it or I'll phone the police' and it was always 'they're not your stairs' ... and he didn't like it so he used to always phone the police and they used to say 'right come on, move on' and that was it (female persister, youngest age group).

The young people interviewed considered the police response to be unfair because 'there's nowhere for us to go and the police don't understand that'. A desister, who claimed to have been moved on when she was just walking to her friend's house, explained: 'you feel like a criminal – different'. A persister was 'really like annoyed because like I live here not them' and another persister who was stopped and searched said: 'I've never ever carried anything like that [weapons or drugs] so I don't think it's right you know. They just stop anybody' (male, youngest age group).

Different approaches to the police when young people are asked to move on appear to provoke different responses from them. A resister explained that the police are 'quite polite about asking you [to move on] as long as you sort of tell them the truth and don't backchat or anything', whereas others (usually persisters or desisters) were less restrained, for example: 'there was a wee bench bit and I was sitting there and I got asked to move and I was like – and this was when I got warned for my cheek as well – I was like 'why do you want me to move? What am

I doing likes?' I got warned for my cheek as well' (female persister, youngest age group).

Police and deterrence: youngest age group

Among the youngest age group, persisters' and desisters' views about deterrence were mixed. Some indicated that the police did act as a deterrent to them as they were 'scared' or 'frightened' of them or because of the consequences: 'the police guy says to us 'see if you get charged again that's it. You'll have a police record, but if you keep your slate clean until you're 18 you'll be wiped clean'' (male persister, youngest age group). Others were less concerned: 'I think they're there to stop it, but there's nothing they can do because everything is just – they can't sit there all night and they're going to do it whether they're there or not' (female persister, youngest age group) or thought that others were not deterred by them: 'I think they just take your name just to scare you, you know, but with most people down here it disnae work' ... it works with me because I knew mum and dad would kill me' (female desister, youngest age group).

A resister was sceptical about the effectiveness of the police:

I know quite a few people who like they are not my friends or anything but they go and hang about at night and drink and just walk about the streets and the police come up to them and just say 'go home' and it doesn't really teach them a lesson because they are out again the next night. I think they really need to kind of take some action kind of thing and punish them in a way instead of just telling them to go home or not to do it because that doesn't really teach them anything and so it's not that bad 'you're not going to get punished for it, but you've got to kind of stop it' (female resister, youngest age group).

The effects of more direct contact with the police on their behaviour varied. Not surprisingly, desisters were more likely to give accounts of its having a deterrent effect, for example 'well I had a bit of a shock because they [police] came to the door and made me go round and apologise and I thought 'well this is humiliation, this is' – all these different things, and I thought 'well, I'm not going through that again'' (male desister, youngest age group). Equally unsurprisingly, more persisters were not deterred by the experience:

Int: Did you get charged or anything?
Boy: Aye, no, not charged. I was only 15 at the time. It was like about this time last year and I got put in the cells ...
Int: How did you feel about that?
Boy: My cousin, he was more bothered about it than I was. I suppose I just look back at it now and laugh ...
Int: And has it made any difference to the way you behave?
Boy: Not really, not a difference because I found it funny at first but aye, I suppose after it, I sat down and thought about it, but in there I felt as if I wanted to burst out laughing' (male persister, youngest age group).

In interviews, the boys talked more about the visibility of the police than the girls: 'you're out at night, you see what's going on and sometimes you see the police but sometimes they're not really there when maybe they should be' and 'they've got a beat now ... that makes it more difficult which means it makes it like you are not likely to do any crimes' (male persisters, youngest age group). The paradox in respect of police presence, particularly for male persisters and desisters in the youngest age group, was that if the police were not visible they were criticised for not deterring potential criminals, yet if they were visible they engendered resentment (as has been discussed above).

Police and deterrence: middle and oldest age groups

The majority of persisters and desisters in the older age groups indicated that the police did *not* act as a deterrent: being caught was the issue for most of them: 'as long as I don't get caught at the time ... see if the polis stopped me and I had drugs on me, so long as they dinnae get it I wouldnae even care. It wouldnae bother me like if they stopped me' (female persister, middle age group) and 'see to tell you the truth, I don't acknowledge the police' (male persister, oldest age group). Others claimed that although a police presence would deter them if they were just about to commit an offence, it did not prevent them from re-offending in the future:

Woman: Well breaking into shops, do you know what I mean? I think it's dead like dodgy and that and the police and that's about and that and things like that or I'm ready to shoplift and somebody's like – could be somebody working in the shop. It's like dead, like if they're going to stick you in, in the back, you'll no touch it.

Int: When you know the police are around and they've maybe been at you does that make you think 'oh I'll not do that again'? Does it make any difference?

Woman: No.

Only a minority of persisters and desisters recalled incidents with the police which they considered would deter them in future, as this persister did:

I'd never get in a stolen car ever again. I mean I've been in umpteen stolen cars but that scared me – when the police started chasing us with the blue light down back streets and that, crashing into a wall and then rolling back into a garden. I was like 'get out of the car'. Oh it was horrible. The police chased me too, running up this hill. Thank god I never got caught (female persister, middle age group).

For others, frequent contact with the police did not deter them until what they considered to be a serious event caused them to reconsider, as this desister explained:

Int: Right so has so much contact with them [the police] made any difference to your offending?

Man: Aye it has, aye. After my last offence, the CID became involved and I got my fingerprints taken that was it. I think it sank in once I got my fingerprints taken.

Int: And what was that for?

Man: Stealing a phone. I think that's when it really sank in and that's when I really decided to settle (male desister, oldest age group).

(ii) COURTS

Tables 7.2a and 7.2b indicate the percentage of persisters (38%) who reported having been to court in relation to charges against them. Fewer desisters, particularly girls and young women, reported having been to court, (28% males; 9% females).

Table 7.2a: Persisters and desisters who had been to court in relation to charges against them: boys and young men

	Been to court (n=34)	Not been to court (n=67)	Total (n=101)
Desisters	12 *(28%)*	31 *(72%)*	43 *(100%)*
Persisters	22 *(38%)*	36 *(62%)*	58 *(100%)*

Table 7.2b: Persisters and desisters who had been to court in relation to charges against them: girls and young women

	Been to court (n=22)	Not been to court (n=60)	Total (n=82)
Desisters	3 *(9%)*	29 *(91%)*	32 *(100%)*
Persisters	19 *(38%)*	31 *(62%)*	50 *(100%)*

How well the courts do their job

Asked what function courts served, four main roles were identified by the young people interviewed: meting out justice, determining whether the accused committed the crime, deciding on the outcome and punishing those who have offended.

Many of the views of those in the youngest age group about the court system were less well developed than those in the older age groups, often comprising a brief response or no opinion at all. Those in the youngest age group who did respond more fully held similar views to those in the older age groups.

The majority of young people – across all age groups – were of the view that the courts could be improved and the main issue that divided them was the leniency or harshness of the sentences. The most commonly held view was that the courts were too lenient in respect of some crimes, while at the same time being too harsh in respect of others, as the following quote illustrates:

I think sometimes they overreact in things that they shouldn't be overreacting in and then go lenient on things they shouldn't be going lenient on, you know. I mean like folk who maybe rape, like a boy raping a wee girl, you know – that's three years you know and then maybe someone who has just broke in somewhere is getting five years (male resister, oldest age group).

Many were of the opinion that that the courts were too lenient, in keeping with the findings of the SCS (1998), for example:

He's forever in and out the jail and no matter what crime he commits it's only like a couple of months they're giving him and I mean it's major offences. He's like hauding [holding] needles that he jags into his arm to people's throats and they're letting him off with stuff like that ... they should jail him for life (male desister, middle age group).

Fewest thought that the courts were too harsh.

The basis for these views differed according to offender type. Resisters were more likely to cite media examples, whereas desisters – and even more so persisters – based their opinion on their own experience and/or that of their family or friends. Persisters, whom it might have been predicted would be antagonistic to the courts, often spoke of having been given many 'chances' (such as probation) or having been fairly treated, for example: '[the courts] do their job fairly I suppose. I've got no grudges against any judge or any lawyers or anything like that, whatever sentence they've passed. Like if I'm up for something I've ... I've deserved it you know what I mean'. A few were cynical or abusive about the courts, for example: 'it's all a fucking big game' (female persister, middle age group).

In terms of deterrence, a minority of persisters and desisters were directly affected by the *process* of being in court. Some remembered their first appearance(s) as having had an impact, but stated that they soon became `immune' from the effects. More relevant was the *outcome* of the court appearance, such as a term of imprisonment.

(iii) PRISONS AND YOUNG OFFENDERS INSTITUTIONS

Tables 7.3a and 7.3b indicate the percentage of persisters and desisters who reported having experienced prison or young offenders institutions (YOI). More persisters than desisters reported incarceration, as did notably more males than females.

Table 7.3a: Whether persisters and desisters have experienced prison: boys and young men

	Some experience of prison (n=22)	No experience of prison (n=76)	Total (n=98)
Desisters	6 *(14%)*	37 *(86%)*	43 *(100%)*
Persisters	16[35] *(29%)*	39 *(71%)*	55 *(100%)*

[35] A further three persisters had been on remand.

Table 7.3b: Whether persisters and desisters have experienced prison[36]: girls and young women

	Some experience of prison (n=5)	No experience of prison (n=77)	Total (n=82)
Desisters	0 *(0%)*	32 *(100%)*	32 *(100%)*
Persisters	5 *(10%)*	45 *(90%)*	50 *(100%)*

How well prisons and young offenders institutions do their job

Prisons and young offender's institutions were referred to largely in terms of punishment, containment and protecting society and less in terms of their re-integrative capacities.

The question of how well prisons and young offenders institutions do their job elicited a more negative response from resisters (than desisters or persisters) as Table 7.4 indicates.

Table 7.4: How well prisons and young offenders institutions do their job

	Positive views (n=62)	Mixed views (n=45)	Negative views (n=120)	No views (n=10)	Total (n=237)
Resisters	12 *(18%)*	10 *(15%)*	43 *(64%)*	2 *(3%)*	67 *(100%)*
Desisters	22 *(28%)*	19 *(24%)*	31 *(39%)*	7 *(9%)*	79 *(100%)*
Persisters	28 *(31%)*	16 *(17%)*	46 *(51%)*	1 *(1%)*	91 *(100%)*

The first yardstick by which prisons and young offenders institutions were evaluated was whether they stopped (rather than reduced) offending. Given many respondents' view that the majority of prisoners re-offended, the system was therefore judged to have failed according to this criterion; they were not considered to act as an effective deterrent. Furthermore, it was argued that prisoners were worse on release, as one resister suggests:

I still think putting them in jail doesn't really help them and I've also read that many of them learn new criminal skills while they're in there or still inmates. Like there was one guy went in, I think he was a standard thief but when he came out he could pick locks and all this sort of thing and could open bank safes and a lot of them meet up [when] they got out and do bigger, going to do much larger crimes so it turns an average offender into a major criminal once they got out (male resister, oldest age group).

Another change in prisoners after their release was thought to be their further antagonism to society. A persister drew on his own experience:

Being locked up all that time you still feel a bit angry at the system and all that you know what I mean? That's what people dae. They sit and grudge and all that and end up fucking angry. It makes me them worse, know what

[36] There are no young offenders institutions for girls/women in Scotland.

I mean? You get oot and you get fucking annoyed and raging (male persister, oldest age group).

A further point, made particularly by desisters, was that prisons were too focused on punishment and not enough on prisoners' welfare or rehabilitation, for example:

Not that impressed to be honest because I mean they are supposed to reform them [prisoners] and things, but they don't work with them ... they don't seem to give them any counselling and find out why they are doing it. They just shut them in a cell and feed them and that's it (female desister, middle age group).

Those who spoke favourably of the prison system argued that it enabled criminals to be removed from society at least for the period of their imprisonment and that it was an effective deterrent.

The prison system and deterrence

Whether the prison system was as an effective deterrent to offending was therefore key to both critics and proponents of the system in this study. Persisters and desisters referred to the threat of incarceration more frequently than other aspects (such as police presence, probation or court appearance). Many of those who had experienced prison, not wanting to return, resolved not to re-offend:

I mean I know a lot of people that's been in there and they're coming back like that 'och, it's cushty, it's this and that'. You've got your ain tv, your ain kettle in your room. You've got MTV ... I'm just scared of going anyway, whether it's got MTV or not' (female persister, middle age group)

I was really scared. I was pretty worried when I knew I was going to [prison]. When I got there it wasn't as bad as what I thought, but it will stop me offending because I wouldn't like to go back (female persister, oldest age group).

It was particularly the deprivation of liberty that was raised by many: 'it was the fear of being locked up, not being able to get out, not having that freedom, you know. It's really freaked me out' (male persister, oldest age group) and:

The thing that really did my nut in, though – I think a couple of things did my nut in – was the door getting shut at the end of the night and not being able to get up and go to the, know, go to the kitchen, make yourself, know, get a drink or whatever, make a piece [sandwich] or whatever. That's what really did my nut in (male persister, oldest age group).

As with the appearance at court, there was a suggestion that for some the impact of prison lessened with time, as is evident from these persister's accounts: 'the jail doesnae bother me noo because I know I've done it and it doesnae fucking bother us so I'm no feart [afraid] of the jail' and 'the first couple of weeks I said I'd never do it again; that was about the only effect. It didn't really have much effect on us' and 'at first I was 'oh god' but now I'm in and out ... no problem at all to me' (male, oldest age group).

Not all those who had experienced prison were deterred from future offending. For example a persister, asked how he felt about the likelihood of going to prison if he breached his probation said 'don't care' and another was resigned: 'nobody likes to go to jail do they [but] if it's got to happen, it's got to happen'. Some who had experienced prison themselves or had relatives who had experienced it, reinforced the view that it was too comfortable, for example: 'prison was a canter' (female persister, middle age group) and 'it's like a holiday because my dad was in a wee while and he was telling me it's not all that bad. They've got a pool room, they've got a tv room, they've got cigarettes, woodwork and all that' (male persister, youngest age group). Whether the threat of prison actually acted as a deterrent at the point of committing an offence was raised; one persister, for example, said:

> I don't go out and do it on purpose. I don't go out and just say 'I'll go out and break a window'. If something happens, like if I get into a fight and that's breaking the law but I won't take that as breaking the law. I wouldn't think about it. If I'm going out and somebody is going to start fighting with me, I'm not going to hold back because I can get the jail for it. Nobody thinks about it that way (male persister, middle age group).

The point was made that for those addicted to drugs, nothing would act as a deterrent.

(iv) CHILDREN'S HEARINGS SYSTEM

Table 7.5a and 7.5b indicate the number of respondents who reported having been referred to the children's hearings system. Persisters reporting most contact (28% males; 30% females).

Table 7.5a: Reported referral to the children's hearings system (CHS): boys and young men

	Referred to CHS (n=24)	Not referred to CHS (n=113)	Total (n=137)
Resisters	2 *(6%)*	34 *(94%)*	36 *(100%)*
Desisters	6 *(14%)*	37 *(86%)*	43 *(100%)*
Persisters	16 *(28%)*	42 *(72%)*	58 *(100%)*

Table 7.5b: Reported referral to the children's hearings system (CHS): girls and young women

	Referred to CHS (n=20)	Not referred to CHS (n=118)	Total (n=138)
Resisters	2 *(4%)*	54 *(96%)*	56 *(100%)*
Desisters	3 *(9%)*	29 *(91%)*	32 *(100%)*
Persisters	15[37] *(30%)*	35 *(70%)*	50 *(100%)*

How well the children's hearings system does its job

The most striking finding with regard to the children's hearings system was that the majority of respondents referred to it as a system solely for dealing with children and young people *who had offended*. A minority were aware that the system dealt with non-attendance at school, but respondents were almost invariably unaware of the child protection element of the system. It was variously considered to be a vehicle for understanding why children had behaved the way they had, meting out punishment, giving warnings and removing children from home and it was frequently referred to as a 'mini court' or a 'court for children'.

In contrast to police, courts and prisons/young offenders institutions, knowledge about the children's hearings system was characterised by its vagueness, misunderstanding as to its role or ignorance of its existence at all. Of 210 respondents asked how well the children's hearings system did its job 38 per cent gave no view at all.

Those who considered the system to be successful thought that it was better than alternatives (such as the courts), that it prevented escalation of crime by bringing children into the system early, 'gave children a fright' or provided them with a fair hearing and a chance to express their views. It was regarded as more successful with 'the ones that have maybe just done one or two offences as it will push them back on the straight and narrow' (female desister, oldest age group). Criticism of the children's hearings system was that it was too lenient and that it would only be effective with offenders if it were more punitive or severe. A male desister gave an example: 'I think they need to do something because this guy, he just went back and did it and they'd [the panel] just sat there and said 'it's bad' and that's it'. A persister, drawing on personal experience, supported this view:

I think it's a good thing but you don't learn your lesson from going to a panel because they treat you with cotton wool gloves. 'oh you poor child, oh' and they are asking you have you come from a broken [home] – 'what has happened?' Asking all sorts of – my social worker was asking me if my dad was my real dad or whatever. I says 'aye' and I mean they treat you with, I don't know, they treat you so carefully. 'oh pat on the head, right okay, be good now, slap on the wrist, right bad go home, know what I mean? You don't learn anything from them, you really don't. And if you are under the pain of a social worker and you are on a home care thing you still go to panels when you're 18, up until you're 18! (female persister, youngest age group)

---

[37] This includes one woman who had been to a hearing in respect of her own children and two who were referred to the reporter to the children's hearing system.

Most of those who had actually been to a hearing were negative about that experience. They were critical of its lay panel (which in other arenas is considered to be its strength), for example:

No, going to panels made me even angrier. I don't know. If I went to a panel I'd end up going out and doing something right after it, just to annoy them in the hope that I'd end up back in front of their faces again. I don't know. I hate panels 'cause like it's like voluntary work. They people they just pick up off the street (female persister, middle age group).

It was also claimed that the panel was out of touch with children's lives, that most of the panel members 'did not care', 'did not to listen' and 'asked hundreds of questions'. Being taken into residential care was the source of the most vehement response, for example:

The choice that they make is not based on compassionate grounds whatever. I mean they didn't take into account that it would affect me quite badly to be put into care ... I mean you see at the end of the day they can go home to their houses and for them nothing has changed, but they've just sent somebody away to a place ... as I say the violence amongst the youths in that place was incredible (male resister, oldest age group).

A few were even of the opinion that having been to a panel and being placed in residential care had made them more likely to offend: 'it was when I was in a home that was what got me on heroin' (female persister, middle age group). Once there, there was seen to be no disincentive to stop: 'as far as myself is concerned I was already in List D school so it more or less made me worse as well as I knew there was nothing else they could do to me, so I carried on (male persister, oldest age group). One or two acknowledged that there had been no alternative but for them to go into care:

Man: I don't think it does you any good. They put you in care and you come out worse than you went in....

Int: So what do they [the panel] do wrong and what should they have done – left you at home?

Man: Well it was the only thing they could do.

Int: Okay, so you don't hold it against them?

Man: No, not at all (male persister, middle age group).

Others who had been involved with the children's hearings system, but not taken into care, were either dismissive of it or mystified by the experience: 'I just come oot the children's panel and I just kind of thought to myself 'what was that all aboot?' (female desister, oldest age group). Very few of those who had been through the system spoke positively about it, as did this persister: 'like after I realised that other people except my family knew and the police and the school. I was like 'oh no, they're going to think I do this all the time and I'm a criminal and I'm only young' (female, youngest age group).

SOCIAL WORKERS

Tables 7.6a and 7.6b indicate how many young people reported social work involvement. There was a notable gender difference, particularly in respect of desisters.

Table 7.6a: Reported social worker involvement: boys and young men

	Some involvement (n=32)	No involvement (n=105)	Total (n=137)
Resisters	5 *(14%)*	31 *(86%)*	36 *(100%)*
Desisters	4 *(9%)*	39 *(91%)*	43 *(100%)*
Persisters	23 *(40%)*	35 *(60%)*	58 *(100%)*

Table 7.6b: Reported social worker involvement: girls and young women

	Some involvement (n=37)	No involvement (n=101)	Total (n=138)
Resisters	0 *(0%)*	56 *(100%)*	56 *(100%)*
Desisters	12 *(38%)*	20 *(62%)*	32 *(100%)*
Persisters	25 *(50%)*	25 *(50%)*	50 *(100%)*

A significant minority of the sample, particularly resisters, were unable to offer any view about social workers, as Table 7.7 indicates. [A typical 'no view' response would be: 'I don't know. I've never really – I don't know anybody that has been to a social worker or anything'].

Table 7.7: How well social workers do their job

	Positive views (n=86)	Mixed views (n=23)	Negative views (n=59)	No views (n=35)	Total (n=203)
Resisters	28 *(44%)*	6 *(9%)*	10 *(16%)*	20 *(31%)*	64 *(100%)*
Desisters	18 *(35%)*	5 *(10%)*	19 *(36%)*	10 *(19%)*	52 *(100%)*
Persisters	40 *(46%)*	12 *(14%)*	30 *(34%)*	5 *(6%)*	87 *(100%)*

The finding that similar proportions of resisters (44%) and persisters (46%) held positive views about social workers belies the fact that they had very different knowledge of the profession. The majority of persisters had experienced social worker involvement and were therefore more likely to draw on their personal experiences, whereas few resisters had and they were therefore more likely to depend on external sources for their information.

Social workers were evaluated in terms of their role in the field of child protection as well as for their work for offenders, particularly by resisters, perhaps an indication of the reliance on the media for information. Apart from issues highlighted by the media (such as removal of children from their homes into care), social workers were criticised for their intrusiveness, being 'wishy washy' and too 'soft', for example: 'a bit too namby pamby for my liking. Less of the holidays and more of the control these young ones need' (female resister, oldest age group).

The fact that criminals re-offended was also regarded by some as a sign of failure on the part of social workers. Resource constraints on social workers were identified as affecting their ability to work more effectively (as they had been in relation to the police). An issue which a number of those without social workers raised about those with social workers was the apparent disparity between the two groups, for example:

> I think they just let them get away with things. I mean there is this girl at school and she has caused so much trouble at school it's unbelievable. If I caused a fight I would be out the door straight away. Because she has a social worker you feel sorry for her. People that have social workers are – who can't afford clothes and that – next thing they are coming out with the latest up to date things, not like normal people trying to save up pocket money to get something really special and they are down at poverty level (female desister, youngest age group).

Social workers were praised by some for being helpful, in particular in the provision of material aid:

> A boy I know, he used to be in a home and all that. He used to be in and out of trouble, so what they [social workers] done for him was they got him a house, helped him decorate, they gave him a tv and all that and now he's just – he's quietened right down, know what I mean, so that's helped him and it means he's not doing it any more (male resister, middle age group);

or activities:

> Woman: Well my wee group was brilliant. I went away to Aviemore and all that wi' them. They were really good. That was brilliant ...
> Int: Oh right. Did it make any difference to your offending?
> Woman: Aye because we were all there; we werenae [offending] (female desister, oldest age group).

Social workers were said by some young people to listen: 'my social worker was all right with me. He gets on brand new with us and I get on brand new with him. He listens to us' (male persister, middle age group). They also took young people out for meals: 'the social worker I had was dead nice and used to take me oot for my dinners and used to take me places' (female desister, oldest age group) or provided advice: 'well the social work department done me proud. I had a great social worker ... I really got to know her and she was brilliant. She helped me out and she was like probation ... she gave me a lot of help and advice' (female persister, oldest age group). Some considered that social workers did help reduce offending behaviour:

> Woman: I know a lot of people, you know older ones in my school that have had social workers and they've helped them a lot .
> Int: In what ways have they helped do you think?

Woman: Just kind of told them all the stuff, what's going to happen to you if you do this, and then people think 'oh there's no point in doing that any more' (female persister, oldest age group).

Others were less enthusiastic. Asked whether his probation was effective a desister said 'not really enough. All you do is just be able to speak to someone for ten seconds 'how are you doing?' 'Okay' 'Are you still using drugs?' 'No. Okay' Then 'bye bye' and that's it' (male desister, oldest age group). Others shared this pessimism: 'probation. They just gi' you more rope to hang yourself anyway because you're only going to go oot and re-offend again' (male persister, oldest age group).

Probation was perceived as 'the end of the line' before incarceration, so the social worker was seen as having a key role in maintaining offenders in the community: 'they just go to social workers to get them out of jail' (female persister, middle age group) and, in relation to community service: 'you say in the court you want it and that but you just say that so you don't get – you just don't want the jail. A waste of time. No effect at all. A waste of space. That doesnae do anything' (male persister, middle age group). Even persisters who did not think highly of social workers acknowledged the role of social workers in preventing imprisonment, for example:

Wom: Like I go to see my social worker and that and because I'm no doing nothing now I've nothing to say to her.
Int: Uhu. You just sit there?
Wom: I'm there for two minutes and back oot. I've no really got strong views on them either.
Int: Right, okay.
Wom: They've never really done anything to help me apart from X [a social worker] stopped us going to jail (female persister, middle age group).

The work done by those at the intensive probation unit in one of the sites in which the research was carried out received much praise, albeit only a minority of the sample had used the service. The following is typical of the attitude of the young people towards the unit:

That is a really good thing intensive probation, [you] know. The statistics and that show that 80 per cent of the people that attend IPU don't commit crimes again, [you] know like, for like two or three years after they've finished it, that they end probation, that they don't just commit a crime right away again, which has been the case with me – I've not committed any crimes since attending it ... if there were more like places like IPU over Scotland, [you] know, for young offending people, [you] know, 'cause it helped me a hell of a lot, [you] know and I know it's helped a lot of other people that's went to it, know what I mean, simply because they show a lot of confidence in you (male desister, oldest age group).

Explanations as to why intensive probation was thought to stop offending were offered: 'They explain things tae you better. I mean I never had anybody telling me half the things, know the way they talk to you, you know, they get through to you better' and 'they make a laugh and a joke aboot it at the same time. It's no deadly all serious ... so you're tuning more into it' (male persister, oldest age group).

VICTIMISATION

Sixty per cent of those asked whether they had been a victim of an offence said they had. The main crimes experienced were: having their house broken into, their property stolen and being physically assaulted. While slightly more female resisters reported being a victim than in others, overall male and female reporting of victimisation was similar. Where the difference became most apparent was in the *type* of victimisation reported, particularly that of physical assault, as Tables 7.8a and 7.8b indicate.

Table 7.8a: Whether male victims had suffered physical assault

	Suffered assault (n=49)	No assault (n=25)	Total (n=74)
Resisters	11 *(48%)*	12 *(52%)*	23 *(100%)*
Desisters	16 *(76%)*	5 *(24%)*	21 *(100%)*
Persisters	22 *(73%)*	8 *(27%)*	30 *(100%)*

Table 7.8b: Whether female victims had suffered physical assault

	Suffered assault (n=29)	No assault (n=54)	Total (n=83)
Resisters	9 *(25%)*	27 *(75%)*	36 *(100%)*
Desisters	5 *(31%)*	11 *(69%)*	16 *(100%)*
Persisters	15 *(48%)*	16 *(52%)*	31 *(100%)*

Overall, more males (particularly persisters and desisters) than females reported that they had been physically assaulted. Many of the tales of victimisation were serious and a significant minority necessitated hospitalisation, including for a broken nose, slashed neck and stab wound in the neck. As with prior research findings (for example the SCS, 1998) strong emotional reactions were reported, including anger, shock, distress and feelings of vulnerability. Females were more likely to report domestic violence from partners, while males often recounted tales of victimisation from men they encountered outside the home; in several instances this was drug related, for example:

Int: So what effect does that have on your life when you do that?
Man: [shows large scar on neck and face]
Int: . Yeah, that looks pretty nasty! How did that happen?
Man: Because I had a run in wi' one of the top drug dealers ...
Int: Were you in hospital?
Man: Three days (male persister, oldest age group).

Asked whether being a victim had an impact on their offending the response varied, particularly across offender type. All but one of the resisters said either that they did not offend anyway – so it had not changed them – or that the experience of victimisation had confirmed their resolve not to offend, for example: 'you know how you feel so you know how other people will feel when it happens to them, so it has probably made it stronger not to commit offences' (male resister, youngest age group) and 'I'm even more against people getting into trouble. I thought that was really bad and it was really upsetting for me and my family' (female resister, middle age group).

A minority of persisters took the view that their experience of being a victim had affected their offending behaviour: 'I've never fought again. That scared me. It just shows you, even them, they could have a knife and everything. I wouldn't risk that' (female persister, middle age group). Others, however, were largely indifferent: 'I didn't really think about it', and 'I didn't really bother: it's just normal'. A number of persisters explained that it had no effect on their offending because the type of offence that they committed was not the same offence as they had experienced as a victim, so they considered the victimisation to be irrelevant:

Man: The only thing I did is stealing.
Int: It's not the same?
Man: It's not in the same category (male persister, oldest age group).

This male persister did not physically assault people, so when he experienced physical assault as a victim it did not have an impact on his offending, which was stealing. The ability to compartmentalise different types of offences (or the inability to consider them generically) in this way enabled persisters to continue offending despite experience of victimisation.

Others empathised with victims as a result of their victimisation, but did not think about it until after they offended, for example:

Even if I'm fighting I still feel crap after. I still feel rubbish because you've went out and fought with somebody. Even if I hate the guy I still feel I shouldn't have done that but at the time you don't think about that. You don't like to see people hurt. You don't like to see stuff getting stolen off them (male persister, middle age group).

Some thought about their victimisation, but it had no effect on their behaviour: 'it made me think about me doing it but it didn't stop me' (male persister, oldest age group). Others claimed that being victimised made them more likely to offend, in retaliation for the victimisation they had suffered: 'I think it would hae an impact on offending if somebody beat you up. You'd think 'I'm going to get him' and that's you going to offend because of it, so I think it would affect in that way' (male persister, middle age group).

Some desisters resembled resisters in their response to victimisation, while others resembled persisters. Many realised in retrospect what their behaviour must have felt like for the victim, for example: 'I think because we used to do – phone people – hoax phone calls when you were young. I think everybody done them and then being the victim of that [made me think] 'what did I do to these people?" (female desister, oldest age group).

Asked what effect, if any, being a victim had on their views of victims, many interviewees indicated that it had indeed changed them. For some it had changed the degree to which they empathised with victims, for example:

I feel more – well I've always felt sympathetic towards the victim but I feel you know even more so because I have been a victim and I'm just so angry about it and I still want to do something about it. I wish there was something I could do you know, but I obviously can't take the law into my own hands (female resister, middle age group).

Those whose views of victims had not changed said either they were already sympathetic to them: 'I think I've always been sympathetic towards them. I don't think it's really at all changed my view' (female resister, youngest age group) or stated that it made no difference, but did not claim to be sympathetic in the first place, for example: 'I don't really care about anybody' (male persister, middle age group) or were resigned to it: 'I feel sorry for people when it happens to them but it happens to most people; it's a fact of life' (male persister, youngest age group) and 'nobody deserves it – it's just one of those things that's always going to be about, but there's always going to be crime' (male persister, middle age group).

Gender differences in the perception of victims were evident in the interviews. More women and girls expressed their own feelings as a victim and their understanding and sympathy towards other victims as a result:

It was a fairly minor thing that happened to me, but I suppose it can help you understand how somebody who suffered a more serious crime would react and feel. The feeling of helplessness and all that, it must be awful (female resister, middle age group);

and:

I think being involved in domestic violence is – well I've always seen other people suffering from domestic violence but I think until you experience something yourself, you don't read right into it. You don't know so much about it until you experience it yourself. I wouldn't say it's changed me crimewise. It hasn't changed my attitude to crime or anything like that, but it's changed my feelings towards victims and stuff like that because I understand it more I suppose (female desister, oldest age group).

Men and boys talked far more about the formal intervention which followed the victimisation incidents, as the following quotes from their interviews illustrate:

Victims as in people that have had beatings and things like that? I suppose nowadays it's not so bad because they've got a – they've got a – I can't remember what it's called, but you get compensation money if you're a victim these days. One of my pals got a doing last year or something like that, got his nose broke like that, got £2,000 for it, I suppose it makes up for it in a way (male resister, youngest age group);

I feel sorry for them because there's no-one you can really turn to, definitely not, because the police are not particularly co-operative (male resister, oldest age group);

I think victims should have more power and you feel that the legal system is on the offender's side because at a hearing if you are the offender and you get convicted you can appeal, but the victim can't appeal if he [the offender] doesn't get convicted (male persister, youngest age group).

Victim blame is a well documented phenomenon (for example, Chambers and Millar, 1983). Boys and men in the current study were more likely to raise the issue of victim blame than their female counterparts: 'I feel sorry for them unless they deserved it', 'it depends on if they were asking for it' (male resisters, youngest age group) and 'I feel a bit sorry for them I suppose if they've not done anything wrong' (male desister, youngest age group).

The sense of anger and need to retaliate as a victim was also evident in (largely) persisters' accounts of their reaction to victimisation: 'I don't agree wi' people getting their bag snatched, [you] know. I just want to see the fucking bastard – like people it's happened to and I'd like to get hold of some of the people that's done it, [you] know' (male persister, oldest age group). The specificity of particular crimes (as discussed above) was reiterated in relation to victims, as this excerpt illustrates:

Int: Do you feel more sympathetic to people who are victims of crime now?
Man: Aye, some crimes, aye.
Int: Some crimes?
Man: Aye, like robberies and things like that, housebreakings and that, the house turned upside doon because I've experienced that myself' (male persister, oldest age group).

PROFESSIONAL PERSPECTIVES ON RESPONSES TO OFFENDING AMONG YOUNG PEOPLE

The police role

The police officers who were interviewed had differing roles within their respective forces. Ultimately, however, the role of the police in relation to young people and offending was said to be to 'guard, watch and patrol', detecting crime and reporting the circumstances to the relevant authority. As one officer explained, 'it's part of the police role to keep individuals safe and society safe and protect them either from themselves or from other people'. In Eastburgh the three possible courses of action once a young person under 16 had been charged were to issue a police warning, report the incident to the reporter to the children's hearings or to report the case to the procurator fiscal, with criteria in respect of the last course of action being described as 'black and white'. In Westburgh the reporter was responsible for deciding in which cases a senior police officer's warning should be issued. Some officers emphasised the limited role of the police – detection and reporting – which, they suggested was at odds with public perceptions of the police as 'judge and jury'. This misunderstanding of the police role could result in public dissatisfaction with the police who were often blamed for the perceived ineffectiveness of other parts of the criminal justice system.

> The public perception of the criminal justice system seems to stop at the police a lot of the time, you know – the police didn't manage to get that guy locked up in the jail so they must have failed in some way. And they forget that you're just the reporting agency for somebody else who decides if they're going to prosecute and conduct the thing in court.

The officers also emphasised their preventive role, though some suggested that resource constraints created a tension between preventive work – including inter-agency initiatives -and 'active policing', with an increasing trend towards the latter type of approach. Nonetheless, various examples were cited of preventive work undertaken by both forces, including police involvement in an offence-focused groupwork programme for 15-17 year olds which was run by the local social work department and a pilot initiative being developed with a local secondary school which aimed to identify young people aged between 12 and 14 years who were offending and 'nip them in the bud'. Another officer described an educational police initiative in primary schools which was aimed at tackling vandalism. This latter initiative was seen as having value beyond it's immediate aims since it enabled young people to view the police in a different role: '...it gets them to identify with the police in another role bar enforcement and maybe it makes us a wee bit more approachable to them'. An increased emphasis upon inter-agency strategies was generally welcomed but some officers were of the view that the police were usually expected to take the lead in the development of inter-agency fora – such as community safety strategies – and the implications which flowed from them, with relatively little input from other agencies.

Relationships between police and young people

Another tension that was said by police officers to arise from limited resources was their inability to develop more effective relationships with young people. As one officer explained:

> You know, they don't see my side of it. What I do, it's always 'in your face' policing they seem to come across.

The barriers which were acknowledged to exist between the police and young people included the perceived unapproachability of the police, their identification as authority figures and an association among young people between speaking to a police officer and 'grassing'. Even if officers were keen to promote a helping role with respect to young people and to encourage increased dialogue with them, negative attitudes towards the police could be instilled in young people at an early age:

> The worst thing for me is when...I'm walking down the street and I've got my uniform on and a woman says [to her small child] 'right, if you don't behave yourself I'll get him to take you away' and I always make a point of going up and saying 'don't say that' if I hear anyone saying that. That annoys me, I have to say. If you're putting that into kids at three and four years old, five years old, what chance have you got when they're older. You know, they identify with the 'oh, he's coming to take me away'. We're not here for that.

The importance of building better relationships with young people and taking a greater interest in them was also stressed by another officer as follows:

> If we don't adopt a stance of being interested in them, then we're not investing in them either – they see us as the authority, the establishment. I mean the police officer in the street has got to be the number one symbol of authority, but it needn't be. He should command respect and friendship for doing his job and do something positive for the child. It's often a case of they want somebody to talk to, somebody to listen to their moan...I want kids to know that we respect them, but I want them to know that there are rules, there are simple society rules that everyone obeys from infancy onwards, you start to disobey them then you're causing a problem, so can we sort of stop doing that, you know, can we maybe do something positive rather than something negative? And I think, if children, if children are, if children are made to feel less the enemy of authority and society then they'll behave better, because that seems to spur them on a wee bit.

The lack of communication between the police and young people may explain why the latter were somewhat mystified by certain actions taken by the former. Officers in both forces had entirely logical explanations for the two types of police behaviour that most often perplexed young people (and may, indeed, have further alienated them): moving groups of young people on and taking down their names in their notebooks.

The officers explained that, unless they directly witnessed offending by a group of young people, they would move them on only in response to a complaint from a member of the public.

> Generally you'll find that the only contact the majority of kids have with the police is when the police are telling them off and when the police are telling them 'get away and move on somewhere else from this street corner' and they don't understand that that's actually causing people annoyance... The police haven't just turned up, in the majority of cases and see a crowd of kids, right, we'll move them on and give them grief. It's because

somebody's phoned in saying 'look, I've got ten kids hanging outside my window and they're making a lot of noise and I'm frightened to go out' and we're duty-bound, we have to do something about that...They don't understand that that's what's actually happened, you know, so all they see is the police are just moving them on and they've got nowhere to go and they've got nothing to do. They can't even stand about and talk. They don't seem to understand that that sometimes causes a fear in people.

The frequent futility of this type of police action was acknowledged by one officer who explained that 'if they're not committing an offence we can only ask them to move on and we know fine well that they're going to go somewhere else and...ten, 15 minutes later we're going to get another call'. Staffing levels and a need to attend to more pressing priorities resulted, it was suggested, in relatively cursory exchanges between officers and young people:

Depending on how much time they've got, they either say 'right, beat it' or they have a short discussion during which they don't really have an opportunity to make much headway and then they resort to 'beat it'.

The fact that the interchange may be fairly brusque and to the point is always going to be the case because people are saying 'my car's been stolen' or 'my house broken into' or 'somebody's assaulted me and I've had to wait an hour because you've been standing chewing the fat with a bunch of neds at the back of the school – what is it we're paying your wages for?'

Improving community relations with young people – through, for example, organising events and activities – could, it was also suggested, result in polarised attitudes towards different types of officer, with the community involvement officers being perceived in a relatively favourable light while the 'real police' are considered to be 'a right shower of bastards' who 'just hunt us all the time'.

Taking names down, on the other hand, was said by police to serve four principal functions. In both areas officers would record the names of young people they encountered in the course of their work as a means of keeping track of repeated contacts with the same young people, a process which was otherwise difficult because a) different officers would be on duty on different days and may not, therefore, be aware that certain young people had been involved in various incidents at other times and b) young people tended to wear similar clothing which made recalling individuals and identifying them from others in a crowd problematic. In this context noting the young person's name would not result in further action – it was simply an aide memoire – unless s/he was being charged which, in the case of those under 16 years of age, could only take place at their home or at the police station in the presence of their parents.

The second purpose of recording names was the operation in Westburgh of a 'contact card system' which was described as being akin to a 'three strikes and you're out' approach. If an incident constituted an offence but was considered not to be sufficiently serious to warrant a report being sent to the reporter, the officer could take the young person home, issue a warning in front of his/her parents and at the station submit a contact card with brief details of the young person, the incident and the police action. The accrual of three contact cards would then result in automatic referral to the reporter on the basis that the child was continually coming to the attention of the police.

A third purpose of taking down young people's names was essentially administrative so that if, for instance, parents complained about their child having been spoken to by the police, it was possible to identify immediately who the officer in question was. Finally, recording the names of young people who were gathered in particular locations might in some instances assist in the detection of crime: if a crime was found to have been committed in an area where a group of young people were hanging about, the young people concerned might be potential witnesses or accused.

Social workers' approaches to young people who offend

A clear distinction emerged between the approach of children and families workers and criminal justice social workers to the supervision of young people who offend. Criminal justice workers – whose approach to supervision was shaped by National Objectives and Standards – tended to adopt a more explicit offending-focused approach ('care and control') whereas children and families workers were keen to stress the importance of working with the young person in relation both to offending and to other problems in the family context:

> We're looking at the relationships and the continuity, trying to get the child into the context of the family...I think we're still addressing the issue of offending and the reason for them to come to our attention in the first place but it's within a broader context.

Given the associations social workers drew between offending and other problems, a focus on these problems still featured clearly in the intervention of criminal justice social workers, though this was generally in the context of addressing the offending itself:

> I think you're trying to reduce offending, you're trying to – there's a whole load of things. You're trying to help some people understand their effect on their victims and you're also trying to deal with what problems they're presenting as well...There's quite a lot involved, you know, in addressing offending.

Criminal justice workers reported adopting a relatively structured, cognitive behavioural approach to supervision, which they considered to be an effective method of effecting personal change:

> I think it really works with people. I think that the clients I have really get a lot from it. It'll influence their thinking and help them to think about their circumstances a lot more.

Children and families workers also reported the use of structured approaches, especially in Westburgh which employed groupwork with young people who were on supervision as a result of offending. The use of groupwork with this age group was seen as a useful way to separate out the offending from the wider family issues. Another approach was to undertake shared work between children and families and criminal justice social workers, with the latter focusing specifically on the offending and the former on providing the young person with more general support. In the absence of structural mechanisms – such as groupwork sessions, IT provision or shared work – which enabled the offending to be directly addressed, children and families workers acknowledged that tensions could arise between their responsibilities for supporting and protecting young people and challenging and confronting delinquent or criminal acts:

There needs to be some sort of clear demarcation so that the two things aren't blurred for the young person...I think it's very difficult to work with a young person for two to three years and to change the approach that you [adopt]. You were in a very supportive role and the, when it comes to offending, you know, you need to be in a much more confrontational, challenging role and sometimes the person just doesn't see you in that role at all.

One criminal justice social worker, who believed the cognitive behavioural approach was relatively effective with young people, also considered that more attention could be paid to providing young people with positive longer-term links into their community after their period on supervision has ended, very much along the lines of the STAC programme in Northern Ireland (Chapman and Maitland, 1995):

I feel that when we do a groupwork programme people come to us for six months and then it's almost like, after that intensive stuff for six months it's 'cheerio' – do you know what I mean?. There's nothing back in the community. I would like to see us being more involved after we deal with people, to get them something in the community...I think we should be trying to socially include people.

PROFESSIONAL PERSPECTIVES ON THE EFFECTIVENESS OF RESPONSES TO YOUNG PEOPLE WHO OFFEND

The effectiveness of policing

Police responses to offending by young people were considered by police officers to be effective with some young people but not with others. Simply taking the young person home or asking their parents to attend the police station could, it was suggested, be a salutary experience for young people who had had no prior contact with the police:

It's good to catch them young where maybe they've shoplifted because of peer pressure or they've went out and got drunk because everybody else is doing it. And the look of disappointment on the parents' faces causes the kids to start crying and we never see these kids again.

The senior police officer's warning – in which the young person would be required to attend the police station with his/her parents for a 'dressing down' by a senior officer – was likewise thought to serve as a deterrent for many young people, especially those who were not particularly 'streetwise':

Although they hate you for evermore for showing them up in front of their parents it's maybe put them back on the right track and maybe you've done a wee bit of good.

In Eastburgh, where the police reported being involved in a range of preventive initiatives with young people – including police initiated organised activities and 'diversion schemes' aimed at giving young people at risk something to do – these were similarly thought to be effective with some young people. However, it was recognised by officers in both areas that there was a 'hard core' of young people involved in repeat offending who were unaffected by various courses of police action and who were, in addition, whether through mistrust or a concern to preserve their image, least likely to participate in social or sporting activities organised by the police.

The effectiveness of social work supervision

As with other responses to young people who offend, social work supervision was thought to be reasonably effective with some young people but not with the 'die hards' who had no interest in 'bettering themselves'. Overall, police officers' appraisals of social workers were relatively positive, with the value of a child-focused approach to supervision in the context of the children's hearings system recognised even if its *effectiveness* was not always apparent.

They say, you know, 'a guy came and took me to McDonald's for a word with me and then he took me home again'. 'What did you talk about?'. 'Well, I can't remember'. So obviously there wasn't anything particularly deep in relation to their concerning behaviour.

The ability of social workers to exercise a monitoring role with respect to young people on their caseloads was thought by some officers to be undermined by the fact that they worked a 9 to 5 shift and were not, therefore, in a position to 'keep tabs' on young people in the evenings and at weekends. More generally, however, there was a widespread perception that social workers' caseloads were such that they could not possibly offer the level of support and supervision to all young people under supervision that they perhaps needed and that a system of prioritisation was required:

A lot of social workers have horrendous workloads. And it's virtually impossible for the social workers to give these kids their attention. There is certain kids get more attention than other kids – you'll probably find that they are the kids that are offending more than the other kids...I think they can suss out the kids who are going to need more attention than others.

Social workers, on the other hand, tended to find it difficult to disentangle the effects of their supervision from the impact of other factors which might impinge positively or negatively upon young people's risk of re-offending, including a 'natural' process of desistance with age: 'is it us that influences their choice not to re-offend or have they made that choice anyway?'. Effectiveness was, it was suggested, 'a longer term thing' and 'the question of effectiveness hasn't been asked very much until now'. The issue of effectiveness was not being side-stepped by social workers, but, rather, the complexity of the issue acknowledged.

The effectiveness of the children's hearings system

Social workers were broadly supportive of the ethos of the children's hearings system which was described by one respondent as being 'the best way to discuss a child's future and make decisions', not least because it endeavoured to encourage parents to accept some responsibility for young people's behaviour. Attending a hearing could serve as a salutary experience for some young people but doubts were expressed about the effectiveness of the system with more persistent young offenders because the 'effectiveness of that immediate impact lessens with familiarity'.

It was suggested that supervision within the context of the children's hearings system might be more effective if dedicated resources were available to develop more structured programmes of intervention with young people who offend. It was also proposed that panel members might have a part to play by 'demanding a much more structured approach...[so that] they know what our plans are for a young person who offends'. The scope under the Children (Scotland) Act 1995 for panel members to request three or six monthly reviews of cases was also thought to be a promising development in that it 'brings families and young people back to be accountable for what's happened in that period of time' and 'focuses social workers on the task to be achieved'.

The current transition from the children's hearings system to the adult criminal justice system was, however, acknowledged to be problematic, with the suggestion being made by some social workers that more focused intervention with young people in the transitional age group was necessary and that this required specific resources and expertise:

I would personally like to see workers who are specifically working with young people that, you know, come in between the court system and the children's hearings system. I think we needs resources and we need people specifically to do that type of work.

The children's hearings system – the concept of which was considered laudable by most police officers interviewed – was thought to vary in its effectiveness depending on the young person concerned. Children's panels were thought most effective with young people who did not have a lengthy history of offending, less so with more 'streetwise' young people who knew how to 'use the system'

> I don't have the figures but I'm led to believe that the vast, vast majority don't re-offend and that the hardy annual – you know the one that's going to keep offending – glides through the system.

The effectiveness of the children's' hearings system was thought by police to be undermined by a limited range of options for dealing with young people who offend and limited power to contain the behaviour of persistent young offenders:

> These guys are just ordinary people – they're going in with their hands tied. It's a hard job for them. It really is a hard job for them. It must be like battering their head off a wall because they're acting to the fullness of their powers and they know that these kids – some of these kids – are just not listening to a word they're saying.

> Once the kids start to re-offend more often, I think that's when the panel loses its effect, because they know there's no real punishment at the end of the day from the children's panel and they know that when they get to 16 that anything they've done before that gets wiped clean.

The effectiveness of residential supervision was questioned by some officers mainly on the grounds that, while some young people might benefit from them, residential units more often functioned as 'schools of crime'. It was also suggested that young people, in any case, continued to offend while living in residential units and that even secure units could not have a complete incapacitation effect since young people could offend when on weekend leave.

The effectiveness of the adult courts

The issue of offending prior to the age of 16 being 'wiped clean' when young people moved into the adult criminal justice system was mentioned as a source of frustration by some officers who believed that it tended to undermine the effectiveness of the courts when dealing with young people who had moved up through the children's hearings system. The courts were thought to be relatively effective but were hampered by having limited powers and being subject to heavy workloads and administrative delays. Whilst the transition from the children's hearings system to the adult courts was said, for many young people, to represent a significant turning point in their attitudes and behaviour, courts and prisons were said to hold limited deterrent value for drug addicts who 'will take their chance no matter what'. One officer suggested that offending behaviour courses should be offered to young people at an earlier point in the system – for instance instead of a fine – rather than functioning as an alternative to custody (as is currently the case) because by that stage patterns of offending had already become relatively entrenched. In this context it is interesting to note the introduction of a pilot supervised attendance order scheme for 16 and 17 year olds in Dundee[38].

Despite the frustration expressed by police officers that courts were unable to take account of offending which had been dealt with via the children's hearings system when passing sentence on young offenders and despite the suggestion by different professionals that the transition from the children's hearings system to the adult courts could encourage desistance from offending among some young people (see also Chapter Eight), social workers voiced concern that young people moving up into the adult courts from the children's hearings system could quickly finding themselves facing the prospect of a custodial sentence, particularly if they failed to appreciate the expectations associated with supervision in the adult context:

> I know that very quickly they get sucked into our system, that they're going to end up in jail very quickly, because they're not going to engage with me as their probation officer if they come through the system at 16. They're going to just keep having the same attitude they've had for a long time.

Opinions were divided with respect to whether female offenders were disadvantaged in the criminal justice system. Some suggested that they were, partly because of a lack of appropriate specialist resources for women who offend (such as bail hostels) and partly because paternalistic attitudes could result in women being more harshly judged and punished for having transgressed both legal and gender codes:

> [It] goes away back to that whole macho perspective as well...It's always much worse when it's a woman, you know. It's that kind of 'well, the woman should know better and shouldn't behave like that'.

On the other hand, it was also recognised that women's offending often escalated rapidly in the context of drug misuse and associated chaotic lifestyles, with the frequency of their offending possibly accounting for the courts' apparent use of relatively severe measures within a short space of time. It was also thought that sheriffs were increasingly reluctant to imprison women following the suicides at Cornton Vale (Scotland's only female prison) and at other local remand institutions and that they occasionally evinced 'astonishing leniency with some women offenders' as a result.

PROFESSIONALS' VIEWS ABOUT THE DEVELOPMENT OF EFFECTIVE STRATEGIES TO REDUCE OFFENDING

Early intervention programmes involving the co-operation of schools and social work departments were thought by some officers to be a promising way forward in the effort to reduce the incidence of youth crime. Others stressed the importance of

---

[38] Supervised attendance orders enable the courts to require offenders to undertake between 10 and 100 hours of supervised activity – which may include life skills courses – as an alternative to imprisonment for fine default. The pilot in Dundee enables the courts to use supervised attendance orders at first sentence with 16 and 17 year olds who are unable to pay a monetary penalty.

tackling drug use through educational programmes or providing young people with a range of outdoor activities, though there was some cynicism with respect to whether initiatives of the latter type would actually be taken up by those young people who were at greatest risk of or most actively involved in crime. One officer believed, however, that the most effective strategy to reduce offending among young people would be to actually listen to the young people themselves:

> We need to organise some means of forums by which children can, either individually or collectively, say their piece and be heard because the message I get is that they come out and everybody hates them, everybody wants to shoo them away: 'go and stand somewhere else' 'go and be somewhere else' 'don't drink' 'don't take drugs'. It's all 'dont's' and 'go aways' and if we can maybe get a strategy going where people have got to listen, set aside some time to listen to them...

Social workers recognised the value of preventive work with families though, despite one worker's view that 'it seems to me a bit senseless that you wait until the problems are so great that people are constantly in crisis', this was considered something of a luxury in the context of limited resources. A greater emphasis on community policing might also, it was suggested, help to reduce some of the tensions that were known to exist between young people and the police, with the former often complaining at being unfairly targeted and dealt with in a heavy handed way by the latter. Inter-agency work in general was seen as one of the most promising ways forward, so long as agencies were willing to share information equally and the enterprise did not become too one-sided. Although multi-agency strategies which could combat social *exclusion* and promote social *inclusion* were thought necessary, these were also acknowledged to be longer term endeavours. In the shorter term there was broad agreement that the incidence of offending among young people was unlikely to decrease without a strategic, multi-agency approach aimed at tackling the issue of drug misuse at the local level, such as the one recently proposed by the Government (Scottish Office, 1999e).

SUMMARY

The majority of persisters and desisters reported involvement with the police. Fewer female resisters (9%) reported involvement than male resisters (36%). More resisters gave a positive response to the question as to how well the police did their job, particularly female resisters (56%). More persisters gave a negative response, particularly male persisters (61%).

Thirty eight per cent of persisters reported having been to court in relation to charges against them and a smaller proportion of desisters. In relation to their view of the courts, the main issue that divided respondents was the leniency or harshness of the sentences. Fewest thought that the courts were too harsh, many were of the opinion that that the courts were too lenient and the most commonly held view was that the courts were too lenient in respect of some crimes while at the same time being too harsh in respect of others. Persisters, whom it might have been predicted would be antagonistic to the courts, often spoke of having been given many chances (such as probation) or having been fairly treated.

More persisters (29% males; 10% females) than desisters (14% males; 0% females) reported having been in prison or in a young offenders institution. Resisters were more negative about the prison service than desisters or persisters, the main reason given being that the majority of prisoners re-offended after their release. Those who spoke favourably of the prison system argued that it enabled criminals to be taken out of society at least for the period of their imprisonment and that it acted as a deterrent. In respect of it being a deterrent, persisters and desisters referred to the threat of incarceration more frequently than other aspects, such as police presence, probation or court appearance.

The most striking finding with regard to the children's hearings system was that the majority of respondents referred to it as a system solely for dealing with children and young people *who had offended*. A minority were aware that the system dealt with non-attendance at school, but respondents were almost invariably unaware of the child protection element of the system. In contrast to police, courts and prisons/young offenders institutions, knowledge about the children's hearings system was characterised by its vagueness, misunderstanding as to its role or ignorance of its existence at all, with 38 per cent of young people offering no view at all about the system.

More women and girls than men and boys reported social work involvement; this was especially notable in respect of desisters. A significant minority of the sample, particularly resisters (31%), were unable to offer any view about how well social workers did their jobs. The finding that similar proportions of persisters and resisters (46% and 44% respectively) held positive views about social workers belies the fact that they had very different knowledge of the profession, with more persisters (50%) reporting social worker involvement.

Sixty per cent of those asked reported that they had been the victim of an offence, mainly having their house broken into, their property stolen or being physically assaulted, with more males (particularly persisters and desisters) reporting the latter. Female interviewees were more likely to report domestic violence from partners, while males were more likely to report victimisation from men outside the home. A minority of persisters took the view that their experience of being a victim had affected their offending behaviour: others, however, were largely indifferent, many because the type of offence that they committed was not the same offence as the offence they had experienced as a victim, so they considered the victimisation to be irrelevant. More women and girls expressed their own feelings as a victim and their resultant understanding and sympathy towards other victims. Men and boys talked far more about the formal intervention which followed the victimisation incidents and were more likely to raise the issue of victim blame than their female counterparts. A sense of anger and need to retaliate was also evident in (largely) persisters' reactions to victimisation.

The professional respondents recognised that relationships between young people and the police could be improved if there was better communication between them, though this was acknowledged as having resource implications. Responses to offending among young people by the police, social workers, the children's hearings system and the adult courts were considered effective with some young people but not with others and all were said to be constrained by workloads and/or a limited range of options. There was universal recognition of the need for co-ordinated multi-agency initiatives aimed at preventing offending among young people, with the development of initiatives to address drug misuse being according the greatest priority.

CHAPTER EIGHT:
UNDERSTANDING RESISTANCE, DESISTANCE AND PERSISTENCE

INTRODUCTION

This chapter discusses the concepts of resistance, desistance and persistence. In particular it discusses young people's explanations for non offending, the cessation of offending and the possibility of continued offending. Also discussed are gender characteristics and moral decision scenarios.

WHY RESISTERS SAY THEY RESIST

Youngest age group

In explaining why they were not involved in offending, resisters (both girls and boys) appeared particularly concerned with the potential consequences of offending, for example: the desire not to caught; the desire not to be imprisoned; the desire not to undermine a 'good reputation'; the perceived inevitability of punishment: 'well I think there's always punishment at the end of it'; or the impact of having a criminal record on future prospects: 'if you've got a criminal record and if you go for a job it is always going to bring you down and not give you as much opportunities as you could have had with that one mistake, so I wouldn't ever do it'. There was also a concern not to arouse parental displeasure. For example, one girl resister commented 'I'd be really killed really if I were to do anything' while another explained ' I don't want to kind of disappoint them [her parents] because they are good to me'. Others empathised with the victims of offending, either specifically: 'you think about the manager [of a store] and how he feels when people take his stuff' or more generally: 'because it's not fair on other folk'.

Despite the fact that peer pressure and boredom were regarded by young people as key explanations of their own offending, only two girls and one boy mentioned that their choice of friends was a reason for not offending (they either avoided people who were involved in offending or they had purposely changed their friends because they were of the opinion that they would get them into trouble) and only one girl and one boy commented that being busy was the reason for their non offending. The girl explained 'because I've got a lot to do, like I've got lots of clubs and stuff and I've got my music practice and I've got homework and things and I'm always busy, I don't have time to think about anything like that'.

Several resisters did not see the point in offending, for example 'if you've got the money to pay for it, why steal?' Others stated that they did not want to offend: 'it's never appealed to me to steal anything or like er break a window or something, you know. It's just silly people do that' (girl) and 'I'm not that kind of person' (boy).

Middle age group

Like their younger counterparts young men and women in the middle age group were also concerned about the potential consequences of offending. This was cited by seven young women and five young men as accounting for why they did not offend. Young women commented that they were afraid of being 'caught' (which one young women thought was an inevitable outcome) and/or 'getting into trouble': 'The fear of, you know, of being caught and because well no matter if it's big or small, you know, what can happen to you, prison and stuff'. Young men were more likely to associate the consequences of offending directly to the impact it could have on their job prospects and career, for example: 'I want a clean, you know a clean record and I want a job and you know I want to get a good job. If you've got a record you'll no get a good job'. One young man, who had been involved with the police in connection with an incident of criminal damage which had occurred when he was drunk, noted that this incident had forced him to seriously consider the consequences offending could have for his future job prospects:

> But you worry about it you know because if you had something like a bigger record you'd have to bring it up in job interviews and I think I'd be worried if I started doing that, if you get caught in a sort of spiral of bigger things.

Eight young women and two of the young men identified their upbringing as being relevant to an understanding of why they did not offend. This was because their parents had taught them 'right from wrong': 'I've been brought up really strictly and told not to offend and told what's right and wrong and what the difference is' (young woman) or because they did not want to upset or elicit the disapproval of their families as one young woman explained:

> I think it was the way I was brought up because my mum always told me if I got into trouble, if I did anything bad at all, like I suppose it's kind of so I don't upset my mum and all that, because like say I went out and shoplifted and got caught that would really hurt my mum and I wouldn't want to do that.

Others (three men and three women) were clearly of the view that offending was 'wrong' and was not, therefore, something that they would do or even consider doing. One young woman explained: 'I realise that deep inside myself, that it is wrong to offend and I would really feel terrible if I did do it, and I knew it was wrong. You would feel so guilty and you would feel so bad'. Five young women also emphasised that they did not offend because they did not associate with people who offended. Others viewed offending as unnecessary (five women and one man), 'pointless' (two women and two men), 'stupid' (one man) and as something they actively chose not to do (two men).

Oldest age group

The majority of young women in the oldest age group explained their resistance to becoming involved in offending in terms of fear. Ten women explained they would be too scared to offend in some cases because of the potential for getting into 'trouble', being 'caught', getting a 'criminal record' or being sent to jail. The latter, it was suggested, could have other repercussions in respect of their families, homes and employment. A few young men in this age group were also concerned about the negative consequences of offending in terms of getting a criminal record and being sent to jail. They also expressed concern about how they would be viewed by family and friends

Upbringing was also identified by five women and four men as a reason why young people in this age group did not offend. As one young woman explained:

> Well I think it's the way I've been brought up. I mean my mum just brought me up to think that that wasn't okay and she was quite clear what was right and what was wrong and she explained it to us and said that wasn't okay and she wouldn't have let us get away with anything.

Some young people (three women and two men) explained that offending was simply not an issue for them and that they had no reason to offend. As one young woman explained:

> I felt it was just silly and I could amuse myself other ways. I didn't get to the degree of boredom that I think they must get to when they want to go and scribble on walls and things like that. [...] I think it's mental. I think because I was more interested in, you know, positive input in my life, I never, it never even really occurred to me.

In contrast to many persisters, one young man, who regularly used heroin and temezepam for pain relief, explained:

> My addiction has never been that bad that I've had to go out and steal to feed it. ... I've always got my painkillers so I don't like rattle. ... I've never needed to go out and steal or rob or anything like that. I condemn it a bit but I know how people feel in a way.

Some young men believed their resistance was attributable to having a conscience, with reference being made to the guilt they would experience if they offended. As one explained: 'It's not something you'd be able to shrug off and say 'oh well I got caught, just bad luck'. I would look on it as a stain on your character and then I'd feel guilty'. Others simply commented that they had no desire to offend (two women), they had 'too much to lose' (two women), they believed offending was wrong (one woman and one man), they 'respected the law' (one woman) and they had the responsibility of bringing up a child (one woman).

WHY DESISTERS SAY THEY DESISTED

Youngest age group

When asked about why they had stopped offending and why they no longer offended the potential negative consequences were a motivating factor for four boy desisters. Particular reference was made to the inevitability of getting caught, parental disapproval, and statutory intervention. Two girl desisters explained their cessation of offending with reference to fear of the police while another expressed fear at the possibility of committing offences: 'Because I'm scared. I think maybe people have got a stronger opinion about everything. It would be no problem but I think I just like – I couldn't imagine myself with a bottle in my hand and smashing it across someone knowing I could kill them'.

Three girl desisters explained that they stopped offending because of others: one because her mother was 'over-protective' and had 'taken me away from people she's saw drinking in the streets'; one because her brother, whom she emulated, had stopped offending; and another because a relative had been in trouble and this had put her off offending. Boys were also influenced by others in their decisions to stop offending. Two commented that their decision to stop offending had been influenced by parental disapproval. For example, one 15 year old explained 'my mum sort of scared me. She told me that if I got into any bother she said she would kick me out of the house. Whether she meant it or not I don't know, but it has stopped me.' One boy attributed his stopping offending to the shame and humiliation he had experienced as a result of an incident when he was twelve years of age which had resulted in police intervention, while another explained that he had stopped because he did not 'like' what was happening to people around him.

Changes in the lives of boy desisters, whether or not self initiated, also appeared significant in their stopping offending. One noted the importance of his moving to a new neighbourhood and making new friends, one thought that the transition to secondary school had been particularly important and another commented that his opportunities to offend had reduced because of his decision to 'stay in more' and to socialise only with friends who did not offend. For three other boys getting older and becoming more mature were identified as contributory factors in stopping offending. As one explained:

I'm more mature now and I understand that like smashing a school window now it would cost the school money and the money is important for education instead of paying for school windows.

Maturity may also have contributed to two boys coming to view offending as pointless, two girls forming the opinion that it was not right to offend and a further two girls realising that they did not need to offend – in this case stealing – because their parents would provide for them if they could not afford things themselves. One girl explained: 'probably I'm different and feel stronger and I know that if I did have a future that [offending] would harm me' while a boy commented that stopping offending was something which 'just kind of happened'.

In accounting for how they had been able to stop offending, personal choice and motivation to desist appeared important considerations. For some, it seems, the decision to stop was enough in itself, although one boy reinforced his personal resolve by informing his peers of his decision and another stopped going out as much as he had done previously.

Middle age group

Growing up was the most common response from both young men (seven cases) and young women (four cases) in explaining their desistance from offending. Maturity was acknowledged both as a factor in itself and also in relation to making adult transitions such as getting a job, going to university, having children, settling down with a partner and leaving home. In keeping with previous research which suggests that having few delinquent friends is associated with desistance (Farrington, 1996; Loeber et al., 1991) some young people (three men and three women) commented on the fact that they had consciously ended friendships with those who had been involved in offending in favour of non offending peers. To a lesser extent factors such as having been caught for previous offending, 'guilt', 'fear', 'common sense' and the consideration of future prospects were referred to by some young people in explaining why they no longer offend. Two male desisters noted that they no longer felt any need to offend since they were in a position to buy whatever they wanted.

Oldest age group

A concern to make amends and protect families featured prominently among young men (nine cases) and to a lesser extent young women (two cases) in explaining desistance amongst the oldest group of desisters. Some young people, who had been allowed back into the family home after a period of absence or had been offered family support and companionship, were concerned not to hurt family members or damage relationships with their families. Young women appeared more concerned with the responsibilities involved in caring for their own children (five cases), though this was also said to have been significant in the decisions made to desist by three young men. In explaining how her children were relevant to an understanding of why she no longer offended, one young woman observed:

> I have got more responsibility, I couldn't afford to take the risk. I mean at the end of the day if I was to do anything stupid and end up locked up or anything ... what happens, what's going to be the outcome, always thinking that bit ahead. ... I have got kids and if I ever done anything stupid or got locked up or anything like that what about the kids, who is going to look after them. It all falls back, this is what holds me back, this is what sort of keeps my head on my shoulders.

A further three young men and one young woman attributed their desistance to stopping or reducing their use of drugs. Support and help from the social work department in respect of homelessness and benefits were said to have proved an important factor in stopping offending for one young man, while another identified medical intervention in the form of access to a methadone programme as important in his situation.

Growing up was a factor more likely to be identified by men (six cases) rather than women (two cases) to explain why they no longer offended and only men (seven cases) attributed their desistance from offending to a personal choice, with one explaining: 'I don't want to go out and commit crime any more ... if I can do it this long I can keep going'. Others believed that they had been motivated to stop offending by the fact they had not been very 'good criminals' in the first case: that is, they had been caught for some or all of the offences they had committed (three men and two women) or they had found offending to be a stressful and frightening experience (one man and one woman). A few young people were motivated to avoid the consequences of offending generally (three women) or a custodial sentence in particular (two men).

WHY PERSISTERS PLAN TO DESIST

The transitory nature of involvement in offending is highlighted in Matza's (1964) theory of delinquency and drift whereby individuals 'drift' into and away from offending. Shover (1997) emphasises that periods of desistance may often be followed by further offending and that 'many, particularly those with criminal identities, may reduce the frequency of their offenses but continue committing crime for months or even years' (1997, p122). This appears to be borne out in the interviews with persisters wherein a variety of accounts and explanations are forwarded on the relative achievements made or planned in respect of stopping offending, often despite having last offended as recently as days or weeks previously. The most striking difference in these accounts across the age range is the relative optimism of the youngest age group, who were most likely to say they had or planned to desist. By comparison, older respondents, while often acknowledging that desistance was something they wished to achieve, were less inclined to say they were not offending or that they planned to stop in the immediate or foreseeable future.

Youngest age group

It was apparent that within the youngest age group many persisters, like desisters, talked about offending as something they had done in the past rather than something in which they continued to be actively involved. For example, one girl persister gives the interviewer the impression that her shoplifting is in the past and she has now stopped. However, on probing, it transpires that she is currently grounded by her parents for shoplifting:

Int:	And what was his – your parents' reaction?
Girl:	I got a row and he was shouting and everything and I got grounded.
Int:	And did that make any difference to what you were doing, the trouble you were getting into?
Girl:	Yeah I can't go out.
Int:	Oh was that quite recent?
Girl:	Yeah.
Int:	So are you grounded at the moment?
Girl:	Yeah.

In trying to explain their desistance several persisters in the youngest age group commented on the deterrent effect of being caught, either personally:

we got caught one time me and my pals went shopping and we got caught shoplifting ... the police said they were coming to my house and we were all greeting [crying] when we were walking home ... we didn't tell our mum and dad and they [the police] didn't come ... I'd never do it again. It was scary because they were pure shouting at us. (girl persister)

or of their friends having been caught:

In the past I have shoplifted, but I found it was stupid. I used to think it was something I really wanted to do, but I found out that my pal got caught – my best pal – and the police were involved and I decided that was it. That was the final straw. (girl persister).

Others identified the potential consequences of offending as being relevant to their plans to desist. For some this included the possibility of the police to coming to their homes, while for one female persister it included the possibility of being sent to a detention centre: 'if I get into bother say something like four more times, I'll be in a detention centre ... my mum says to us detention centres don't look as nice as what they are. They treat you bad, treat you as if you're in jail'. In more general terms a male persister commented:

It was just me realising that if I do anything wrong I'm going to get into serious trouble and more trouble than what I'm in already. So then I just stop myself from doing it because basically all I'm thinking about is my future now.

Others thought that offending had been a phase that had now passed, either because they had 'grown out it' or because they had, without necessarily realising it, 'not done it for a while'. Other explanations forwarded to account for planned desistance among this group included changing their friendship groups; a wish to avoid parental hurt and disappointment; friends' disapproval; and a sudden realisation (unexplained) that they were being 'stupid' or 'untrue'. In some cases strategies were instituted to make desistance more likely. One boy, for instance, claimed that he now stayed at home more in order that there would be fewer temptations for him to become involved in offending. One girl, who admitted that her offending had reduced in frequency rather than having stopped, explained: 'I think – I know this sounds stupid, but the buzz like wore off me'.

Middle age group

Young men and women in the middle age group were most often motivated towards desistance through concern about the potential consequences of continuing to offend. Reference was variously made to the wish to avoid being caught; police involvement; the risks associated with breaching probation; and the possibility of being sentenced to custody. Several others noted that the decision to stop offending reflected an active choice on their part: that is, they 'wanted to' or they 'wouldn't want that happening to me'. Not using drugs had been instrumental in facilitating desistance in two young women while the use of methadone had made possible a cessation in offending by two men. Parenthood was identified by one young man and one young women as being a motivating factor in their decisions to stop offending. As the former explained: 'I wouldn't want him [son] looking up to us, know what I mean, and us going to jail and that.'

It was more common for young women to initiate avoidance strategies to facilitate their desistance. These included staying in, getting a job, going to college or breaking away from friends who were involved in offending and drug use. One young man had changed his circle of friends and another was attempting to stay at home more. However, in marked contrast to young women of the same age, one young man who had stopped offending for a few months commented that although he would not actively seek out trouble, he would certainly react to it because 'sometimes you've got to do it'. Furthermore, although both young men and young women in this age group recognised the importance of family in respect of desistance it seemed that they did so for quite different reasons: young women were motivated by concerns about the adverse impact their offending would have on their family while young men relied on families to provide them with support and help of both a practical and emotional kind.

Oldest age group

Stopping drug use appeared the most significant factor in stopping offending for young men and women in the oldest age group. The most common scenario was that if they were not using drugs they were not forced to offend to support their habit. Several young men also credited receiving medical help and support for their drug use as having made it possible for them to stop offending. For example:

Man: Well for the last four months, three to four months, I've not committed a crime.

Int: For what reason?

Man: Well I'm off drugs now, so I don't need money to pay for my habit any more, so I'm not pressured to get out and get money.

Int: Was it a conscious decision, I mean how did you succeed?

Man: Well I had the support of my family, my pals, my girlfriend, I had help from the doctor. So I had quite a lot of people all involved in it to help me out.

One young man, who was a registered addict, commented that he was able to stop offending only for those periods of time when he was given or could borrow money from family, friends and money-lenders to support his habit.

Other young men observed that stopping offending had been facilitated by breaking away from friends who were involved in offending or by moving away from an area where they were involved in or known for offending. One young woman also noted the importance of ending the relationship with a partner who offended while another attributed her success at stopping offending to getting and keeping a job.

The consequences of offending did not appear to feature as a major concern for those who had or planned to stop offending in this age group. However, one young man suggested that the risk of being sentenced to custody had contributed to his desistance, one young woman did not want to breach her probation order and another young woman was concerned about the effect of further offending on the outcome of her outstanding charges.

The support of families (one young man) and partners (one young man and one young woman) had proved important in helping some young persisters stop offending. Simply having children had proved influential for one young woman, while for another the realisation that she might lose her children was a motivating factor. The latter explained: 'say I get caught, I've been told by the social worker next time I get lifted by the police my kids will get took away'.

PERSISTENCE

Graham and Bowling (1995) conclude that the transition to adulthood, particularly in terms of marriage and forming relationships, is more significant in terms of desistance from offending for women than it is for men. While women are less likely to offend than men in the first place they are more likely to desist by the time the reach their twenties since by this stage they are also more likely than young men to have acquired symbols of adult status. This conclusion is one which seems very pertinent to the findings in respect of persistence given that the experiences and accounts of young men and young women seem quite different.

Youngest age group

Amongst this youngest age group girls appeared more concerned than boys to be viewed as desisting and succeeding in this whereas boys, while also trying to desist, acknowledged that this process was by no means straightforward. One boy for example, commented that while he did not actively seek out fights with others, he would fight if provoked. Another explained that while it was his intention to stay out of trouble, he would rarely back down from a fight and often had no control over his actions when drunk. Others who indicated that they often did not offend for quite long periods of time suggested that they actively avoided situations in which they could offend. As one boy explained, 'sometimes I just avoid it I just go where I know no one else is going to be or if there is a big crowd I just carry on' (boy persister).

Overall it appeared that many boy persisters believed that continued involvement in offending was an inevitable part of their lifestyle and when pressed as to whether they had actually considered stopping offending the majority, while having considered this particular scenario, were doubtful of their ability to do so. Four boy persisters were adamant that they were unlikely to stop fighting as they would not – and indeed could not – avoid provocation in this respect:

It's always somebody else who wants to fight or else wants to fight with your mate and you canny walk past or whatever.

One boy simply concluded that his efforts to stop offending in the past had proved unsuccessful and that this was unlikely to change. Another thought that stopping offending at his age was not feasible. As he explained:

I don't think anyone my age could actually give up, well for the next four years or something like that. I don't think I'll be able to give up like doing things wrong. Because I mean it's just sheer boredom and peer pressure and stuff like that.

Middle age group

In the middle age group young women were again more keen to be viewed as desisting than were young men, though the gender difference was not as marked as in the youngest age group. Just under two thirds of female persisters (five cases) and just under a fifth of male persisters (three cases) in the middle age group considered themselves to have stopped offending. Drug addiction, largely to heroin, was the reason young men and young women most commonly gave for continued offending. A common story was that young people had to steal to get money to fund their drug habit. One young men explained this as follows: '[you've] got to steal to get money. If you've got a drug habit, you've got to feed your drug habit. Everything you get goes on your drugs. So you've got to offend to get money to feed your habit. That's you stuck'. The most common means of generating money for drug use was shoplifting and a range of other offences which varied somewhat by gender. Young women reported being involved in reset, drug dealing or fraud while young men, in addition to perpetrating these offences, reported also having been involved in breaking into shops and muggings.

Drug use was, of course, not the only reason offered for persistence in offending. Another common explanation offered – by both sexes – was self defence, defence of friends or retaliation in cases of fighting and assault. For example:

That last one [assault] a couple of months ago, there was one of my pals standing outside a club in the town and somebody came through and started shouting and bawling at him and started hooking right into him ... and he was getting hammered and the guy was just punching right into him and his pal was trying to attack him to, so I just busted him on the head with a bottle. (young man)

I mean I don't go out looking for fights or that. If I have to fight someone I will. Then weeks later, like see their pals or their sisters will try and attack us for fighting with them and I'll end up in another fight and it's just they keep always coming back on us. (young woman)

Others ascribed their continued offending to: diminished responsibility as a result of excessive alcohol use (three young men and one young woman); boredom (two young men and one young woman); peer pressure (three young woman and one young man); impulsiveness (two young men); lack of money (two young men) and stupidity (one young man).

Oldest age group

In the oldest age group young women were again more likely than young men to indicate that they were desisting. Only a quarter of female persisters claimed that they were still actively offending and that they were likely to continue doing so compared with just over two thirds of young men. Drug use and addiction were considered responsible for all of the young women's and the majority of young men's continued involvement in offending. One young man explained: 'It's just the drug scene. I can't stay away from it and I never will'. Theft was again seen as a necessary means by which to fund drug use which, for all in this age group was considered an addiction, mostly to heroin and in one case to temazepam. Shoplifting was again the favoured means of offending for this purpose (five young men and two young women), although one young woman explained that she preferred to steal from her own family and friends. In addition to shoplifting young men were also involved in stealing money from other addicts (two cases), reset (one case) and housebreaking (one case). The potential severity of this offending is illustrated in one young man's description of how he uses a knife to demand money or drugs from other users:

> If you pull a knife out, you're no intending to stick that in them, you're only trying to frighten them. ... What I say is 'There's an easy way and a hard way. Why no just give us the easy way. Give me it and go home. Just walk away'. Or the hard way is just to offer them [the knife] and get it over and done with. At the end of the day I know I'm going to get it whether it's five minutes or ten minutes struggle.

Two young men also attributed some of their offending – in this case fighting – to provocation or revenge. The only young man who did make a direct connection between his offending and drug use was involved in repeat theft from his workplace in respect of which he explained: 'things like tools and that, they just come under miscellaneous. It can be written off. There's that much, ... they're no labelled, they're no counted. They don't look for the tools, it's just one of those things. If it goes missing, nobody knows it's missing and that'.

EFFECT OF OFFENDING ON YOUNG PERSON THEMSELVES

Persisters and desisters varied in the extent to which offending had an impact on them personally, partly due to the extent and severity of their offending but also because they varied with respect to whether or not their offending had resulted in any kind of intervention. It is not surprising, therefore, that offending was seen to have more serious cumulative consequences with increasing age. The youngest desisters and persisters talked about the impact of offending in terms of getting caught and punished (largely by parents rather than statutory agencies) and in terms of feeling guilty about their actions. In the middle age group the consequences of offending had become more serious, especially for persisters, and the outcomes which seemed of most concern to them were those which involved contact with the criminal justice system, most notably the police. While many young people in the middle age group expressed embarrassment at their involvement in offending it was apparent that for others offending was having increasingly serious repercussions, particularly in terms of estrangement from family and friends. In the oldest age group many persisters were starting to recognise some quite serious consequences of their offending. A higher proportion of the oldest age group, particularly persisters, had acquired a criminal record and some had, in addition, served custodial sentences. The consequences of offending on the personal lives of some persisters included losing partners, children, homes and contact with families and having few employment prospects or opportunities.

However, it was also clear that many young people in all age groups did not feel themselves to have been affected in any way by their involvement in offending. In the youngest age group and among desisters this was most commonly attributed to the fact they had not been caught or because the offending in which they were involved was not particularly serious. Many persisters in the middle and oldest age groups also commented that offending had no effect on their lives. Some attributed this to the fact that they had never received a custodial sentence while for others offending had become an integral part of a lifestyle which often involved regular drug use and it had, as a consequence, become a means to an end.

EFFECT OF OFFENDING ON OTHERS

Parents were most commonly cited by young people as having been adversely affected by their involvement in offending. Many persisters and desisters of all ages recognised that when their offending was known about or became public this caused their parents and families to experience distress, hurt, anger, disappointment, shock and despair. A loss of trust was a recognised parental and family reaction for all groups of young people. Obviously however, parental reactions varied by age, with the youngest age group most likely to be subjected to punishments which included restrictions on where, when, how often and with whom they could spend leisure time. By contrast, for the older two age groups punishment in any form was often not a consideration given their adult status. That said, many commented that their offending had seriously damaged relationships with their families. For a few this had resulted either in their exclusion from the family home or in their families severing all ties with the young person.

PROFESSIONAL PERSPECTIVES ON DESISTANCE AND PERSISTENCE

Desistance

Just as a variety of factors were said by police officers to be associated with the causation of crime, so were various factors acknowledged by the police to be related to desistance from offending. These included 'maturation', which was frequently accompanied by a recognition that offending was 'pointless', finding employment and entering into a stabilising relationship with a partner. Reference was also made to young people 'taking a tumble' and recognising the potential personal consequences of continued offending. A police warning or an appearance before a children's hearing was considered sufficient to deter many young people from further involvement in delinquency, but reference was most commonly made to the impact made upon young people by their transition from the children's hearings system to the adult criminal justice system at 16 years of age:

There's some guys and girls at school who for bravado offend to show off to their friends, go to the children's panel and they just shut their ears when this is on. But when they go to court for maybe one or two times they suddenly realise this is a slippery slope here, and they could stop offending. I think the coming of age – the 16 year old thing – is a barrier for a lot of kids to stop offending.

They get into a pattern of offending when they're a juvenile and they know the system backwards. And they know that as soon as they get to three months before their 16th birthday it all goes to the fiscal. And that's when you can start getting fined. Its with the 'big boys' now – you can go to jail.

Teachers formed the impression that many pupils began to desist from offending around the end of the fourth year at school when they 'grow up' and 'realise that their education is important', with this process being more likely among children from middle class backgrounds who had become involved in offending 'for a bit of dare devil fun'. Many young people, it was said, were reluctant to jeopardise their prospects of a good job by accumulating a criminal record. By the time they reached school leaving age it was also hoped that many pupils would have acquired the inter-personal skills necessary to deal with situations which might result in offending in more appropriate ways.

The process of desistance from offending was thought by social workers to be influenced by a range of factors, though these could be broadly grouped into three categories: lifestyle changes; relationships; and deterrence. First, it was suggested that over time young people matured and began to identify the need to replace their existing lifestyle – including, where relevant, the use of drugs – with something else. This could often mean spending more time with a smaller circle of friends, rather than 'hanging around with the crowd'. 'Settling down' with a partner could also serve as a positive stimulus to change, and for young women this was said often to be accompanied by the desire to have children. Finally, if young people were not otherwise deterred by contact with the children's hearings system or the criminal justice system – with the transition between the two being considered a significant source of motivation towards desistance – the wish to maintain other lifestyle changes could result in the stakes associated with continued offending becoming too high.

Persistence

Young people were thought by teachers to be at risk of becoming persistent offenders if they had no aspirations and limited opportunities for employment and if they therefore began to view offending – including drug dealing – as an attractive financial option:

If crime puts money in your pocket and you have not got any great prospects of a reasonably paid job anyway, that's much harder to give up because everybody likes to have money in their pocket.

Whilst it was agreed by the police officers who were interviewed that most young people would, for various reasons, 'grow out of crime', others would continue to offend well into adulthood. Persistence in crime was thought to be a result of three principal factors. First, it was suggested that some young people had been brought up in families where crime was inter-generational and that they therefore knew of no other way of life. Second, some young people were said to become institutionalised in the child care and penal systems with the result that they were unable to function effectively in the community. Third, continued involvement in crime was, for some, essentially utilitarian: the outcome of a deliberate and conscious choice to pursue a criminal lifestyle for financial gain (see, for example, Shover, 1996).

SELF-ESTEEM

There is a rather mixed and inconclusive literature on the relationship between self esteem and offending. While some have suggested that offending may be associated with low self-esteem (e.g. Fischer and Bersani, 1979) others, such as Andrews (1995) have argued that self-esteem is a poor criminogenic target since increasing self-esteem is likely simply to lead to more self-assured criminals unless other criminogenic needs have been addressed.

In view of the conflicting data about the relationship between self-esteem and offending a decision was reached to explore this relationship in the present study. The most commonly used validated measure of self-esteem is Rosenberg's (1965) self-esteem Scale. It consists of ten statements of varying polarity (that is, half are negative statements and half are positive) and young people were asked to indicate the extent of their agreement or disagreement with each statement (strongly agree, agree, disagree, strongly disagree). An overall score was derived by assigning a score of between one and four to responses to individual items (with scores reversed in the case of negative statements) and summing the scores on each item. A higher score indicated a higher level of self esteem.

Analysis of the Rosenberg Self-esteem Scale revealed no significant differences in mean scores between persisters (29.5), desisters (30.2) and resisters (31.1) in the youngest age group. There was, however, a significant gender difference, with boys having a higher mean score (31.1) than girls (29.3) (t=2.2, p<.05). In other words, boys exhibited higher levels of self-esteem on average than did girls. This finding may lack explanatory potential in the present context but it is consistent with other studies (e.g. Chubb et al., 1997) which have pointed to lower levels of self-esteem among adolescent girls.

Table 8.1: Self esteem by age, gender and offender category

	Resisters	Desisters	Persisters
YOUNGEST AGE GROUP Male (n=48)	31.8	31.1	30.7
Female (n=50)	30.6	29.1	28.1
MIDDLE AGE GROUP Male (n=39)	32.8	29.5	28.6
Female (n=45)	29.2	29.0	26.5
OLDEST AGE GROUP Male (n=37)	34.5	29.0	26.6
Female (n=37)	31.7	29.4	23.9

There was no difference in mean self-esteem score between the two older age groups (29.2 and 29.1 respectively). There was, however, a significant difference in self esteem between young men and women in the middle age group (30.5 compared with 28.1, p<.05) but not among young people in the oldest age group. More importantly, however, the mean self esteem scores for resisters, desisters and persisters differed significantly in both age groups, with the lowest score observed among persisters and the highest among resisters. As Table 8.1 shows, this relationship held true for both young men and women. The highest mean score was found among young male resisters in the oldest age group whilst the lowest mean level of self esteem was observed among young women in the same age group who were actively involved in offending. The greatest difference in self esteem scores between resisters, desisters and persisters was found among the oldest age group. Lower levels of self esteem among persisters in this age group may be associated with the social exclusion apparently experienced by many of these young people, especially those who were also involved in drug misuse.

GENDER ATTITUDES

In recent years there has been increasing attention paid within the criminological literature to the relationship between masculinities and crime (e.g. Messerchmidt, 1994; Newburn and Stanko, 1994; Collier, 1998). Within these analyses, criminal activity in various forms is reconstructed within a discourse of hegemonic masculinity[39] (Connell, 1987) which, as in feminist analyses, is intrinsically related to power. Buckley (1995) for instance, has argued that masculinity is associated with 'curtailing emotion, success, fighting and sexual competence...It is possible to see offending as a rational response to the messages of how to construct one's masculinity. In other words, crime is a way of expressing

[39] The academic literature recognises that masculinity is not a unitary concept but that, rather, different masculinities exist. The concept of megemonic masculinity refers to the traditional and dominant form of masculinity in western societies.

masculinity and behind that emphasising one's gender...To show that you are a man you must show that you: a) are strong and tough, lacking sensitivity; b) are successful/popular/one of the gang – a real 'lad'; c) have no feelings, or if you have they must not be shown; d) are ready to fight; e) regard women as subordinates and objects of gratification' (pp. 101-102).

An exploration in the interview of young people's attitudes towards gender roles indicated that most young people did not, in fact, ascribe different expectations to men and women. Young people, in the main, failed to identify behaviours which they considered were appropriate for men but not for women and vice versa. This issue was also examined through the administration of a questionnaire on the laptop which sought to explore whether young people perceived different attributes as being more appropriate for men and women. The questionnaire consisted of 20 adjectives, ten of which might be broadly defined – in accordance with traditional stereotypes – as 'feminine' and ten as 'masculine'. Respondents were asked to indicate the extent to which they agreed or disagreed that people[40], men and women respectively should possess each characteristic. A five point Likert scale was employed, enabling young people to indicate whether they agreed strongly, agreed, neither agreed nor disagreed, disagreed or disagreed strongly with each example. The categories were then further collapsed to indicate agreement, disagreement or neutrality.

As Table 8.2 shows, certain characteristics were more often thought appropriate for one sex than for another. Boys and girls in the youngest age group more often agreed that women should be dependent, emotional, sensitive, successful and warm and that men should be daring. Whilst these findings suggest the existence of attitudes which tend to accord with traditional gender stereotypes it is also notable that most characteristics were considered equally appropriate to men and women.

There were relatively few differences between boys and girls in terms of the attributes they considered appropriate for men and women but several differences emerged between resisters, desisters and persisters. Persisters were least likely to agree that men should be caring, sympathetic and sensitive while resisters were most likely to not to agree that women should be aggressive and dependent. Although any conclusions must be tentative, these differences point to persisters in the youngest age group having more stereotyped views about men and women which accord to traditional conceptions of masculinity and femininity.

[40] Young people's views about people – as opposed to men or women specifically – have been excluded to simplify interpretation. Had stark differences in beliefs about men and women emerged it would have been interesting to explore whether people were perceived more in masculine or feminine terms. In the absence of such differences, however, analysis of this sort would serve to confuse rather than elucidate the issue.

Table 8.2: Agreement that men and women should possess certain characteristics - youngest age group[41]

	Men should be...	Women should be...
Aggressive	15 (15%)	12 (12%)
Ambitious	92 (94%)	92 (93%)
Caring	89 (90%)	96 (97%)
Controlling	37 (37%)	41 (41%)
Daring	33 (34%)	22 (22%)
Dependent	48 (48%)	60 (61%)
Emotional	67 (68%)	83 (84%)
Independent	88 (89%)	90 (91%)
Loving	90 (91%)	92 (94%)
Powerful	42 (42%)	44 (44%)
Rational	55 (56%)	58 (59%)
Sensitive	70 (71%)	80 (81%)
Strong	72 (73%)	73 (74%)
Submissive	21 (21%)	22 (22%)
Successful	72 (73%)	84 (85%)
Sympathetic	75 (76%)	80 (81%)
Thoughtful	92 (93%)	94 (95%)
Unassertive	12 (12%)	17 (17%)
Unemotional	7 (7%)	10 (10%)
Warm	78 (79%)	92 (93%)

In the absence of differences between the older age groups with respect to the perceived appropriateness of different attributes for men and women, the relevant data have been combined in Table 8.3. Whilst it was more often thought that women should be warm, there were otherwise no differences in the perceived appropriateness of characteristics for men and for women.

There were, however, differences between young men and women with respect to the perceived appropriateness of certain attributes for men and women. In particular, in comparison with the young women, the young men in the sample tended to adhere to more stereotyped 'macho' views of men. For instance, young women were more likely not to agree that men should be aggressive and unemotional whereas young men were more likely than young women to agree that men should be controlling, daring and powerful and were less likely to agree that men should be caring, emotional, loving, sensitive and warm.

There were, similarly, some differences in views between resisters, desisters and persisters in the older age groups. Persisters were more likely to agree that men should be controlling and unemotional and less likely to agree that men should be rational and sympathetic.

[41] N = 98 or 99.

Table 8.3: Agreement that men and women should possess certain characteristics - middle and oldest age group[42]

	Men should be...	Women should be...
Aggressive	**20** *(13%)*	**12** *(8%)*
Ambitious	**132** *(85%)*	**127** *(84%)*
Caring	**144** *(94%)*	**147** *(96%)*
Controlling	**37** *(24%)*	**34** *(22%)*
Daring	**57** *(37%)*	**47** *(31%)*
Dependent	**61** *(40%)*	**74** *(48%)*
Emotional	**112** *(73%)*	**121** *(80%)*
Independent	**135** *(88%)*	**135** *(88%)*
Loving	**145** *(94%)*	**151** *(98%)*
Powerful	**64** *(41%)*	**69** *(45%)*
Rational	**99** *(64%)*	**96** *(63%)*
Sensitive	**127** *(83%)*	**138** *(90%)*
Strong	**120** *(77%)*	**109** *(72%)*
Submissive	**22** *(14%)*	**15** *(10%)*
Successful	**116** *(75%)*	**119** *(78%)*
Sympathetic	**130** *(84%)*	**134** *(88%)*
Thoughtful	**142** *(92%)*	**144** *(94%)*
Unassertive	**11** *(7%)*	**13** *(9%)*
Unemotional	**17** *(11%)*	**13** *(9%)*
Warm	**128** *(83%)*	**146** *(95%)*

Two general observations are worthy of note in the present context. First, these findings, whilst certainly not conclusive, suggest that persisters had a greater tendency to adhere to gendered stereotypes, especially those which emphasise the emotional detachment of men, lending some support to the proposition that a relationship exists between crime and masculinity.

Second, it was found – especially, though not exclusively, amongst the older age groups – that young people believed, on the whole, that men and women should possess broadly similar characteristics, though young men tended to adopt slightly more stereotyped views of men. The fact that attributes which have traditionally been perceived as 'masculine' – success, ambition, independence, strength – were as likely to be thought 'desirable' for women may, we would wish to argue, take us some way towards understanding the common perception among police officers, teachers and social workers that girls were becoming increasingly involved in crime[43]. More specifically, we would contend that crime and delinquency may for

[42] N varies between 151 and 155.

[43] Although there was also a perception of increased offending amoung young women, this was usually attributed directly to an increase in drug use: we believe that different explanations are required for offending amongst women and offending among girls and will return to this in the final chapter.

many boys and young men be a mechanism for confirming a masculine identity in the absence of other 'legitimate' means, access to which may, in themselves, be socially, economically and culturally defined. If attributes which previously were perceived as masculine are now becoming perceived instead as universally desirable – that is, equally relevant for men and women – then we might expect girls to adopt similar approaches to boys in the pursuit of common identities. Such an argument, which we will develop more fully in the final chapter, would be consistent with perceptions that a) girls were increasingly adopting similar attitudes, appearances and behaviours to boys and b) this was most marked among girls who were described as being 'low achievers' in school.

MORAL DILEMMA QUESTIONS

It has been suggested that young people who believe strongly in the importance of complying with the law are less likely to violate the law (Braithwaite,1989). When exploring young people's likely reactions to a number of moral dilemmas, ranging from shoplifting to finding £10 in the street, it certainly appeared that resisters and persisters approached the various scenarios from very different perspectives. Tables 8.4 to 8.6 illustrate the percentage of young people in each offender category who answered the questions in what can be viewed as the 'morally responsible' manner.

Table 8.4: Percentage of young people in the youngest age group who answered the moral dilemma questions in the morally responsible manner

	Resisters		Desisters		Persisters	
	Boys (n=13)	Girls (n=20)	Boys (n=14)	Girls (n=14)	Boys (n=21)	Girls (n=18)
Wouldn't cheat at cards?	46	65	57	43	33	33
Wouldn't shoplift?	100	95	71	86	52	78
Would hand in £10?	46	50	7	7	9	-
Would hand in £100 ?	77	80	43	71	24	22
Wouldn't sell friend's CDs?	100	95	93	93	100	83
Wouldn't accuse someone of stealing?	100	100	93	64	90	100
Would hand in handbag?	100	95	93	100	95	89
Would remind friend of £10 loan?	85	80	57	71	33	55
Would tell shopkeeper of too much change?	85	90	28	57	9	5
Wouldn't take credit for making up tapes?	77	70	28	43	62	72
Wouldn't accuse person of breaking window?	100	100	86	93	71	89

Table 8.5: Percentage of young people in the middle age group who answered the moral dilemma questions in the morally responsible manner

| | Resisters | | Desisters | | Persisters | |
	Men (n=14)	Women (n=15)	Men (n=12)	Women (n=7)	Men (n=17)	Women (n=16)
Wouldn't cheat at cards?	57	13	58	14	35	13
Wouldn't shoplift?	100	100	83	100	70	44
Would hand in £10?	7	87	-	-	-	-
Would hand in £100 ?	57	80	17	43	29	7
Wouldn't sell friend's CDs?	100	100	100	100	94	75
Wouldn't accuse someone of stealing?	86	100	92	100	94	94
Would hand in handbag?	86	100	75	100	65	69
Would remind friend of £10 loan?	79	80	58	29	59	31
Would tell shopkeeper of too much change?	42	80	8	43	18	7
Wouldn't take credit for making up tapes?	71	67	75	86	47	69
Wouldn't accuse person of breaking window?	100	100	100	86	65	94

Table 8.6: Percentage of young people in the oldest age group who answered the moral dilemma questions in the morally responsible manner

	Resisters		Desisters		Persisters	
	Men (n=14)	Women (n=15)	Men (n=12)	Women (n=7)	Men (n=17)	Women (n=16)
Wouldn't cheat at cards?	50	81	35	25	-	10
Wouldn't shoplift?	62	100	88	100	33	40
Would hand in £10?	-	12	12	8	-	-
Would hand in £100 ?	12	75	12	33	-	-
Wouldn't sell friend's CDs?	100	100	100	100	67	80
Wouldn't accuse someone of stealing?	100	100	88	100	94	90
Would hand in handbag?	87	100	76	83	22	30
Would remind friend of £10 loan?	87	100	65	67	17	50
Would tell shopkeeper of too much change?	12	50	-	33	-	-
Wouldn't take credit for making up tapes?	62	93	88	83	78	60
Wouldn't accuse person of breaking window?	100	100	76	100	78	70

Overall, there were clear differences in young people's responses to how they would deal with these various situations, with resisters being most likely and persisters least likely to respond in a morally appropriate way. Resisters and desisters of all ages were relatively consistent in their approaches to various situations, while for persisters there was a clear difference in the responses of the youngest and the oldest age groups, with the latter being less likely to respond to the various situations in what can be viewed as the 'morally responsible' way. There also appeared to be some examples in which girls and young women were more likely to respond in a 'morally responsible' way than young men and boys. This is particularly apparent in respect of: not taking the opportunity to shoplift in an unsupervised shop; handing in £100 found on the street (for resisters and desisters); and handing in a handbag found on the bus (oldest two age groups).

Gilligan (1982) suggests that male and female perceptions of what is right and what is wrong differ. Women's moral reasoning, she suggests, tends to be informed with regard to the effects of a particular course of action on others, while men tend to view things as right or wrong almost regardless of the circumstances and potential effects on other people. However, in explaining their responses to the various hypothetical situations, empathy for others was commonly cited by both young men and young women to explain why they would behave in a 'morally responsible' way. For example, when explaining why they would hand in money or a handbag that they found, many young people suggested that the person who had lost the property might be elderly or in greater need than themselves. This attitude was in stark contrast to the 'finders keepers' view which was common to those who would not hand in such items. Similarly those situations involving shoplifting or taking too much change from a shop elicited concerns that small shopkeepers work hard to make money while in larger shops taking too much change might result in the cashier being reprimanded or having the amount deducted from their wages. Reluctance to sell a friend's CDs or cheat them out of money was put down to not treating people in ways they would not want to be treated in themselves.

SUMMARY

Resisters of all ages generally explained their non offending in terms of the potential consequences of offending, particularly statutory intervention and the undermining of job or career prospects. Their upbringing and their desire not to upset or elicit family disapproval were also thought by resisters to have contributed to their non offending.

In explaining why they had stopped offending desisters in the youngest age group identified the risk of getting caught, parental disapproval and the deterrent effect of the police or other statutory intervention. Some also commented on the importance of family influence, a change of friendship groups, moving to a different area and maturity. Desisters in the middle age group generally explained their desistance in terms of maturity and making adult transitions, such as getting a job, having children, forming a relationship with a partner and leaving home. A major concern for male desisters in the oldest age group was that of making amends to or protecting their families whereas young women in this age group were more concerned with the responsibilities involved in caring for their own children. 'Growing up' was more likely to be identified by men than women as having influenced their decisions to desist. The cessation or reduction of drug use was also considered to have played a part in desistance among young people in the oldest age group.

Persisters often made reference to attempts they had made to desist or plans they had to do so, even though they had, by their own admission, offended very recently. The youngest persisters were most optimistic about their ability to desist, with many viewing their offending as a transitory 'phase'. Female persisters in the middle age group were most likely to initiate avoidance strategies to facilitate their desistance. Stopping the use of drugs appeared to be the most significant factor associated with desistance among young people in the oldest age group.

Female persisters were more likely than male persisters to portray themselves as desisting or trying to desist. Male persisters in the youngest age group often believed that desistance was unlikely, either because they could not be seen to back down from provocation or because they perceived offending as an inevitable part of their lifestyle. Drug addiction was the most common explanation offered for continued offending by persisters in the older age groups.

Police officers believed desistance was related to 'maturation', finding employment, entering a stabilising relationship with a partner, recognising the potential personal consequences of offending and the deterrent effect of statutory interventions. Teachers believed that many young people stopped offending around the end of fourth year at school because they were reluctant to jeopardise job prospects by accumulating a criminal record. Social workers thought that the process desistance was influenced by young people making lifestyle changes and by the deterrent effect of the transition from the children's hearing system to the adult criminal justice system.

Teachers thought that young people were at risk of becoming involved in persistent offending if they had no aspirations and limited opportunities for employment. Police officers attributed persistence in offending to intergenerational family involvement in crime and the effects of institutionalisation by the child care and penal systems. They also thought that for some young people persistent offending represented a deliberate and conscious choice to pursue a criminal lifestyle for financial gain.

Analysis of the Rosenberg Self-esteem Scale revealed no significant differences in self esteem between persisters, desisters and resisters in the youngest age group though boys, on average, exhibited higher levels of self esteem than did girls. In the middle and oldest age groups persisters had the lowest levels of self esteem and resisters the highest. Lower levels of self-esteem among persisters may be a response to the social exclusion apparently experienced by many of these young people, especially those who were involved in the misuse of drugs.

Completion of an adjective checklist revealed that young people, on the whole, believed that men and women should possess broadly similar characteristics. Young men tended to adopt slightly more stereotyped views of men than did young women. Persisters also had a greater tendency to adhere to gendered stereotypes, especially those which emphasise the submissiveness of women and the emotional detachment of men, lending some support to the relationship that has been postulated to exist between crime and masculinity.

In response to eleven moral dilemma scenarios there were clear differences in young people's responses to how they would deal with these various situations with resisters being most likely and persisters least likely to respond in a 'morally responsible' manner.

CHAPTER NINE: CONCLUSIONS

INTRODUCTION

This concluding chapter begins by summarising the main findings from the research, with a particular emphasis upon age and gender related patterns of offending and in differences in behaviour and attitudes between young people classified as resisters, desisters and persisters. It then considers these findings in the context of several broader conceptual frameworks – risk, identity, social inclusion/exclusion and deterrence – which have emerged from the experiences of the young people interviewed in this study as being relevant to an increased understanding of the issue of youth crime in Scotland. Finally, the implications of the data presented are considered and the explanations invoked by them for the development of effective strategies to prevent offending among children and young people.

SUMMARY OF MAIN FINDINGS

The study focused upon three primary variables in attempting to explore and understand the nature of offending among young people in Scotland. Rather than attempting to obtain a 'representative' sample of young people, it was decided instead to seek a stratified sample which enabled the significance of age and gender to be explored in relation to young people's decisions to resist involvement in offending, to desist from offending and to persist in continued offending behaviour. In this section we therefore consider the relationships between offending and age and gender before considering the nature of resistance, desistance and persistence and their relationship to gender and age.

Age related patterns in offending

By focusing upon three different age groups the study permitted an exploration and analysis of offending among young people by age. The school-based survey of self-reported offending among 3rd and 4th year secondary pupils in the two research sites revealed that the majority of pupils had committed one or more offences, with most claiming to have done so within the previous 12 months. Most of this offending was, however, apparently of a relatively minor nature. The fact that most young people had already offended by the time they were 14 or 15 years old suggests that many began offending at a younger age – around 11 or 12. It also appeared that boys' offending changed somewhat in severity between 13 and 15 years of age, with a greater incidence among older boys of violent offences and various property offences such as handling stolen goods, breaking into property and stealing from cars.

Comparable self-report data were not available in respect of the older age groups. However, there was evidence from the interviews with young people in the three age groups that young people's attitudes towards offending changed with age, with increased tolerance for property crimes of an essentially utilitarian nature and less tolerance for offences – such as street fights or vandalism – which tended to be associated with younger people. Stealing to alleviate poverty, for instance, was often considered to be acceptable by those in the middle and oldest age groups who were also more likely than the youngest age group – perhaps because they engaged in it themselves – to consider drug-related crime to be acceptable.

The main difference between the three age groups with respect to their reasons for offending was drug use and the middle and oldest age groups were more likely than the youngest age group to attribute other people's offending to this factor. Young people's use of drugs increased dramatically with age, being relatively uncommon among the youngest age group where, with the exception of alcohol and cannabis, few young people admitted to having used drugs, and none attributed their drug use to addiction. By contrast, more than half of the young people in the oldest age group said they had used amphetamines, LSD and temazepam and just under half had used heroin. Among the middle and oldest age groups offending was often necessary to support the daily use of heroin, especially since the majority of users were either unemployed or claiming sickness benefit.

Alcohol use, in comparison, was more often associated with their offending by boys and girls in the youngest age group, though this was more often linked to the illegality of purchasing alcohol or drinking in public places than to offending which had been triggered by the consumption of excess alcohol. In the middle and oldest age groups alcohol was not, on the whole, associated with criminal activity, though it was acknowledged sometimes to contribute to young people becoming involved in fights, disorderly behaviour or vandalism.

Gender differences in offending

The data derived from the self-report study of 3rd and 4th year pupils were broadly consistent with the international literature insofar as they pointed to a higher rate and frequency of offending among boys than among girls (e.g. Elliot et al., 1989; Junger-Tas et al., 1994; Graham and Bowling, 1995). Girls were more likely than boys to report having never offended and were less likely than boys to be classified as persistent offenders, while boys were more likely than girls to have committed all but the least common offences among the youngest age group. However, set against this clear 'gender ratio' in offending (e.g. Triplett and Myers, 1995) was the striking *similarity* in the types of offences committed by boys and girls. That is, those offences most commonly and least commonly committed by girls were the same as those most and least commonly committed by boys. Any explanations of offending among this youngest age group therefore need to capable of accounting for the similarities in boys' and girls' offending as well as the differences.

From the interviews conducted with a sub-sample of 14 and 15 year olds who had previously completed a self-report questionnaire it became apparent that the similarity in the types of offences committed by boys and girls – if not in the rate of offending – was accompanied by no obvious differences between them with respect to their perceptions of the seriousness of different types of offences. Both boys and girls tended to take a more tolerant view of offences in which they were more commonly involved. It has been suggested that involvement in minor offending influences moral beliefs about offending (that is, rendering certain types of offences acceptable from the perspective of the perpetrator) to a greater extent than prior moral beliefs impact on the propensity towards crime (Matseuda, 1989).

Young women in the middle and oldest age groups tended to be less tolerant of a range of offences than did young men. However, this may have been attributable to the higher proportions of female resisters and male persisters in the oldest age group. Male respondents more often than female respondents emphasised the personal consequences of offending for the offender, suggesting, perhaps, that the former adopted a more individualistic and the latter a more relational approach to moral reasoning (Gilligan, 1982). Indeed, young women and girls more often emphasised relational factors in their explanations of offending by others – family influences, peer pressure, the influence of friends and the desire to attract attention or notoriety – while boys and young men more often attributed others' offending to the misuse of drugs. Young women and girls were, in addition, more likely to express sympathy towards victims as a result of their own personal experience of victimisation while young men were more likely to engage in 'victim blaming' and to place more emphasis upon formal interventions which had followed their experiences of victimisation than upon the feelings they had experienced at the time.

There was a commonly held perception among the professional respondents that girls were becoming increasingly involved in offending, though still to a lesser extent than boys. This was attributed at least partly to media influences which encouraged girls to behave like and compete with boys in areas that were traditionally the province of the latter. Offending among young women, on the other hand, which was also said to have increased significantly in recent years, was attributed largely to drug addiction, with young women being introduced to drugs and to offending through their relationships with young men. Amongst the study sample, young women and girls were as likely to have used a range of illegal drugs as were young men and boys. However, most young women and girls who had offended reported having a partner who had offended, while offending was less common among the female partners of male offenders and was relatively rare among the partners of male and female resisters.

Resisters, desisters and persisters

On the basis of the nature and recency of their self-reported offending (whether in the school-based survey or, in the case of the older age groups, through discussion of their offending in interviews) the respondents in this study were classified as 'resisters' (young people who had never offended or who had committed one or two offences of a very trivial nature); 'desisters' (young people who had offended in the past but who had refrained from doing so for at least 12 months); and 'persisters' (young people who were still actively offending or who had done so within the previous 12 months). As we note in Chapter Two, these categories are, of course, temporally specific, fluid and subject to change: resisters and desisters might, at some point in the future become persisters and persisters might eventually desist. That being the case, a remarkable degree of consistency was observed in the experiences, views and attitudes of young people allocated to the three categories, with desisters almost invariably occupying a middle position, albeit sometimes more similar to resisters and sometimes more similar to those young people who continued to offend.

With respect to attitudes towards offending, for instance, it was found that persisters took a less serious view of certain types of offences than did resisters, with desisters occupying a position somewhere between the two, for some offences having attitudes more similar to the former and for other offences appearing more similar to the latter. Desisters and resisters generally construed offending in broad terms as immoral, futile or both, whereas few persisters considered offending to be wrong as such, emphasising instead that this was conditional upon a variety of factors including the seriousness of the offence or the circumstances of the offender.

Resisters, desisters and persisters were also differentiable in terms of a range of other factors. Persisters, for example, were most likely and resisters least likely to have misused drugs, while the former were most likely and the latter least likely to consider engaging in a range of risk-taking behaviours. Resisters and desisters were more likely than persisters to report engaging in social activities or hobbies, while 'hanging about' amongst the youngest age group was an activity confined to young people who were currently offending or who had done so in the past. Persisters were least likely to evince a commitment towards education, with more leaving school at 16 years of age and more having been excluded or suspended from school. Persisters were also most likely to be unemployed. Although resisters, desisters and persisters had broadly similar, and on the whole fairly conventional, aspirations, persisters were less optimistic than either desisters or persisters that in the longer term these would be fulfilled.

Persisters were most likely to report having a family member who had offended and resisters were least likely to do so. Persisters were also most likely and resisters least likely to have friends who offended. Although young people did not in the main think that their friends' views about offending made any difference to their own behaviour, clearly an association between peer networks and offending did exist. However, it was not possible from the available data to establish the direction of the association between having friends who offend and offending oneself: that is, does having friends who offend encourage young people to offend or do young people actively seek out friends who have similar attitudes towards offending to their own?

With respect to their perceptions of the acceptability or otherwise of offending, the location of desisters in relation to resisters and persisters changed with age, with desisters in the youngest age group more closely resembling resisters and those in the oldest age group more closely resembling persisters. A similar pattern was apparent in relation to drug use, with the pattern of drug use among desisters in the youngest age group similar to that among resisters. In the oldest age group, however, desisters were as likely as persisters to have used a range of recreational drugs, with the patterns of drug use among desisters and persisters being distinguishable largely by the more prevalent use of opioids and opiates among the latter. These age related differences in the location of desisters relative to desisters and persisters suggests that the process and nature of desistance differs with age.

As we saw in Chapter Eight, desistance among boys and girls in the youngest age group was often associated with the consequences – actual or potential – of offending or with a growing recognition – attributed to increased maturity – of the pointlessness of continued involvement in offending behaviour. Increased maturity was likewise invoked as a reason for desisting by young people in the middle age group, though this was often linked to the transition to adulthood, as characterised by events such as getting a job, going to college or university, entering into a relationship with a partner or leaving home. Among the oldest age group desistance was more often said to have been encouraged by the assumption of family responsibilities, especially among young women, or by a conscious lifestyle change. Persisters in the youngest age group were more optimistic about their ability to desist while for older respondents, who may have become more entrenched in patterns of offending and drug use, desistance was rarely considered to be an immediate or achievable goal.

Across all three age groups it was found that female persisters more often than male persisters were keen to be perceived as desisting, even if they acknowledged having recently offended. This may be because of the existence of more socially disapproving attitudes towards female offending wherein the woman who offends is viewed as having broken both the law and the 'gender contract' (Worrall, 1990). Assigning the offending to the past rather than acknowledging it as a current or future reality may enable young women and girls better to cope with any ensuing conflict or guilt.

UNDERSTANDING AND EXPLAINING OFFENDING AMONG YOUNG PEOPLE

Through the accounts provided by the young people who were interviewed in this study and from the observations made by different professionals who regularly come into contact with young people who offend, a number of broad themes emerged which are relevant to understanding offending among young people: family, identity, social exclusion and legitimacy and deterrence. Moreover, the relative salience of these themes – with the exception, perhaps, of deterrence – varies with age, allowing us to account for changes in the nature of offending among children and young people of different ages.

Family

The literature on risk and protective factors identifies the family as central to an understanding of why some young people offend while others do not. Family factors which are said to place young people at greater risk of offending include poor parental supervision and discipline, family conflict, a family history of problem behaviour and parental condoning of or involvement in offending (e.g. Utting et al., 1993; Farrington, 1996). Conversely, strong affectionate relationships within the family and parental interest in their children's education can increase resilience in children who are otherwise living in adverse social circumstances:

The importance of family risk factors was highlighted by police officers, teachers and social workers in their explanations of why young people offend and family factors featured strongly among those considered by professional respondents to protect young people from involvement in offending and other problem behaviours. Young people themselves did not make an association between their *own* offending and their upbringing but this was the reason they most commonly cited reason for offending by *other people.*

Young people appeared to be more at risk of offending if they came from families where other family members had offended. By contrast, the importance of their family's positive influence, including the values they imparted, was more often identified by resisters and desisters. However the impact of families on their offending appeared to vary somewhat with the age of the young person. For those in the youngest age group families exerted their influence through the communication of pro-social views and through the desire of young people not to arouse parental disapproval. Among the middle and oldest age groups the desire not to hurt other family members was more apparent and the assumption of family responsibilities featured prominently in the accounts of desistance offered by young people in the oldest age group.

The concept of inter-generational offending – that is, offending among successive generations within a family – appeared relevant both to an understanding of why young people started offending and to an understanding of why some continued to do so beyond an age at which most young people have effectively grown out of crime. Whilst offending among the oldest age group in particular was often linked to drug misuse, poverty and disadvantage – and could, as such, be construed at least partly as a survival strategy – persistence in offending was also thought by professional respondents to be more likely when offending was condoned within the family – or, indeed, even the norm – because young people knew of no other alternatives. While young people in the former group would fit into the 'coping' or 'lifestyle' categories in the typology of offending developed by Stewart et al. (1994), those in the latter group would be more appropriately located in the category of 'social norm'.

Family factors are, therefore, crucial to an understanding of offending among young people. They should be a central focus of preventive strategies aimed at reducing young people's exposure to risk and of attempts to impact on the behaviour of younger people who have begun to offend. However, family factors alone cannot explain why most young people in Scotland have offended by the time they reach their mid-teens, albeit often in a minor way. Positive family influence was clearly significant in the accounts of young people who had not offended and in some young people's explanations of desistance, but such an influence was not necessarily absent in the lives of the majority of young people in the present study who had offended at some point in time. An understanding of the prevalence of minor offending among young people requires, we would argue, attention to the transition from childhood to young adulthood and, in particular, the part played by offending and other related behaviours in the creation of an adult identity.

Identity

Adolescence represents an intermediate stage in the transition from childhood to adulthood. It is characterised, among other things, by a diminution in the role of parents as a reference point for young people and their increased identification with other young people of their own age in the process of forming an adult identity. The peer group consequently exerts greater influence over young people's attitudes and behaviour and interventions which seek to neutralise the influence of or to mobilise a young person's peer group become more relevant and effective than those which seek to involve parents directly in efforts to reduce offending among their children (McIvor, 1990).

The importance of peer group influence was acknowledged by young people and professionals alike. It was considered particularly relevant to an understanding of why young people began offending in their early teens, less so for explaining offending among young adults. In this context offending by young people can be conceptualised as deriving from a desire to conform to pressures from friends to engage in a range of risk-taking behaviours which signal increasing independence from parental and other adult influences. An increased propensity towards risk-taking was evident among young people who were offending or who had done so in the past which is consistent with the finding in other studies that offending is associated with increased behavioural impulsivity. Rutter et al. (1998) argue that cognitive impulsivity – measured by standardised tests which assess responses to tasks – is a relatively poor predictor of delinquency whereas behavioural impulsivity – as indicated by a tendency to do things without planning or thinking – is a stronger predictor of such behaviour.

In this context offending can be viewed as one of a number of risk-taking behaviours that young people may engage in in the search for an adult identity. In the present study, for instance, young people who offended were more likely than those who did not to have used a range of illegal substances and – in the case of those in the youngest age group for whom the purchasing of alcohol if not its consumption was illegal – to have consumed alcohol in the absence of parental supervision.

It also appeared that the identities to which young people aspired – and, indeed, their personal aspirations for the future – were broadly similar for boys and girls. This, we would argue, takes us some way towards understanding the apparent increase in girls' involvement in offending. Offending may be viewed as one means by which young people attempt to achieve an adult identity which increasingly encompasses attributes such as competitiveness, independence and success and which may be pursued, both by young men and young women, principally through employment. With this avenue not yet open to them some young people may accord importance to educational achievement which will reap benefits in the labour market in the longer term. Others, whose prospects of doing well at school are less assured, may look to other less conventional ways to achieve self-confidence and respect. Gaining the respect of like-minded peers may, for these young people, be achieved through a willingness to engage in behaviour which is daring, risky or challenges authority. If girls are keen to attain an adult identity which shares many or most of the qualities aspired to by boys, then it is likely that they will adopt increasingly similar strategies – including offending and associated behaviours – to achieve that end.

This explanation is capable of accounting for some of the similarities in patterns of offending among boys and girls but it less readily embraces the differences, either in the nature of girls' offending or in their experiences. It does not, in particular, explain the existence of the gender ratio in offending, that is the fact that fewer girls than boys offend and when they do the offences they commit tend to be less serious. This may be because girls still tend to be subject to greater parental supervision than boys which is reflected in 'the greater controls placed on girls about where they can go, the friends with whom they associate, [and] the time they can stay out until' (Social Work and Prisons Inspectorates, 1998, p.6). Such an explanation is, as we have already indicated, consistent with the 'routine activities' theory of crime (e.g. Felson, 1987). It receives some support from research which suggests that girls offend in fewer contexts than boys – arguably because they have more limited opportunities to do so – and that the types of offences committed by boys and girls are strongly influenced by the contexts in which they occur (Triplett and Myers, 1995).

There is also evidence of wide differences in the level and nature of offending among young men and women. To account for these differences it has been suggested that continued adherence and reference to traditional gender stereotypes means that offending remains largely acceptable among young men but among young women results in their ability to fulfil various gender roles being called into question. As a recent Scottish Office report on women offenders notes:

Whilst offending may be a socially inclusive experience for many men and they may gain prestige amongst their friends for their criminal behaviour, this is rarely the case for women and this may be a partial explanation of why so few women offend.

(Social Work and Prisons Inspectorates, 1998, p.6)

It appears therefore that the relationship between offending and identity diminishes with age and that this may occur sooner for girls than for boys. The association between offending and the transition from childhood to adulthood helps us to understand the temporary nature for many young people of their involvement in offending: once other more legitimate ways have been found to construct their identities the need for young people to engage in offending in order to do so declines. At this point further offending may threaten rather than bolster the adult identities that they have newly found.

The fact that offending is, for most young people, a transitory phenomenon linked to their social development rather than being construed as fundamental to their identity and sense of self may explain why many of the young people in the present study engaged in what Maruna et al. (1997) have described as 'narrative strategies' to justify or excuse their behaviour. Young people variously excused their behaviour by attributing it to loyalty to others or provocation, justified it on the grounds that offending is universal and their own behaviour is less serious than others' or refused to acknowledge that the behaviour they had engaged in was wrong.

Social inclusion and exclusion

It is now widely accepted that offending among young people may be influenced by a range of social and economic factors. Low income, poor housing and disadvantaged neighbourhoods may place young people at increased risk of offending and may, we will argue, make it more difficult for those who do so subsequently to desist.

While offending appears a fairly common pursuit among young people the risk factors commonly associated with criminal activity include a disadvantaged neighbourhood, community disorganisation and neglect, availability of drugs, high turnover and lack of neighbourhood attachment, alienation and lack of social commitment, in short those factors commonly associated with multiple deprivation. The current discourse for the consideration of multiple deprivation is that of social exclusion. Social exclusion is thought to be a dynamic process which occurs as the result of the interaction of many processes, encompassing economic, social and policy elements, which combine with discrimination on the grounds of race or gender to trap people in disadvantaged positions. The result of this process is multiple deprivation wherein different elements of social exclusion reinforce one another to exclude those affected from lifestyles – in terms of work, leisure, and well-being – enjoyed by wider society. The relevance of social exclusion to the consideration of young people and crime revolves around the question of whether there is a link between the processes of social exclusion and young people's involvement in criminal activity.

The economic and social factors which have been identified as having an association with crime are, in turn, influenced by policy makers and those responsible for the implementation and administration of policy. Graham and Bowling (1995) concluded that there was a strong association between more serious offences and social class, for both male and females. This finding is in keeping with studies of convicted offenders where a strong social class effect is discernible (Walmsley et al., 1991). It would appear therefore that while offending among young people appears a normal activity, more serious offending and offending which results in criminal justice intervention is more strongly associated with lower socio-economic groups who are more likely to be socially excluded. This, however, is likely to reflect, to an unknown degree, crime control and prevention policies and their implementation.

Indeed, the association between multiple deprivation and crime is not without contention. Crime prevention and crime control policies inevitably mean that official statistics are more likely to reflect street crimes rather than white collar and corporate crime, such as tax evasion. Furthermore, there are those who would argue that the latter are more damaging to society and the economy (Box, 1983) and such arguments are difficult to ignore given that in 1995/6 DSS fraud detection accrued savings of £1,222 million while tax fraud, labelled yield from compliance, accrued to £5,242 million (Cook, 1997).

We have already made reference to the importance of participation in the labour market for the construction of an adult identity and have seen how young people in the present study generally had traditional aspirations focused upon employment and family life. Despite the observation by teachers that many young people tended to shun opportunities for further education in favour of the prospect of employment, their entry into the labour market will be constrained by the economic climate and availability of paid work. For young people who have limited income and little opportunity to partake in social, leisure and cultural activities which are enjoyed by others, offending may become increasingly linked to financial gain, sometimes simply for the purpose of survival.

In economic terms the major change in the last two decades with respect to young people has been the near collapse of the youth labour market which in turn has witnessed an end to traditional patterns which involved leaving school, getting a job, forming a family and gaining independence. For many young people transitions to adulthood have become 'extended' and 'protracted', delayed by unemployment, youth training and further education. Family formation and leaving home have, in turn, been similarly delayed and are now embarked upon at a later age. Craine and Coles (1995) argue that for some young people such fractured transitions will mean there are significant periods of their lives when they do not have secure work in the formal labour market, nor stable personal relationships, nor secure accommodation independent of the parental home. At the extreme this could result in long term unemployment, social isolation and homelessness, with the experience of exclusion in economic and social terms leading some young people to offend. Craine and Coles (1995) further argue that because employment is a distant and diminished possibility for some young people, alternative routes to income and identity are matters of economic and psycho-social survival. This being so, it is of no surprise that some young people become involved in the alternative economy and crime which includes benefit fraud, illegal marketing, drug dealing, forgery, shoplifting, burglary, property theft, robbery and armed robbery.

Amongst the youngest and middle age groups in the present study especially, drinking with friends, smoking cannabis or using other 'recreational drugs' were, in the main, activities which helped young people to feel socially included with respect to their peers. Alcohol and drug misuse may, however, become for some young people a means of escape from the personal and social consequences of economic disadvantage or, particularly in the case of young women, previous sexual or emotional abuse. Moreover the widespread availability and use of heroin, with its addictive potential, was acknowledged both by professionals and young people to have resulted in an increase among both young men and women of drug-related crime. For these young people, whose lives were characterised by a daily ritual of obtaining and using drugs, drug use had in itself become a vehicle for their increased exclusion from society.

The gendered nature of continued criminal involvement was apparent in Graham and Bowling's (1995) study which found that successful completion of school, domestic and housing transitions was associated with an abrupt and conscious end to offending among young women. However, young men tended to drift away from crime much more gradually and remained susceptible to peer group pressure for some time after making key transitions. Furthermore, they found that many young male offenders were offending well into their twenties (albeit at a reduced rate) and concluded that if they became involved in regular drug use and alcohol misuse there were few opportunities or incentives to encourage them to stop offending during the transition to adulthood. A number of writers have linked male criminality to difficulties in establishing masculine identities in a changing economic context. Meserschmidt (1994) argues that with a growth in educational participation, young men who fail to excel academically see schooling as frustrating their masculinity. Moreover the decline in manual employment opportunities means that young men today are forced to define their masculinities in new ways, with crime offering one route through which positive identifies can be established.

Craine and Coles (1995) also identify the growing closeness of the relationship between youth cultures and consumerism as another key change that is likely to have an impact on crime. They argue that whereas during the 1950s and 1960s youth was a period of affluence – especially for young people from working class backgrounds who had relatively high disposal incomes soon after leaving school – today few young people have the same sort of access to consumer goods and some are in danger of long term exclusion from consumer society. Although most juvenile crime is expressionistic rather than instrumental, criminologists have argued that the relative deprivation which stems from exclusion can lead to the development and prolongation of criminal careers as young people begin to appreciate that crime provides the potential for the enhancement of lifestyles and the means of access to consumer culture.

The experience and impact of social exclusion was also reflected in the present study in young people's confidence and self esteem. Whilst similar levels of self esteem were found among boys and girls who were offending and those who were not, self esteem was lowest in the middle and oldest groups among those young people who were still involved in offending, most of whom were also regularly misusing drugs. Although a direct association between offending and self esteem has yet to be clearly established it seems likely that young people who have a limited sense of self worth will have lower aspirations and fewer opportunities to participate fully in society.

The significance of community was highlighted in the study by the territoriality which existed in both of the research sites and which had the effect of limiting young people's access to resources and facilities which lay outside their own territorial areas. Some of these communities were characterised by deprivation, disadvantage and social exclusion. The concept of community re-integration has been variously invoked as a protective mechanism against offending among young people and adults (see, for example, Haines, 1990). However, its potential in this regard is called into question when the community into which a young person is integrated has high levels of social exclusion reflected in poverty, unemployment and the widespread use of illegal drugs.

The assertion that community integration may be a less potent factor than social inclusion in preventing offending among young people receives further support from the finding that resisters, desisters and persisters were equally likely to say that they felt a part of their community. In other words there was no evidence that young people who offended felt any more alienated from their communities than did other young people, even if they were in many respects more marginalised in society. Nor did most young people consider their community's views about offending to impact significantly upon them, although some did acknowledge that tolerance for minor offending and drug use and the existence of peer group pressure within their community could have contributed in some way to their own involvement in delinquent or criminal behaviour.

These findings, therefore, point to the development of policy initiatives which aim to promote social inclusion and seek to reduce the economic and social inequalities which are increasingly recognised as contributing to crime (e.g. Downes, 1993). It is worth noting in this context that juvenile justice group conferencing, which is becoming increasingly popular on account of its appeal to communitariansim and promise of improved access to justice for minority ethnic groups, has been fundamentally criticised for its failure to take cognisance of and to impact upon wider institutional processes which contribute to marginalisation and exclusion (Polk, 1994).

Deterrence and legitimacy

The relationship between deterrence and crime is one which has been widely discussed in the criminological literature, with the evidence pointing to detection being a greater deterrent against offending than the severity of the resulting punishment. In the present study professional respondents and young people alike made reference to the deterrent impact of contact with the criminal justice system, though that impact was largely confined to young people whose involvement in offending was of a relatively minor nature. To understand why the criminal justice system has an apparently limited deterrent influence on offending it is useful to consider the concept of legitimacy, which has been invoked to account for people's willingness to obey the law (Tyler, 1990). As Bottoms and Rex (1998) explain, obedience to the law is derived partly from 'a morally-based perception that legal authorities have a right to expect that their demands will be met simply because *they are the demands of legitimate authority'* (p.20, original emphasis). Moreover, the procedures adopted by agents of the criminal justice system – such as the police – have important implications for their perceived legitimacy: people are less likely to respect the law and behave legally if they perceive its administration to demonstrate a lack of respect or to be inconsistent or unfair. For instance Paternoster et al. (1997) found some evidence of lower re-arrest rates among individuals accused of domestic violence when police officers acted in a procedurally fair manner. They argued that the procedural factors which appeared to be associated with legitimacy were: representation; consistency; impartiality; accuracy; correctability; and ethicality.

The relevance of legitimacy was most apparent in the views young people expressed about the police, with those who had had contact with the police tending to express less favourable views. Whilst some young people – especially resisters – reported having been treated politely in their dealings with the police most were critical of their lack of visibility, their failure to concentrate on the 'real criminals' or what was construed as their intrusive and unwarranted 'surveillance' of young people. Young people variously made reference to having been charged unnecessarily or wrongly, to having been stopped and searched for weapons, stolen goods or drugs or to having been treated without respect. In short, many young people's perceptions of the police were such that they were unlikely to be deemed as having the necessary legitimacy to encourage adherence to the law. This was recognised by most of the police officers who were interviewed, with some emphasising the importance of developing relationships with young people which were characterised by greater openness and respect. The apparent lack of legitimacy accorded to the police may explain why the majority of young people – especially those who had come into contact with the police as a consequence of their offending – did not believe that the police served as an effective deterrent against offending.

Legitimacy also pertains at other points in the criminal or juvenile justice process. Children's hearings – like different aspects of the criminal justice system – were thought by professionals to be effective with some young people who offended but not with others, either as a result of the deterrent impact of appearing before a hearing or the supervision received. However, young people themselves tended to have limited knowledge about the children's hearings system and those who had appeared before a children's panel tended to be mystified by or dismissive of the experience. Some questioned the legitimacy of the lay panel members, some believed that children's hearings were too lenient and others felt that appearing before a panel made it more likely that a young person would re-offend. In an important sense, therefore, the children's hearings system could be said to lack legitimacy in the eyes of many young people, thereby limiting its potential to serve as a deterrent to offending.

Young people's views about the effectiveness of the courts were mixed, though many believed that courts were inconsistent in their responses to similar types of crime. This perceived inconsistency may detract from the legitimacy ascribed by young people to the courts and account at least partly for the observation that court processes were less often considered to serve as a deterrent against further offending than were the outcomes. Various views were expressed about the effectiveness of prisons and community based disposals, with the former being construed, on the whole, as less effective than the latter with respect to the reduction of offending. The limited effectiveness of prisons was said to derive from them according prisoners too many privileges while serving as 'universities of crime' and failing to place sufficient emphasis upon rehabilitation. Among those young people who did consider prisons to be an effective response to crime, reference was made to their incapacitative effects or their capacity for individual as opposed to general deterrence.

Although social work supervision was thought by some young people to be too soft or too intrusive, others identified several features of social work supervision which were helpful. These included being provided with material assistance, being listened to, being given access to a range of activities and being given advice. Intensive probation was singled out for particular praise by young people who had attended such a programme or who knew others who had done so. The specific features of intensive probation which were highlighted included the clarity with which information was conveyed – enabling young people better to gain an insight into their behaviour – and the respect which was accorded to young people on the programme. The importance of clear boundary setting, a structured approach and staff relating to offenders in ways which are enthusiastic, open and caring has been similarly highlighted in recent studies of intensive probation in Scotland (Jamieson, 1997a, b). These are also features which have been identified by Andrews (1995) as being integral to effective offender supervision.

The concept of legitimacy has recently been developed in the arena of offender supervision by Rex and Bottoms (1998) who argue that probation officers who are consistent and fair in their exercising of authority, who convey rules and expectations clearly to offenders and who treat them with respect are more likely to motivate offenders towards positive attitudinal and behavioural change because they are perceived as having greater legitimacy to do so. On the basis of her research into offenders on probation Rex (1997) has concluded that offenders are willing to receive a greater degree of structure and guidance than their supervising probation officers imagine if the latter are perceived to have legitimacy in expecting their probationers to change. An approach to offender supervision which based upon a broad definition of pro-social modelling – such as the one advanced by Trotter (1993, 1999) – is, according to Rex, more likely to confer such legitimacy on the supervising officer. Within this framework, pro-social modelling includes clarity of expectations, the challenging of anti-social and rewarding of pro-social attitudes and behaviours, and the demonstration on the part of the probation officer of genuine concern for the probationer and belief in his/her capacity to change.

PREVENTING OFFENDING AMONG YOUNG PEOPLE

There is a growing literature on effective approaches to the prevention of offending among young people and a growing consensus as to which approaches are more likely to make a difference in terms of reducing the incidence of youth crime. Within this broad literature a distinction is made between primary, secondary and tertiary prevention, with different approaches considered appropriate to each. Primary prevention is aimed at preventing offending amongst a particular population and may be universal in its application or targeted more specifically upon groups who are considered to be more at risk; secondary prevention is aimed at those young people who have already been identified as being at risk of offending; and tertiary prevention aims to reduce the risk of re-offending among young people who have already come into contact with the criminal justice agencies as a consequence of their behaviour.

The findings from the present study confirm the relevance to the Scottish context of those interventions which were identified in Chapter One as having shown some promise with respect to the prevention or reduction of offending among young people. However, this study has also shown that the causes of offending among young people are complex and varied and defy simplistic solutions. A strategic approach to the issue of youth crime will, accordingly, require responses at a variety of levels if offending and related problems are to be successfully addressed.

At the individual level there is growing evidence that theoretically informed structured approaches which actively engage offenders in the process of change are more likely to impact positively upon recidivism. Moreover the relationship between offender and social worker – characterised by clarity of expectations, openness and genuine concern – appears to be central to efforts to motivate offenders towards positive attitudinal and behavioural change. Such an approach stands in rather stark contrast to aspects of the criminal justice system and the children's hearings system which were perceived by young people as lacking clarity, consistency and, consequently, legitimacy. The introduction of more structured interventions with young people who are referred on offence grounds to the children's hearings system may, for instance, serve to increase the effectiveness of supervision in this context. Any such developments must, however, guard against over-intrusiveness (after all, for many young people an appearance at a children's panel will in itself serve as a deterrent to further offending) and be guided by the principles of need and risk which were described in Chapter One.

At the local level a particular need was identified for initiatives which aimed to improve parenting skills, to increase parental involvement in their children's education and to tackle the issue of drug misuse, with the latter being accorded the greatest immediate priority. Effective prevention programmes were widely recognised as requiring a co-ordinated, multi-agency approach to harness the resources available within communities to best effect. Recent developments in Scotland which represent a more co-ordinated approach to preventive service provision at the local level include the introduction of community schools, Social Inclusion Partnerships and the Communities That Care programme.

Finally, at the national level there is a need for policies which are aimed at tackling social exclusion and reducing inequalities in society through increasing access to what Worrall (1995) has described as the structural pre-determinants of social justice, such as income, housing, employment, health services and education. In this respect the Government's social inclusion strategy (Scottish Office, 1999b) is a welcome move away from previous piecemeal approaches to social policy which failed to recognise the intrinsic inter-connectedness of social problems and their capacity to coalesce in a spiral of disadvantage.

The methodological approach adopted in the present study derived from our belief that an enhanced understanding of offending among children and young people would be achieved most effectively by hearing the accounts of the young people themselves. The approach yielded material of a richness and depth that would have been impossible to achieve had the respondents not been given the opportunity to frame their experiences within their own personal terms of reference. These accounts have further increased our knowledge about why young people in Scotland start offending, continue offending, stop offending and avoid offending altogether. We have also in the process become even more convinced of the importance of young people being listened to and having a direct voice in the formulation of local and national policies which impact upon their lives.

REFERENCES

Anderson, S., Kinsey, R., Loader, I. and Smith, C. (1994) *Cautionary Tales: Young People, Crime and Policing in Edinburgh,* Aldershot: Avebury.

Andrews, D.A. (1995) The Psychology of Criminal Conduct and Effective Treatment, in J. McGuire (Ed.) *What Works: Reducing Reoffending – Guidelines from Research and Practice,* Chichester: Wiley.

Asquith, S. and Samuel, E. (1994) *Criminal Justice and Related Services for Young Adult Offenders,* Edinburgh: HMSO.

Asquith, S., Buist, M., Loughran, N., Macauley, C. and Montgomery, M. (1998) *Children, Young People and Offending in Scotland,* Edinburgh: Scottish Office Central Research Unit.

Audit Commission (1996) *Mis-spent Youth: Young People and Crime,* London: The Audit Commission.

Bottoms, A. and Rex, S. (1998) Pro-social modelling and legitimacy: their potential contribution to effective practice, in S. Rex and A. Matravers (Eds.) *Pro-Social Modelling and Legitimacy: The Clarke Hall Day Conference,* Cambridge: Institute of Criminology.

Box, S. (1983) *Power, Crime and Mystification,* London: Tavistock.

Braithwaite, J. (1989) *Crime, Shame and Integration,* Cambridge: Cambridge University Press.

Buckley, K. (1995) Masculinity, the Probation Service and the causes of offending behaviour, in T. May and A.A. Vass (Eds.) *Working with Offenders: Issues, Contexts and Outcomes,* London: Sage.

Burnett, R. (1992) *The Dynamics of Recidivism,* Oxford: University of Oxford Centre for Criminological Research.

Canter, R. (1982) Sex differences in self-report delinquency, *Criminology,* 20, 373-93.

Cernkovich, S.A., Giordano, P.C. and Pugh, M.D. (1985) Chronic offenders: the missing cases in self-report delinquency research, *Journal of Criminal Law and Criminology,* 76, 705-32.

Chambers, G. and Millar, A. (1983) *Investigating Sexual Assault,* Edinburgh: The Scottish Office.

Chapman, T. and Hough, M. (1998) *Evidence Based Practice: A Guide to Effective Practice,* London: The Home Office.

Chapman, T. and Maitland, A. (1995) *Stop, Think and Change: An Integrated and Progressive Programme of Change for High Risk Offenders,* Belfast: probation Board for Northern Ireland.

Chubb, N.H., Fertman, C.I. and Ross, J.L. (1997) Adolescent self esteem and locus of control: a longitudinal study of gender and age differences, *Adolescence, 32,* 113-29.

Cook, D. (1997) *Poverty, Crime and Punishment,* London, Child Poverty Action Group.

Coote, A. (ed) (1994) *Families, Children and Crime,* Institute for Public Policy Research: London.

Collier, R. (1998) *Masculinities, Crime and Criminology,* London: Sage.

Communities That Care (1997) *Communities That Care (UK): A New Kind of Prevention Programme,* London: CTC.

Connell, R.W. (1987) *Gender and Power,* Cambridge: Polity Press.

Craine, S. and Coles, B. (1995) Alternative Careers: Youth Transitions and Young People's Involvement in Crime, *Youth and Policy, 1995, 48, Spring,* 6-26.

Dobash, R.P., Dobash, R.E. and Ballantyne, S. (1987) *Young people and the Criminal Justice System,* Edinburgh: Scottish Office Central Research Unit.

Downes, D. (1993) *Employment Opportunities for Offenders,* London: HMSO.

Elliot, D., Huizinga, D. and Menard, S. (1989) *Multiple Problem Youth,* New York: Springer Verlag.

Farrall, S. and Bowling, B. (1997) *Structuration, Human Development and Desistance from Crime,* paper presented at the British Criminology Conference, The Queen's University, Belfast.

Farrington, D.P. (1986) Stepping stones to adult criminal careers, in D. Olweus, J. Blockand and M.R. Yarrow (Eds.) *Development of Antisocial and Prosocial Behavior,* New York: Academic Press.

Farrington, D.P. (1996) *Understanding and Preventing Youth Crime,* York: Joseph Rowntree Foundation.

Farrington, D., Barnes, G. and Lambert, S. (1996) The concentration of offending in families, *Legal and Criminological Psychology,* 1, 47-63.

Farrington, D.P., Ohlin, L.E. and Wilson, J.Q. (1986) *Understanding and Controlling Crime: Towards a New Research Strategy,* New York: Springer-Verlag.

Farrington, D.P. and West, D.J. (1981) The Cambridge study in delinquency development, in S.A. Mednick & A.E. Baert (Eds.) *Prospective Longitudinal Research,* Oxford: Oxford University Press.

Felson, M. (1987) Routine activity and crime prevention in the developing metropolis, *Criminology, 25,* 911-32.

Felson, M. and Cohen, L.E. (1980) Human ecology and crime: A routine activity approach, *Human Ecology, 8,* 389-406.

Fischer, B.J. and Bersani, C.A. (1979) Self esteem and institutionalized delinquent offenders: The role of background characteristics, *Adolescence, 14,* 197-214.

Gendreau, P. and Ross, R.R. (1987) Revivification of rehabilitation: Evidence from the 1980s, *Justice Quarterly, 4,* 349-407.

Gilligan, C. (1982) *In a Different Voice,* Cambridge, MA: Harvard University Press.

Gottfredson, D.C. (1997) School-based crime prevention in L. Sherman et al. (Eds.), *Preventing Crime: What Works, What Doesn't, What's Promising,* Report to the US Congress, Washington D.C.: National Institute of Justice.

Gottfredson, D.C., Sealock, M.D. and Koper, C.S. (1996) Delinquency, in R. DiClemente et al. (Eds.), *Handbook of Adolescent Health Risk Behaviour,* New York: Plenum.

Graeff, R. (1993) *Living Dangerously: Young Offenders in their Own Words,* London: Harper Collins.

Graham, J. and Bowling, B. (1995) *Young People and Crime,* Home Office Research Study 145, London: The Stationery Office.

Haines, K. (1990) *After-care Services for Released Prisoners: A Review of the Literature,* Cambridge: University of Cambridge Institute of Criminology.

Hawkins, J.D., Catalano, R.F. and Miller, J.Y. (1992) Risk and protective factors for alcohol and other drug problems in early adulthood: Implications for substance abuse prevention, *Psychological Bulletin, 112,* 64-105.

Hendry, L. (1993) *Young People's Leisure and Lifestyles,* London, Routledge.

Hirschi, T. (1969) *Causes of Delinquency,* Berkley, CA: University of California Press.

Home Office (1999) What's Effective?, *Newsletter of the Effective Practice Initiative, 1/99.*

Hood, R. (1993) *Psychosocial Interventions in the Criminal Justice System: Draft Conclusions and Recommendations,* 20th Criminological Research Conference, Council of Europe, Strasbourg.

Howell, J.C., Krisberg, B., Wilson, J.J. and Hawkins, J.D. (1995) *A Sourcebook on Serious, Violent, and Chronic Juvenile Offenders,* Newbury Park, CA: Sage

Hubert, R.P. and Hundleby, J.D. (1993) Pathways to desistance: How does criminal activity stop?, *Forum on Corrections, 5,* 1.

Jamieson, J. (1997a) *An Evaluation of the Community Alternatives Unit, Paisley,* Stirling, Social Work Research Centre, University of Stirling.

Jamieson, J. (1997b) *An Evaluation of the NCH Inverclyde Intensive Probation Unit,* Stirling, Social Work Research Centre, University of Stirling.

Junger-Tas, J. (1994) *Delinquent Behaviour Among Young People in the Western World,* Amdersdam: Kugler.

Junger-Tas, J., Terlouw, G-J. and Klein, M.W. (1994) *Delinquent Behaviour Among Young People in the Western World: First Results of the International Self-report Delinquency Study,* Amsterdam: Kugler.

Kennedy, R. and McIvor, G. (1992) *Young Offenders in the Children's Hearings and Criminal Justice Systems,* Dundee: Tayside Social Work Department.

Klein, M.W. (1994) Epilogue, in J.Junger-Tas (Ed.) *Delinquent Behaviour Among Young People in the Western World,* Amsterdam: Kugler.

Leibrich, J. (1993) *Straight to the Point: Angles on Giving up Crime,* Dunedin, New Zealand: University of Otago Press.

Lipsey, M.W. (1992) Juvenile delinquency treatment: A meta-analytic enquiry into variability of effects, in T.D. Cook et al. (Eds.) *Meta-analysis for Explanation,* New York: Russell Sage Foundation.

Lipsey, M.W. (1995) What do we learn from 400 research studies on the effectiveness of treatment with juvenile delinquents?, in J. McGuire (Ed.) *What Works: Reducing Reoffending – Guidelines from Research and Practice,* London: Wiley.

Loeber, R.T. and Dishion, T. (1983) Early predictors of male delinquency: A review, *Psychological Bulletin, 93,* 68-99.

Loeber, R., Stouthamer-Loeber, M., Van Kammen, W. and Farrington, D.P. (1991) Initiation, escalation and desistance in juvenile offending and their correlates, *Journal of Criminal Law and Criminology, 82,* 36-82.

Loeber, R. and Waller, D. (1988) Artefacts in delinquency: specialisation and generalisation studies, *British Journal of Criminology, 28,* 461-77.

Mac an Ghaill, M. (1996) *Understanding Masculinities,* Buckingham: Open University Press.

Maguire, M. and Norris, C. (1992) *The Conduct and Supervision of Criminal Investigations* (Royal Commission on Criminal Justice Research Study no. 5), London: HMSO.

Maruna, S. (1997) *Desistance and Development: The Psychosocial Process of Going Straight,* paper presented at the British Criminology Conference, The Queen's University, Belfast.

Maruna, S. (1998) *Deconstructing Deviant Adaptations: When the 'Inner-Logic' of Deviance Breaks Down,* paper presented at the Annual Meeting of the American Society of Criminology, Washington, D.C.

Maruna, S. (forthcoming) *Going Straight,* Washington D.C.: American Psychological Association Press.

Maruna, S. Alison, L. and Porter, L. (1997) Reports, concessions, excuses, justifications and refusals in offender narratives, in S. Maruna (1998), *Redeeming One's Self: How Reformed Ex-offenders Make Sense of their Lives,* unpublished PhD thesis, Northwestern University.

Matseuda, R.L. (1989) The dynamics of moral beliefs and minor deviance, *Social Forces, 68,* 428-57.

Matza, D. (1964) *Delinquency and Drift,* New York: John Wiley & Sons.

May, T. (1993) *Social Research: Issues, Methods and Process,* Milton Keynes: Open University Press.

McConville, M., Sanders, A. and Leng, R. (1991) *The Case for the Prosecution,* London: Routledge.

McGuire, J. and Priestley, P. (1995) Reviewing 'what works': Past, present and future, in J. McGuire (Ed.) *What Works: Reducing Reoffending – Guidelines from Research and Practice,* London: Wiley.

McGuire, J. and Priestley, P. (1985) *Offending Behaviour: Skills and Stratagems for Going Straight,* London: Batsford.

McIvor, G. (1990) *Sanctions for Serious or Persistent Offenders: A Review of the Literature,* Stirling: Social Work Research Centre, University of Stirling.

McIvor, G. (forthcoming) Exploring diversity: Understanding and responding to offending among young women and girls, in M. Barry and J. Curran (Eds.) *Children, Young People and Crime in Britain and Ireland: From Exclusion to Inclusion,* Edinburgh: Scottish Office Central Research Unit.

McIvor, G. and Barry, M. (1998) *Social Work and Criminal Justice Volume 6: Probation,* Edinburgh: The Stationery Office.

MacKenzie, D.L. (1997) Criminal justice and crime prevention, in L. Sherman et al. (Eds.), *Preventing Crime: What Works, What Doesn't, What's Promising,* Report to the US Congress, Washington, DC: National Institute of Justice.

Menard, S. and Elliot, D.S. (1994) Delinquent bonding, moral beliefs and illegal behaviour: A three-wave panel model, *Justice Quarterly, 11,* 173-88.

Messerschmidt, J.W. (1993) *Masculinities and Crime: Critique and Reconceptualization of Theory,* Lanham, MD: Rowman and Littlefield.

MVA (1998) *Main Findings from the 1996 Scottish Crime Survey,* Edinburgh: Scottish Office Central Research Unit.

NACRO (1995) *Crime and Social Policy,* Report of the Crime and Social Policy Committee, London: NACRO.

Newburn, T. and Stanko, E.A. (1994) *Just Boys Doing Business?: Men, Masculinities and Crime,* London: Routledge.

Omodei, R.A. (1979) Delinquency in girls in South Australia, *Australian and New Zealand Journal of Sociology, 15,* 81-85.

Paternoster, R., Bachman, R., Brame, R. and Sherman, L.W. (1997) Do fair procedures matter? The effect of procedural justice on spouse assault, *Law and Society Review, 31,* 163-204.

Polk, K. (1994) Family conferencing: theoretical and evaluative concerns, in C. Alder and J. Wundersitz (eds.) *Family Conferencing in Juvenile Justice: The Way Forward or Misplaced Optimism?,* Canberra: Australian Institute of Criminology.

The Prince's Trust (1997) *Young People and Crime in Scotland,* Edinburgh: The Prince's Trust.

Pulikkinen, L. (1986) The role of impulse control in the development of antisocial and prosocial behavior, in D. Olweus, J. Block and M. Radke-Yarrow (Eds.) *Development of Antisocial and Prosocial Behavior,* Orlando, FL: Academic Press.

Ramsay, M. And Percy, A. (1996) *Drug Misuse Declared: Results of the 1994 British Crime Survey,* Home Office Research Study 151, London: HMSO.

Reiss, A.J. (1988) Co-offending and criminal careers, in M. Tonry and N. Morris (Eds.) *Crime and Justice: A Review of Research Volume 10,* Chicago: University of Chicago Press.

Rex, S. (1997) *Desistance from Offending: Experiences of Probation,* paper presented at the British Criminology Conference, The Queen's University, Belfast.

Rouse, L. and Eve, R. (1991) Explaining delinquent behaviour among adolescent girls: Internal social control and differential association, *Clinical Sociology Review, 9,* 162-77.

Rosenberg, M. (1965) *Society and the Adolescent Self-image,* Princeton, N.J.: Princeton University Press.

Rutherford, A. (1986) *Growing out of Crime: Society and Young People in Trouble.* Harmondsworth: Penguin.

Rutter, M. and Giller, H. (1983) *Juvenile Delinquency: Trends and Perspectives,* Harmondsworth: Penguin.

Rutter, M., Giller, H. and Hagell, A. (1998) *Antisocial Behaviour by Young People,* Cambridge: Cambridge University Press.

Save the Children (1997) *The Milton Youth Survey,* Edinburgh: Save the Children.

Scottish Office (1997) *Referrals of Children to Reporters and Children's Hearings 1995-6,* Edinburgh: The Scottish Office.

Scottish Office (1999a) *Criminal Proceedings in Scottish Courts 1997,* Edinburgh: The Scottish Office.

Scottish Office (1999b) *Social Inclusion – Opening the Door to a Better Scotland,* Edinburgh: The Scottish Office.

Scottish Office (1999c) *A Safer Scotland: Tackling Crime and its Causes,* Edinburgh: The Scottish Office.

Scottish Office (1999d) *Scottish Economic Bulletin No 58,* Edinburgh: The Scottish Office.

Scottish Office (1999e) *Tackling Drugs in Scotland: Action in Partnership,* Edinburgh: The Scottish Office.

Sherman, L. (1997) Thinking about prevention, in L. Sherman et al. (Eds.), *Preventing Crime: What Works, What Doesn't, What's Promising,* Report to the US Congress, Washington D.C.: National Institute of Justice.

Sherman, L., Gottfredson, D., MacKenzie, D., Eck, J., Reuter, P. and Bushway, S. (1997) *Preventing Crime: What Works, What Doesn't, What's Promising,* Report to the US Congress, Washington D.C.: National Institute of Justice.

Shover, N. (1985) *Ageing Criminals,* Beverly Hills, CA: Sage.

Shover, N. (1996) *Great Pretenders: Pursuits and Careers of Persistent Thieves,* Oxford: Westview Press.

Social Work and Prisons Inspectorates (1998) *Women Offenders – A Safer Way: A Review of Community Disposals and the use of Custody for Women Offenders in Scotland,* Edinburgh: The Scottish Office.

Steffensmeier, D and Allan, E. (1996) Gender and crime: toward a gendered theory of female offending, *Annual Review of Sociology, 22,* 459-87.

Stewart, G. and Stewart, J. (1993) *Social Circumstances of Younger Offenders Under Supervision,* London: Association of Chief Officers of Probation.

Stewart, J., Smith, D. and Stewart, G. (1994) *Understanding Offending Behaviour,* Harrow: Longman.

Tarling, R. (1993) *Analysing Offending: Data, Models and Interpretation,* London: HMSO.

Thornberry, T.P. and Krohn, M.D. (1997) Peers, drug use and delinquency, in D. Stoff, J. Breiling and J.D. Master (Eds.) *Handbook of Antisocial Behaviour,* New York: Wiley.

Thornberry, T.P., Lizotte, A.J., Krohn, M.D., Farnworth, M. and Jang, J.S. (1994) Delinquency peers, beliefs and delinquency behaviour: A longitudinal test of interactional theory, *Criminology, 32,* 47-83.

Triplett, R. and Myers, L.B. (1995) Evaluating contextual patterns of delinquency: gender-based differences, *Justice Quarterly, 12,* 59-84.

Tyler, T.R. (1990) *Why People Obey the Law,* New Haven CT: Yale University Press.

Underdown, A. (1998) *Strategies for Effective Offender Supervision: Report of the HMIP What Works Project,* London: Home Office.

Utting, D. (1996) *Reducing Criminality Among Young People: A Sample of Relevant Programmes in the United Kingdom,* Home Office Research Study 161, London: Home Office.

Utting, D., Bright, J. and Henricson, C. (1993) *Crime and the Family: Improving Child-rearing and Preventing Delinquency,* London: Family Policy Studies Centre.

Walklate, S. (1995) *Gender and Crime: An Introduction,* London: Prentice Hall.

Walmsley, R., Howard, L. and White, S. (1991) *The National Prison Survey 1991: Main Findings,* Home Office Research Study No.128, London, HMSO.

West, D.J. and Farrington, D.P. (1973) *Who Becomes Delinquent?,* London: Heinemann Educational.

West, D.J. and Farrington, D.P. (1977) *The Delinquent Way of Life,* London: Heinemann Educational

White, J.L., Moffitt, T.E., Caspi, A., Jeglum, D., Nettles,D. and Stouthamer-Loeber, M. (1994) Measuring impulsivity and examining its relationship to delinquency, *Journal of Abnormal Psychology, 103,* 192-205.

Worrall, A. (1990) *Offending Women: Female Lawbreakers and the Criminal Justice System,* London: Routledge.

Worrall, A. (1995) Gender, justice and the probation service, in G. McIvor (ed.) *Working with Offenders,* London: Jessica Kingsley.

APPENDIX

The use of the laptop computer

A variety of schedules were administered via a laptop computer as a mechanism for breaking up a lengthy interview and maintaining young people's interest in the interview process. As discussed elsewhere in this report, these schedules focused upon the following issues:

- risk-taking and impulsiveness;
- nature and frequency of substance abuse;
- attitudes towards offending;
- self esteem;
- gender attitudes: masculinity/femininity.

Laptop computers have been used in other studies of offending among young people as a means of inputting data from structured interviews with young people (Ramsay and Percy, 1996). As far as authors are aware, however, none of these studies have engaged young people directly in the use of the laptop as part of the interview process. Comments made by young people on completion of their interviews suggested that the use of the laptop was a useful feature of the study. In view of the innovative nature of this element of the research a decision was therefore made to seek young people's views about using the laptop in a more systematic way. A brief questionnaire was designed and sent by post to all young people who had been interviewed up to that point (around a quarter of those in the youngest study age group). Thereafter all interviewees were given a questionnaire at the end of their interview, along with a pre-paid envelope in which to return it to the university.

The questionnaire consisted of 10 statements about the use of the laptop. Young people were asked to indicate on a 5-point likert scale the extent to which they agreed or disagreed with the statements (strongly agree; agree; neither agree nor disagree; disagree; strongly disagree). To reduce the likelihood of response set a combination of six positive statements and four negative statements was employed, with the latter interspersed throughout the questionnaire.

Seventy-two young people in the youngest study age group completed questionnaires, representing a response rate of 69 per cent. The response rate for boys and girls was identical, with an equal number of questionnaires returned (36 each).

The young people's responses are summarised in Tables 1 and 2. To facilitate interpretation the responses have been re-grouped into three categories representing agreement with the statement, disagreement with the statement or a neutral response.

Table 1: Agreement with positive statements about using the laptop - youngest age group

	Agree	Neutral	Disagree
The laptop was fun to use	63 *(87%)*	8 *(11%)*	1 *(1%)*
The laptop helped to break up the interview	60 *(83%)*	8 *(11%)*	4 *(5%)*
The laptop was easy to use	66 *(92%)*	4 *(5%)*	2 *(3%)*
The laptop made the interview more interesting	60 *(83%)*	9 *(12%)*	3 *(4%)*
Without the laptop the interview would have seemed too long	35 *(49%)*	19 *(26%)*	18 *(25%)*
Using the laptop helped to keep me interested in the interview	52 *(72%)*	13 *(18%)*	7 *(10%)*

Table 2: Agreement with negative statements about using the laptop - youngest age group

	Agree	Neutral	Disagree
The laptop was difficult to use	2 *(3%)*	4 *(5%)*	66 *(92%)*
The laptop made the interview too long	3 *(4%)*	12 *(49%)*	57 *(47%)*
I couldn't see the point in using the laptop	2 *(3%)*	5 *(7%)*	65 *(90%)*
Using the laptop was boring	2 *(3%)*	2 *(3%)*	68 *(94%)*

Clearly the laptop was viewed by most respondents as a useful addition to the interview process which was interesting to use and which served to break up the interview and maintain young people's interest in it. Moreover, there were no gender differences in this respect. The only ambivalence appeared to centre upon the impact of the laptop on the duration of the interview. Although a few young people agreed that the use of the laptop had made the interview too long, fewer than half disagreed with this statement. On the other hand, around a quarter of respondents believed that the interview would have seemed too long if the use of the laptop had not been included. In other words, it seems that some young people recognised that the use of the laptop may have made the interview longer in real terms, but that this was offset by the interview being more interesting and enjoyable as a result.

Twenty-seven young people took the opportunity to provide additional comments in the questionnaire. As with the responses to the specific questions, these were largely positive. Three of the four respondents who made negative comments referred to the fact that there were too many questions; that some of the questions were difficult; and that the laptop was difficult to use at first. This latter comment most likely alludes to the operation of the mouse[44], which the fourth respondent suggested should be changed. More commonly, however, young people took the opportunity to reinforce their view that the laptop was 'fun', 'easy to use', 'interesting', 'cool' and a 'very good use of resources' and that it should be used more widely in the interviewing of people their age.

[44] The laptop had a touchpad mouse which moved the cursor very quickly and was difficult to control.

Fewer completed questionnaires (30 in total) were returned by young people in the middle and oldest age groups and the responses are therefore combined in Tables 3 and 4. Again there was a high level of agreement with the positive statements though, in comparison with the younger respondents, respondents in the middle and oldest age groups were less likely to agree that without the laptop the interview would have seemed too long and that the use of the laptop helped to maintain interest in the interview. More young people in the middle and oldest age groups, however, disagreed with the proposition that using the laptop made the interview too long.

Table 3: Agreement with positive statements about using the laptop - middle and oldest age groups

	Agree	Neutral	Disagree
The laptop was fun to use	22 *(73%)*	7 *(23%)*	1 *(3%)*
The laptop helped to break up the interview	24 *(80%)*	6 *(20%)*	-
The laptop was easy to use	28 *(93%)*	1 *(3%)*	1 *(3%)*
The laptop made the interview more interesting	22 *(73%)*	4 *(13%)*	4 *(13%)*
Without the laptop the interview would have seemed too long	7 *(23%)*	12 *(40%)*	11 *(37%)*
Using the laptop helped to keep me interested in the interview	12 *(40%)*	10 *(33%)*	8 *(27%)*

Table 4: Agreement with negative statements about using the laptop - middle and oldest age groups

	Agree	Neutral	Disagree
The laptop was difficult to use	-	2 *(7%)*	28 *(93%)*
The laptop made the interview too long	1 *(3%)*	5 *(17%)*	24 *(80%)*
I couldn't see the point in using the laptop	3 *(10%)*	6 *(20%)*	21 *(70%)*
Using the laptop was boring	1 *(3%)*	5 *(17%)*	24 *(80%)*

The additional comments made by this group of young people were mixed. Four young people offered positive comments, stating that the use of the laptop made the interview 'more private and easier' and made them 'feel more part of the interview', that the laptop was 'straightforward and user-friendly' and that 'without it it would have been a long process'. Two young people were neutral in their appraisal, with one stating that the laptop was 'awkward at times but OK' and the other that it was 'neither a good or bad thing'. The most critical comments came from two young people, one of whom 'couldn't see the point' of using the laptop while the other considered it to have been 'unnecessary'. A third negative comment centred on the manageability of the mouse ('an easier input device would speed things up') while a fourth respondent echoed a concern of the researchers that the laptop might have become a target for opportunistic thieves in commenting that 'forms are a better idea for security of interviewer'.

Table 3.7a: Number of times boys and girls had been involved in a fight

	Boys (n=413)	Girls (n=309)	Total (n=722)
1-2	145 *(35%)*	155 *(50%)*	300 *(42%)*
3-5	121 *(29%)*	83 *(27%)*	204 *(28%)*
6-10	68 *(16%)*	44 *(14%)*	112 *(16%)*
11 or more	79 *(19%)*	27 *(9%)*	106 *(15%)*

p<.001

Table 3.7b: Number of times boys and girls had set fire to something

	Boys (n=357)	Girls (n=174)	Total (n=531)
1-2	161 *(45%)*	104 *(60%)*	265 *(50%)*
3-5	78 *(22%)*	40 *(23%)*	118 *(22%)*
6-10	54 *(15%)*	14 *(8%)*	68 *(13%)*
11 or more	64 *(18%)*	16 *(9%)*	80 *(15%)*

p<.01

Table 3.7c: Number of times boys and girls had hurt someone with a weapon

	Boys (n=269)	Girls (n=121)	Total (n=390)
1-2	148 *(55%)*	91 *(75%)*	239 *(61%)*
3-5	65 *(24%)*	17 *(14%)*	82 *(21%)*
6-10	26 *(10%)*	4 *(3%)*	30 *(8%)*
11 or more	30 *(11%)*	9 *(7%)*	39 *(10%)*

p<.01

Table 3.7d: Number of times boys and girls had beat someone up

	Boys (n=396)	Girls (n=221)	Total (n=617)
1-2	120 *(30%)*	120 *(54%)*	240 *(39%)*
3-5	120 *(30%)*	57 *(26%)*	177 *(29%)*
6-10	81 *(20%)*	23 *(10%)*	104 *(17%)*
11 or more	75 *(19%)*	21 *(10%)*	96 *(16%)*

p<.01

Table 3.7e: Number of times boys and girls had stolen from school

	Boys (n=293)	Girls (n=264)	Total (n=557)
1-2	112 *(38%)*	135 *(51%)*	247 *(44%)*
3-5	86 *(29%)*	78 *(30%)*	164 *(29%)*
6-10	38 *(13%)*	24 *(9%)*	62 *(11%)*
11 or more	57 *(20%)*	27 *(10%)*	84 *(15%)*

p<.01

Table 3.7f: Number of times boys and girls had stolen something else

	Boys (n=266)	Girls (n=149)	Total (n=415)
1-2	148 *(56%)*	99 *(66%)*	247 *(60%)*
3-5	64 *(24%)*	31 *(21%)*	95 *(23%)*
6-10	32 *(12%)*	16 *(11%)*	48 *(12%)*
11 or more	22 *(8%)*	3 *(2%)*	25 *(6%)*

p<.01

Table 3.13a: Number of times stole a bike by study area

	Westburgh (n=113)	Eastburgh (n=114)	Total (n=227)
1-2	82 *(73%)*	60 *(53%)*	142 *(63%)*
3-5	23 *(20%)*	33 *(29%)*	56 *(25%)*
6-10	5 *(4%)*	6 *(5%)*	11 *(5%)*
11 or more	3 *(3%)*	5 *(13%)*	18 *(8%)*

p<.01

Table 3.13b: Number of times damaged property by study area

	Westburgh (n=457)	Eastburgh (n=330)	Total (n=787)
1-2	181 *(40%)*	107 *(32%)*	288 *(37%)*
3-5	146 *(32%)*	82 *(25%)*	228 *(29%)*
6-10	60 *(13%)*	53 *(16%)*	113 *(14%)*
11 or more	70 *(15%)*	88 *(28%)*	158 *(20%)*

p<.01

Table 3.13c: Number of times involved in a street fight by study area

	Westburgh (n=435)	Eastburgh (n=302)	Total (n=737)
1-2	182 *(42%)*	122 *(40%)*	304 *(41%)*
3-5	136 *(31%)*	69 *(23%)*	205 *(28%)*
6-10	71 *(16%)*	46 *(15%)*	117 *(16%)*
11 or more	46 *(11%)*	56 *(22%)*	111 *(15%)*

p<.001

Table 3.13d: Number of times set fire to something by study area

	Westburgh (n=291)	Eastburgh (n=256)	Total (n=547)
1-2	166 (57%)	106 (41%)	272 (50%)
3-5	65 (22%)	58 (23%)	123 (22%)
6-10	31 (11%)	40 (16%)	71 (13%)
11 or more	29 (10%)	52 (20%)	81 (15%)

p<.001

Table 3.13e: Number of times hurt someone with a weapon by study area

	Westburgh (n=199)	Eastburgh (n=201)	Total (n=400)
1-2	118 (59%)	124 (62%)	242 (60%)
3-5	51 (26%)	32 (16%)	83 (21%)
6-10	11 (6%)	21 (10%)	32 (8%)
11 or more	19 (10%)	24 (12%)	43 (11%)

p<.001

Table 3.13f: Number of times beat someone up by study area

	Westburgh (n=363)	Eastburgh (n=268)	Total (n=631)
1-2	146 (40%)	97 (36%)	243 (39%)
3-5	117 (32%)	63 (24%)	180 (28%)
6-10	56 (15%)	51 (19%)	107 (17%)
11 or more	44 (12%)	57 (21%)	101 (16%)

p<.01

Table 4.3a: Young people in each offender category who considered particular offences to be very serious - youngest age group

	Resister (n=34)	Desister (n=26)	Persister (n=43)
PROPERTY OFFENCES			
Steal a car	33 *(97%)*	25 *(96%)*	38 *(88%)*
Sell a stolen bank/credit card	34 *(100%)*	26 *(100%)*	36 *(84%)*
Use a stolen bank/credit card	31 *(91%)*	24 *(92%)*	36 *(84%)*
Handle stolen goods	34 *(100%)*	23 *(88%)*	29 *(67%)*
Steal a moped/motorcycle	25 *(74%)*	20 *(77%)*	32 *(74%)*
Snatch a bag	28 *(82%)*	17 *(75%)*	29 *(67%)*
Break into property	26 *(77%)*	20 *(77%)*	23 *(54%)*
Set fire to something	28 *(82%)*	18 *(69%)*	17 *(40%)*
Make a false insurance/benefit claim	21 *(62%)*	19 *(73%)*	21 *(50%)*
Steal from a car	20 *(61%)*	15 *(58%)*	21 *(50%)*
Steal something else	24 *(71%)*	11 *(44%)*	15 *(36%)*
Pick someone's pocket	20 *(59%)*	11 *(42%)*	18 *(42%)*
Steal from work	17 *(50%)*	7 *(27%)*	17 *(40%)*
Steal a bicycle	16 *(47%)*	8 *(31%)*	15 *(36%)*
Shoplifting	17 *(50%)*	5 *(19%)*	8 *(19%)*
Damage property/vandalism	14 *(41%)*	4 *(15%)*	7 *(16%)*
Steal from school	11 *(32%)*	5 *(19%)*	8 *(19%)*
Steal from a machine	7 *(21%)*	7 *(27%)*	5 *(12%)*
VIOLENT OFFENCES			
Hurt someone using a weapon	33 *(97%)*	24 *(92%)*	35 *(81%)*
Mug someone	32 *(94%)*	22 *(85%)*	32 *(74%)*
Beat up a family member	28 *(82%)*	14 *(54%)*	22 *(51%)*
Beat someone up	24 *(71%)*	8 *(31%)*	9 *(21%)*
Street fight	13 (38%)	5 *(19%)*	7 *(16%)*

Table 4.3b: Young people in each offender category who considered particular offences to be very serious - middle age group

	Resister (n=35)	Desister (n=19)	Persister (n=34)
PROPERTY OFFENCES			
Steal a car	29 *(83%)*	13 *(68%)*	20 *(59%)*
Sell a stolen bank/credit card	30 *(86%)*	16 *(68%)*	18 *(53%)*
Use a stolen bank/credit card	29 *(83%)*	13 *(68%)*	18 *(53%)*
Handle stolen goods	17 *(49%)*	4 *(21%)*	3 *(9%)*
Steal a moped/motorcycle	21 *(60%)*	7 *(37%)*	17 *(50%)*
Snatch a bag	27 *(77%)*	14 *(77%)*	28 *(82%)*
Break into property	28 *(80%)*	8 *(42%)*	13 *(38%)*
Set fire to something	19 *(54%)*	9 *(47%)*	17 *(50%)*
Make a false insurance/benefit claim	19 *(54%)*	6 *(32%)*	9 *(26%)*
Steal from a car	20 *(57%)*	9 *(47%)*	8 *(24%)*
Steal something else	22 *(63%)*	7 *(37%)*	8 *(24%)*
Pick someone's pocket	23 *(66%)*	9 *(47%)*	15 *(44%)*
Steal from work	14 *(40%)*	5 *(26%)*	7 *(21%)*
Steal a bicycle	10 *(29%)*	4 *(21%)*	9 *(27%)*
Shoplifting	15 *(43%)*	3 *(16%)*	4 *(12%)*
Damage property/vandalism	10 *(29%)*	4 *(21%)*	6 *(18%)*
Steal from school	5 *(14%)*	2 *(11%)*	2 *(6%)*
Steal from a machine	13 *(37%)*	1 *(5%)*	4 *(12%)*
VIOLENT OFFENCES			
Hurt someone using a weapon	34 *(97%)*	17 *(90%)*	23 *(68%)*
Mug someone	30 (86%)	16 *(84%)*	20 *(59%)*
Beat up a family member	20 *(57%)*	11 *(58%)*	18 *(53%)*
Beat someone up	25 *(71%)*	8 *(42%)*	6 *(18%)*
Street fight	15 (43%)	6 *(32%)*	2 *(6%)*

Table 4.3c: Young people in each offender category who considered particular offences to be very serious - oldest age group

	Resister (n=24)	Desister (n=28)	Persister (n=25)
PROPERTY OFFENCES			
Steal a car	17 *(71%)*	19 *(68%)*	6 *(24%)*
Sell a stolen bank/credit card	17 *(71%)*	15 *(54%)*	6 *(24%)*
Use a stolen bank/credit card	15 *(62%)*	13 *(46%)*	7 *(28%)*
Handle stolen goods	5 *(21%)*	2 *(7%)*	2 *(8%)*
Steal a moped/motorcycle	12 *(50%)*	12 *(43%)*	7 *(28%)*
Snatch a bag	18 *(75%)*	25 *(89%)*	20 *(80%)*
Break into property	16 *(67%)*	15 *(54%)*	11 *(44%)*
Set fire to something	18 *(75%)*	16 *(57%)*	14 *(56%)*
Make a false insurance/benefit claim	8 *(33%)*	6 *(21%)*	4 *(16%)*
Steal from a car	13 *(54%)*	10 *(36%)*	1 *(4%)*
Steal something else	8 *(33%)*	9 *(32%)*	3 *(12%)*
Pick someone's pocket	14 *(58%)*	15 *(54%)*	8 *(32%)*
Steal from work	8 *(33%)*	7 *(25%)*	4 *(16%)*
Steal a bicycle	8 *(33%)*	3 *(11%)*	3 *(12%)*
Shoplifting	5 *(21%)*	-	2 *(8%)*
Damage property/vandalism	8 *(33%)*	12 *(43%)*	5 *(20%)*
Steal from school	6 *(25%)*	4 *(14%)*	-
Steal from a machine	5 *(21%)*	3 *(11%)*	3 *(12%)*
VIOLENT OFFENCES			
Hurt someone using a weapon	24 *(100%)*	26 *(93%)*	19 *(76%)*
Mug someone	24 (100%)	23 *(82%)*	17 *(68%)*
Beat up a family member	17 *(71%)*	21 *(75%)*	11 *(44%)*
Beat someone up	18 *(75%)*	11 *(39%)*	4 *(16%)*
Street fight	12 (50%)	10 *(36%)*	7 *(28%)*

Table 5.1a: Drug and alcohol use – boys in youngest age group

	Resisters (n=14)	Desisters (n=14)	Persisters (n=24)	Total (n=52)
Alcohol	7 *(50%)*	13 *(93%)*	18 *(75%)*	38 *(73%)*
Amphetamines	-	-	1 *(4%)*	1 *(2%)*
Cannabis	-	2 *(14%)*	10 *(42%)*	12 *(23%)*
Ecstasy	-	-	1 *(4%)*	1 *(2%)*
Glue/gas	-	1 *(7%)*	-	1 *(2%)*
Heroin	-	-	-	-
LSD	-	-	3 *(12%)*	3 *(6%)*
Magic mushrooms	-	-	2 *(8%)*	2 *(4%)*
Methadone	-	-	-	-
Temazepam	-	-	2 *(8%)*	2 *(4%)*
Tranquillisers	-	-	-	-
Other substance	-	-	1 *(4%)*	1 *(2%)*

Table 5.1b: Drug and alcohol use – girls in youngest age group

	Resisters (n=20)	Desisters (n=12)	Persisters (n=20)	Total (n=52)
Alcohol	11 *(55%)*	10 *(83%)*	20 *(100%)*	41 *(79%)*
Amphetamines	-	-	1 *(5%)*	1 *(2%)*
Cannabis	3 *(15%)*	1 *(8%)*	15 *(75%)*	18 *(37%)*
Ecstasy	-	-	1 *(5%)*	1 *(2%)*
Glue/gas	-	-	6 *(30%)*	6 *(12%)*
Heroin	-	-	1 *(5%)*	1 *(2%)*
LSD	-	-	3 *(15%)*	3 *(6%)*
Magic mushrooms	-	-	2 *(10%)*	2 *(4%)*
Methadone	-	-	1 *(5%)*	1 *(2%)*
Temazepam	-	-	3 *(15%)*	3 *(6%)*
Tranquillisers	-	-	1 *(5%)*	1 *(2%)*
Other substance	1 *(5%)*	-	2 *(10%)*	3 *(6%)*

Table 5.1c: How recently boys and girls had used drugs and alcohol – youngest age group

	Never used	Used more than 12 months ago	Used within the last 12 months
Alcohol	25 *(24%)*	11 *(11%)*	68 *(65%)*
Amphetamines	102 *(98%)*	1 *(1%)*	1 *(1%)*
Cannabis	73 *(70%)*	7 *(7%)*	24 *(23%)*
Ecstasy	102 *(98%)*	-	2 *(2%)*
Glue/gas	97 *(93%)*	1 *(1%)*	6 *(6%)*
Heroin	103 *(99%)*	-	1 *(1%)*
LSD	98 *(94%)*	1 *(1%)*	5 *(5%)*
Magic mushrooms	101 *(97%)*	3 *(3%)*	1 *(1%)*
Methadone	103 *(99%)*	-	1 *(1%)*
Temazepam	99 *(95%)*	2 *(2%)*	3 *(3%)*
Tranquillisers	103 *(99%)*	-	1 *(1%)*
Other substance	100 *(96%)*	1 *(1%)*	3 *(3%)*

Table 5.1d: Frequency of use of alcohol and drugs - youngest age group

	Alcohol (n=74)[45]	Cannabis (n=29)[46]	Other drugs (n=16)[47]
Once or twice	22 *(30%)*	10 *(35%)*	11 *(69%)*
Once every couple of months	18 *(24%)*	4 *(14%)*	9 *(56%)*
1-3 times a month	26 *(35%)*	8 *(28%)*	6 *(38%)*
1-5 times a week	8 *(11%)*	5 *(17%)*	4 *(25%)*
Daily	-	2 *(7%)*	1 *(6%)*

[45] Information about frequency of use was missing in five cases.
[46] Information about frequency of use was missing in two cases.
[47] The column total exceeds 16 since six young people had used more than one type of drug.

Table 5.2a: Drug and alcohol use – young men in middle age group

	Resisters (n=15)	Desisters (n=11)	Persisters (n=16)	Total (n=42)
Alcohol	15 *(100%)*	10 *(91%)*	16 *(100%)*	41 *(98%)*
Amphetamines	3 *(20%)*	4 *(36%)*	10 *(62%)*	17 *(40%)*
Cannabis	8 *(53%)*	9 *(82%)*	13 *(81%)*	30 *(71%)*
Cocaine	-	1 *(9%)*	4 *(25%)*	5 *(12%)*
Crack	-	1 *(9%)*	-	1 *(2%)*
Ecstasy	2 *(13%)*	3 *(27%)*	10 *(62%)*	15 *(36%)*
Glue/gas	-	1 *(9%)*	3 *(19%)*	4 *(10%)*
Heroin	-	2 *(18%)*	6 *(38%)*	8 *(19%)*
LSD	5 *(33%)*	5 *(45%)*	11 *(69%)*	21 *(50%)*
Magic mushrooms	-	2 *(18%)*	6 *(38%)*	8 *(19%)*
Methadone	-	2 *(18%)*	4 *(25%)*	6 *(14%)*
Temgesic	-	-	1 *(6%)*	1 *(2%)*
Temazepam	-	4 *(36%)*	7 *(44%)*	11 *(26%)*
Tranquilisers	-	2 *(18%)*	4 *(25%)*	6 *(14%)*
Other substance	2 *(13%)*	1 *(9%)*	3 *(19%)*	5 *(12%)*

Table 5.2b: Drug and alcohol use – young women in middle age group

	Resisters (n=20)	Desisters (n=8)	Persisters (n=19)	Total (n=47)
Alcohol	20 *(100%)*	8 *(100%)*	18 *(95%)*	46 *(98%)*
Amphetamines	1 *(5%)*	3 *(38%)*	11 *(58%)*	15 *(32%)*
Cannabis	8 *(40%)*	7 *(88%)*	16 *(84%)*	31 *(66%)*
Cocaine	-	2 *(25%)*	4 *(21%)*	6 *(13%)*
Crack	-	-	3 *(16%)*	3 *(6%)*
Ecstasy	1 *(5%)*	3 *(38%)*	12 *(63%)*	16 *(34%)*
Glue/gas	-	1 *(12%)*	6 *(32%)*	7 *(15%)*
Heroin	-	1 *(12%)*	11 *(58%)*	12 *(26%)*
LSD	-	3 *(38%)*	12 *(63%)*	15 *(32%)*
Magic mushrooms	-	1 *(12%)*	3 *(16%)*	4 *(8%)*
Methadone	-	-	6 *(32%)*	6 *(13%)*
Temgesic	-	-	7 *(37%)*	7 *(15%)*
Temazepam	-	1 *(12%)*	12 *(63%)*	13 *(28%)*
Tranquilisers	1 *(5%)*	1 *(12%)*	10 *(53%)*	12 *(26%)*
Other substance	-	-	1 *(5%)*	1 *(2%)*

Table 5.2c: How recently young people had used drugs and alcohol – middle age group

	Never used	Used more than 12 months ago	Used within the last 12 months
Alcohol	2 *(2%)*	3 *(3%)*	84 *(94%)*
Amphetamines	57 *(64%)*	13 *(15%)*	19 *(21%)*
Cannabis	28 *(31%)*	17 *(19%)*	44 *(49%)*
Cocaine	78 *(88%)*	7 *(8%)*	4 *(4%)*
Crack	85 *(96%)*	4 *(4%)*	-
Ecstasy	58 *(65%)*	20 *(22%)*	11 *(12%)*
Glue/gas	78 *(88%)*	9 *(10%)*	2 *(2%)*
Heroin	69 *(78%)*	3 *(3%)*	17 *(19%)*
LSD	53 *(60%)*	26 *(29%)*	10 *(11%)*
Magic mushrooms	77 *(86%)*	9 *(10%)*	3 *(3%)*
Methadone	73 *(82%)*	4 *(4%)*	12 *(13%)*
Temgesic	76 *(85%)*	6 *(7%)*	7 *(8%)*
Temazepam	65 *(73%)*	7 *(8%)*	17 *(19%)*
Tranquilisers	61 *(68%)*	4 *(4%)*	14 *(16%)*
Other substance	83 *(93%)*	1 *(1%)*	5 *(6%)*

Table 5.2d: Frequency of drug and alcohol use - middle age group

	Once or twice	Once every couple of months	1-3 times per month	1-5 times per week	Daily
Alcohol	7	9	30	37	-
Amphetamines	11	9	2	1	
Cannabis	15	8	3	10	11
Cocaine	9	2	-	-	-
Crack	2	-	-	-	-
Ecstasy	11	5	4	1	-
Glue/gas	5	1	-	-	-
Heroin	-	3	3	1	10
LSD	14	3	5	-	-
Magic mushrooms	8	-	-	-	-
Methadone	5	3	2	-	3
Temazepam	5	4	3	3	3
Tranquillisers	5	1	5	1	2
Other substance	3	2	-	-	1

Table 5.3a: Drug and alcohol use – young men in oldest age group

	Resisters (n=8)	Desisters (n=17)	Persisters (n=17)	Total (n=41)
Alcohol	8 *(100%)*	15 *(88%)*	14 *(82%)*	37 *(90%)*
Amphetamines	4 *(50%)*	10 *(59%)*	13 *(76%)*	27 *(66%)*
Cannabis	4 *(50%)*	17 *(100%)*	16 *(94%)*	37 *(90%)*
Cocaine	2 *(25%)*	10 *(59%)*	8 *(47%)*	20 *(49%)*
Crack	1 *(12%)*	3 *(18%)*	4 *(24%)*	8 *(20%)*
Ecstasy	2 *(25%)*	13 *(76%)*	15 *(88%)*	30 *(73%)*
Glue/gas	2 *(25%)*	3 *(18%)*	7 *(41%)*	12 *(29%)*
Heroin	1 *(12%)*	9 *(53%)*	14 *(82%)*	24 *(58%)*
LSD	2 *(25%)*	12 *(71%)*	12 *(71%)*	26 *(63%)*
Magic mushrooms	2 *(25%)*	8 *(47%)*	11 *(65%)*	21 *(51%)*
Methadone	1 *(12%)*	8 *(47%)*	14 *(82%)*	23 *(56%)*
Temgesic	1 *(12%)*	8 *(47%)*	13 *(76%)*	22 *(54%)*
Temazepam	2 *(25%)*	10 *(59%)*	14 *(82%)*	26 *(63%)*
Tranquilisers	2 *(25%)*	4 *(24%)*	12 *(71%)*	18 *(44%)*
Other substance	1 *(12%)*	-	1 *(6%)*	2 *(5%)*

Table 5.3b: Drug and alcohol use – young women in oldest age group

	Resisters (n=16)	Desisters (n=12)	Persisters (n=11)	Total (n=39)
Alcohol	15 *(94%)*	12 *(100%)*	11 *(100%)*	38 *(97%)*
Amphetamines	5 *(31%)*	7 *(58%)*	10 *(91%)*	22 *(56%)*
Cannabis	11 *(69%)*	9 *(75%)*	10 *(91%)*	30 *(77%)*
Cocaine	1 *(6%)*	-	9 *(82%)*	10 *(26%)*
Crack	-	1 *(8%)*	6 *(54%)*	7 *(18%)*
Ecstasy	4 *(25%)*	5 *(42%)*	9 *(82%)*	18 *(46%)*
Glue/gas	1 *(6%)*	4 *(33%)*	8 *(73%)*	13 *(33%)*
Heroin	-	3 *(25%)*	11 *(100%)*	14 *(36%)*
LSD	6 *(38%)*	6 *(50%)*	10 *(91%)*	22 *(56%)*
Magic mushrooms	-	2 *(17%)*	8 *(73%)*	10 *(26%)*
Methadone	-	3 *(25%)*	11 *(100%)*	14 *(36%)*
Temgesic	-	2 *(17%)*	7 *(64%)*	9 *(23%)*
Temazepam	3 *(19%)*	5 *(42%)*	10 *(91%)*	18 *(46%)*
Tranquilisers	-	2 *(17%)*	9 *(82%)*	11 *(28%)*
Other substance	-	1 *(8%)*	2 *(18%)*	3 *(8%)*

Table 5.3c: How recently young people had used drugs and alcohol – oldest age group

	Never used	Used more than 12 months ago	Used within the last 12 months
Alcohol	6 *(7%)*	11 *(14%)*	64 *(74%)*
Amphetamines	32 *(40%)*	25 *(31%)*	24 *(30%)*
Cannabis	14 *(17%)*	15 *(19%)*	52 *(64%)*
Cocaine	51 *(63%)*	19 *(37%)*	11 *(14%)*
Crack	66 *(82%)*	8 *(10%)*	7 *(9%)*
Ecstasy	32 *(40%)*	27 *(33%)*	22 *(27%)*
Glue/gas	64 *(79%)*	25 *(31%)*	-
Heroin	51 *(63%)*	4 *(5%)*	34 *(42%)*
LSD	33 *(41%)*	41 *(51%)*	7 *(9%)*
Magic mushrooms	50 *(62%)*	28 *(35%)*	3 *(4%)*
Methadone	44 *(54%)*	8 *(10%)*	29 *(36%)*
Temgesic	50 *(62%)*	18 *(22%)*	13 *(16%)*
Temazepam	37 *(46%)*	11 *(14%)*	33 *(41%)*
Tranquilisers	52 *(64%)*	7 *(9%)*	22 *(27%)*
Other substance	76 *(94%)*	3 *(4%)*	2 *(3%)*

Table 5.3d: Frequency of drug and alcohol use - oldest age group

	Once or twice	Once every couple of months	1-3 times per month	1-5 times per week	Daily
Alcohol	11	17	17	27	-
Amphetamines	10	7	6	4	-
Cannabis	8	4	11	13	18
Cocaine	11	3	-	1	-
Crack	8	1	-	-	-
Ecstasy	8	13	4	1	-
Glue/gas	6	1	-	1	-
Heroin	2	-	1	2	27
LSD	10	5	2	-	-
Magic mushrooms	9	2	-	1	-
Methadone	5	6	3	3	13
Temazepam	1	7	8	12	2
Tranquillisers	4	1	8	7	4
Other substance	-	1	1	-	1

Interviewee number ☐   **Age** ☐

Gender ☐   **Location** ☐

I am now going to ask you how you would react if a number of things happened to you …

If you got an unexpected windfall of money – say £100 – from somewhere, how likely would you be to spend it fairly soon afterwards rather than hang on to it for a while?
☐ Absolutely certain   ☐ very likely   ☐ quite likely   ☐ not very likely   ☐ not at all likely

If you saw something you wanted to buy and had the cash on you at the time, how likely would you be to buy it rather than shop around to see if there's something better?
☐ Absolutely certain   ☐ very likely   ☐ quite likely   ☐ not very likely   ☐ not at all likely

In general, how likely are you to say what you think whenever it comes into your head, regardless of where you are and who is listening?
☐ Absolutely certain   ☐ very likely   ☐ quite likely   ☐ not very likely   ☐ not at all likely

Suppose someone dared you to do something a bit dangerous, like climb up onto the roof of a two storey house for instance. How likely would you be to do it?
☐ Absolutely certain   ☐ very likely   ☐ quite likely   ☐ not very likely   ☐ not at all likely

If you are buying something second-hand (e.g. a ghetto-blaster) and what looks like a real bargain turns up, how likely would you be to settle for it on the spot rather than wait to have it checked over?
☐ Absolutely certain   ☐ very likely   ☐ quite likely   ☐ not very likely   ☐ not at all likely

Imagine that you talking to a group of friends who've all got more money than you. They are arranging to go together to quite an expensive club and want you to go too but you can't really afford it? How likely would you be to go?
☐ Absolutely certain   ☐ very likely   ☐ quite likely   ☐ not very likely   ☐ not at all likely

You really need some money to pay off a few debts. You meet a well-known local criminal who offers to lend it to you interest free provided you 'do some work for him sometime'. Is it likely you would accept?
☐ Absolutely certain   ☐ very likely   ☐ quite likely   ☐ not very likely   ☐ not at all likely

A group of friends turn up at your house one night with a car and invite you to go for a spin. You didn't even know any of them had a car. How likely would you be to just go?
☐ Absolutely certain   ☐ very likely   ☐ quite likely   ☐ not very likely   ☐ not at all likely

Imagine that you are walking past a pub late at night when you notice that a side window has been left slightly open. How likely is it that you would try to go in?
☐ Absolutely certain   ☐ very likely   ☐ quite likely   ☐ not very likely   ☐ not at all likely

You are sitting at home watching television when you hear some sort of commotion going on a couple of streets away. How likely would you be to go around to see what's happening?
☐ Absolutely certain   ☐ very likely   ☐ quite likely   ☐ not very likely   ☐ not at all likely

Which of the following have you used ever and or in the last twelve months?

Cannabis	☐ Ever	☐ In the last 12 months
Heroin	☐ Ever	☐ In the last 12 months
Cocaine	☐ Ever	☐ In the last 12 months
Methadone	☐ Ever	☐ In the last 12 months
Crack	☐ Ever	☐ In the last 12 months
Ecstasy	☐ Ever	☐ In the last 12 months
Acid/LSD	☐ Ever	☐ In the last 12 months
Tranquillisers	☐ Ever	☐ In the last 12 months
Amphetamines	☐ Ever	☐ In the last 12 months
Temazepam	☐ Ever	☐ In the last 12 months
Temgesic	☐ Ever	☐ In the last 12 months
Magic Mushrooms	☐ Ever	☐ In the last 12 months
Glue/gas	☐ Ever	☐ In the last 12 months
Alcohol	☐ Ever	☐ In the last 12 months
Other	☐ Ever	☐ In the last 12 months

How often have you used these drugs in the last twelve months?

Cannabis
- [ ] Once/twice
- [ ] once every couple of months
- [ ] 1-3 times a month
- [ ] 1-5 times a week
- [ ] every day

Heroin
- [ ] Once/twice
- [ ] once every couple of months
- [ ] 1-3 times a month
- [ ] 1-5 times a week
- [ ] every day

Methadone
- [ ] Once/twice
- [ ] once every couple of months
- [ ] 1-3 times a month
- [ ] 1-5 times a week
- [ ] every day

Cocaine
- [ ] Once/twice
- [ ] once every couple of months
- [ ] 1-3 times a month
- [ ] 1-5 times a week
- [ ] every day

Crack
- [ ] Once/twice
- [ ] once every couple of months
- [ ] 1-3 times a month
- [ ] 1-5 times a week
- [ ] every day

Ecstasy
- [ ] Once/twice
- [ ] once every couple of months
- [ ] 1-3 times a month
- [ ] 1-5 times a week
- [ ] every day

Acid/LSD
- [ ] Once/twice
- [ ] once every couple of months
- [ ] 1-3 times a month
- [ ] 1-5 times a week
- [ ] every day

Tranquillisers
- [ ] Once/twice
- [ ] once every couple of months
- [ ] 1-3 times a month
- [ ] 1-5 times a week
- [ ] every day

Amphetamines
- [ ] Once/twice
- [ ] once every couple of months
- [ ] 1-3 times a month
- [ ] 1-5 times a week
- [ ] every day

Temazepam
- [ ] Once/twice
- [ ] once every couple of months
- [ ] 1-3 times a month
- [ ] 1-5 times a week
- [ ] every day

Temgesic
- [ ] Once/twice
- [ ] once every couple of months
- [ ] 1-3 times a month
- [ ] 1-5 times a week
- [ ] every day

Magic Mushrooms
- [ ] Once/twice
- [ ] once every couple of months
- [ ] 1-3 times a month
- [ ] 1-5 times a week
- [ ] every day

Glue/gas
- [ ] Once/twice
- [ ] once every couple of months
- [ ] 1-3 times a month
- [ ] 1-5 times a week
- [ ] every day

Alcohol
- [ ] Once/twice
- [ ] once every couple of months
- [ ] 1-3 times a month
- [ ] 1-5 times a week
- [ ] every day

Other
- [ ] Once/twice
- [ ] once every couple of months
- [ ] 1-3 times a month
- [ ] 1-5 times a week
- [ ] every day

I am now going to describe a number of offences that people might commit in each case I would like you to indicate how serious you think the offence is ...

Damaging or destroying, on purpose or recklessly, something belonging to somebody else (for example, telephone box, bus shelter, car, house window etc.)

☐ Very serious   ☐ Quite serious   ☐ Not very serious   ☐ Not serious at all

Setting fire on purpose or recklessly to something not belonging to you. It might be to paper or furniture, to a barn, a car, a forest, a basement, a building or something else.

☐ Very serious   ☐ Quite serious   ☐ Not very serious   ☐ Not serious at all

Stealing money from a gas or electricity meter, public telephone, vending machine, video game or fruit machine.

☐ Very serious   ☐ Quite serious   ☐ Not very serious   ☐ Not serious at all

Stealing anything from a shop, supermarket or department store.

☐ Very serious   ☐ Quite serious   ☐ Not very serious   ☐ Not serious at all

Stealing anything in school.

☐ Very serious   ☐ Quite serious   ☐ Not very serious   ☐ Not serious at all

Stealing anything from the place where you work.

☐ Very serious   ☐ Quite serious   ☐ Not very serious   ☐ Not serious at all

Taking away a bicycle without the owner's permission.

☐ Very serious   ☐ Quite serious   ☐ Not very serious   ☐ Not serious at all

Taking away a motorcycle or moped without the owner's permission.

☐ Very serious   ☐ Quite serious   ☐ Not very serious   ☐ Not serious at all

Taking away a car without the owner's permission.

☐ Very serious   ☐ Quite serious   ☐ Not very serious   ☐ Not serious at all

Stealing anything out of or from a car.

☐ Very serious   ☐ Quite serious   ☐ Not very serious   ☐ Not serious at all

Pickpocketing anything from anybody.

☐ Very serious   ☐ Quite serious   ☐ Not very serious   ☐ Not serious at all

Snatching from a person a purse, bag or something else.

☐ Very serious   ☐ Quite serious   ☐ Not very serious   ☐ Not serious at all

Women should be …

Strong
☐ Strongly agree ☐ Agree ☐ Neither agree nor disagree ☐ Disagree ☐ Strongly disagree

Warm
☐ Strongly agree ☐ Agree ☐ Neither agree nor disagree ☐ Disagree ☐ Strongly disagree

Dependent
☐ Strongly agree ☐ Agree ☐ Neither agree nor disagree ☐ Disagree ☐ Strongly disagree

Successful
☐ Strongly agree ☐ Agree ☐ Neither agree nor disagree ☐ Disagree ☐ Strongly disagree

Daring
☐ Strongly agree ☐ Agree ☐ Neither agree nor disagree ☐ Disagree ☐ Strongly disagree

Emotional
☐ Strongly agree ☐ Agree ☐ Neither agree nor disagree ☐ Disagree ☐ Strongly disagree

Submissive
☐ Strongly agree ☐ Agree ☐ Neither agree nor disagree ☐ Disagree ☐ Strongly disagree

Rational
☐ Strongly agree ☐ Agree ☐ Neither agree nor disagree ☐ Disagree ☐ Strongly disagree

Ambitious
☐ Strongly agree ☐ Agree ☐ Neither agree nor disagree ☐ Disagree ☐ Strongly disagree

Loving
☐ Strongly agree ☐ Agree ☐ Neither agree nor disagree ☐ Disagree ☐ Strongly disagree

Independent
☐ Strongly agree ☐ Agree ☐ Neither agree nor disagree ☐ Disagree ☐ Strongly disagree

Sensitive
☐ Strongly agree ☐ Agree ☐ Neither agree nor disagree ☐ Disagree ☐ Strongly disagree

Controlling
☐ Strongly agree ☐ Agree ☐ Neither agree nor disagree ☐ Disagree ☐ Strongly disagree

Unassertive
☐ Strongly agree ☐ Agree ☐ Neither agree nor disagree ☐ Disagree ☐ Strongly disagree

Powerful
☐ Strongly agree ☐ Agree ☐ Neither agree nor disagree ☐ Disagree ☐ Strongly disagree

Sympathetic
☐ Strongly agree ☐ Agree ☐ Neither agree nor disagree ☐ Disagree ☐ Strongly disagree

Aggressive
☐ Strongly agree ☐ Agree ☐ Neither agree nor disagree ☐ Disagree ☐ Strongly disagree

Caring
☐ Strongly agree ☐ Agree ☐ Neither agree nor disagree ☐ Disagree ☐ Strongly disagree

Thoughtful
☐ Strongly agree ☐ Agree ☐ Neither agree nor disagree ☐ Disagree ☐ Strongly disagree

Unemotional
☐ Strongly agree ☐ Agree ☐ Neither agree nor disagree ☐ Disagree ☐ Strongly disagree

Printed for The Stationery Office, c8 11/99